METADATA AND ITS APPLICATIONS IN THE DIGITAL LIBRARY

Approaches and Practices

Jia Liu

LIBRARIES UNLIMITED

A Member of the Greenwood Publishing Group

Westport, Connecticut • London

Library of Congress Cataloging-in-Publication Data

Liu, Jia.
 Metadata and its applications in the digital library : approaches and
practices / Jia Liu.
      p. cm.
 Includes bibliographical references and index.
 ISBN-13: 978–1–59158–306–6 (alk. paper)
 1. Metadata. 2. Digital libraries. I. Title.
 Z666.7L58 2007
 025.3—dc22   2007013572

British Library Cataloguing in Publication Data is available.

Library of Congress Catalog Card Number: 2007013572
ISBN-13: 978–1–59158–306–6

First published in 2007

Libraries Unlimited, 88 Post Road West, Westport, CT 06881
A Member of the Greenwood Publishing Group, Inc.
www.lu.com

Printed in the United States of America

The paper used in this book complies with the
Permanent Paper Standard issued by the National
Information Standards Organization (Z39.48–1984).

10 9 8 7 6 5 4 3 2 1

Dedicated to all the people whom I love and who love me

Contents

Illustrations

TABLES

Preface

Metadata is data about data. Though the term metadata has been used for no more than 20 years, its practices have a long history of operating under other names. Metadata has drawn increasing attention since the dramatic increase in the number of network information resources.

I majored in library science, the domain with the longest and most successful history of dealing with metadata. Based on my knowledge background, I have conducted a lot of research on metadata, which constantly expands my views on the subject. In addition to gaining an understanding of the latest developments in library metadata, I continually attempt to extend my field of knowledge to the practices of and approaches to metadata in other domains. I've especially paid attention to metadata in the digital library. As a researcher, I believe the best way to express my own viewpoint, summarize my knowledge, and communicate with the widest possible range of colleagues is to publish a book. These were my original motivations for writing this book. This book is also the main product of my project that is financially supported by the Alexander von Humboldt Foundation in Germany and implemented in the Lower Saxony State and Goettingen University Library. In the book, I try to provide an overview of the basic and latest metadata knowledge, as well as its implementation and applications in the digital library.

Most of the materials referenced in this book were accessed on the Internet. Fortunately, with the support of the Alexander von Humboldt Foundation, I've had the opportunity to visit three European institutions (including the host institute) to obtain more first-hand materials and gain experience directly from the related experts and resources that are not accessible from the network. Therefore, this book is a little different from previous books on the subject of metadata because it describes many practices in Europe and other countries, rather than just those in the United States. Though I have made an effort to choose the most representative examples for this book, my choice of samples was sometimes restricted because of the unavailability of some materials.

I am confident that the variety of metadata will coexist in the foreseeable future. A harmonizing structure for different kinds of metadata is especially necessary in the hybrid library. Metadata-related research and practice is ongoing. I will continue to explore the magical world of metadata together with others who share my passion.

Dr. Jia Liu

Acknowledgments

After nearly three years of work, this book is completed in the autumn, which is a season for harvesting. Before I begin to appreciate the fruit of my work, I'd like to say thanks to a lot of people. Without their support and help, I would have met many more difficulties during my research. The book is really an achievement for international cooperation.

First of all, I'm very thankful to the Alexander von Humboldt Foundation. From October 2000 until November 2004, the powerful financial support from the AvH Foundation enabled me to not only come to Germany to do my research, but also to take part in several academic activities and visit two institutions outside of Germany. I do appreciate the Humboldt Foundation's endeavor in promoting the scholarly communication between Germany and other countries so as to accelerate the development of science all over the world.

At the same time, I'm very thankful for the support and help coming from my host institute during my stay in Germany, the Goettingen State and University Library. It was so kind of Prof. Dr. Elmar Mittler to accept my invitation to act as my supervisor during my project, and to support me in participating in a variety of academic activities. Additionally, I'd like to take this opportunity to express my thanks to the colleagues in the library, who are Heike, Thomas, Holger, Margo, Claudia, Reccada, Pertra, and other persons who have given me help on a wide range of aspects. Thanks a lot to the acquisitions editor at Libraries Unlimited, Dr. Sue Easun, for her continuous guidance to me on publishing this book.

I'm also very grateful for help from the two institutions I visited during the last two years, which are the NetLab, Lund University, Sweden, and the Oxford Digital Library, United Kingdom. I very much appreciate the kind attention and pretty helpful assistance from Traugott, Colm, Michael, Nick, and many other people.

In addition, I'm grateful for the support from the Department of Information Management, Peking University, China. Thanks a lot to the leaders of the department for allowing me to come to Germany and focus on my research on metadata and its applications in the digital library.

Finally, I'd like to say thanks to the following people: my parents and younger brother; Dr. Yuansu Luo; my former supervisors Prof. Weihan Diao, Prof. Wenjun Zhou and his wife; and Dr. Victor C. Young and his wife, Mr. Tinghe Lu and his wife, et al. Their endless love is one of the most important strengths supporting me all the time.

There is a Chinese idiom saying that when one person presents me a drop of water, I should repay him a fountain. I do hope this book can express my gratitude to the people who once helped me and contribute a little to the development in the field related to metadata.

Abstract in English

This book deals not only with the general knowledge of metadata and metadata projects, but also its applications in the digital library. Basically, the purpose of the writer is to provide an outline about the approaches and practices about metadata so as to lay a fundament for further research and practice in the subject.

The text of the book is divided into two parts, and further subdivided into six chapters. In the first part, the writer elaborates the general and latest knowledge about metadata and its implementations. In the second part, the book discusses the practices related to metadata, including metadata projects and its applications in the digital library.

In the first part, Metadata in General, there are four chapters. In the first chapter, "Metadata Basics," in addition to elucidating the forms and attribute of the term metadata, the writer provides a brief overview about the variety of definitions of metadata. Then the new implications under the current circumstance and functions of metadata are described one by one. In the second chapter, "Metadata Types," a general typology of metadata is given at first. In the following sections, four kinds of metadata are introduced in detail. Not only the definitions, but also practical examples of different kinds of metadata are mentioned here. In the third chapter, "Metadata Encoding Standards," five kinds of encoding standards for metadata and one infrastructure for containing and exchanging metadata are discussed. Among them, the latest metadata encoding standards, METS, might be interpreted for the first time in a book. In the fourth chapter, "Metadata Implementation," some issues such as namespace, application profile, metadata schema registry, metadata working flow, as well as others, are discussed. In this chapter, a lot of practical examples are also given during the description.

In the second part, Metadata Projects and Applications in the Digital Library, practices about metadata all over the world are dealt with. There are two chapters in this part. In the fifth chapter, "Metadata Projects," four typical metadata projects are introduced briefly, which all have worldwide influence and took place in different parts of the world. Firstly, the BIBLINK project is a European project between libraries and publishers. Next is the MetaLib project, which is the first metadata project implemented in Germany, and also a model of earlier metadata project. MetaWeb project is taking place in Australia, where there have been a lot of approaches to metadata. The last one is the Nordic Metadata Project, which is the biggest metadata project launched in northern Europe and plays an important role in popularizing and improving Dublin Core. In the final chapter, "Metadata Applications in the Digital Library," a brief general introduction to the digital library and metadata applications in the digital library is given first. Then some representative examples of the metadata applications in the digital library projects occurring in the different parts of the world are elaborated on in the sections following. It might also be the first print introduction to DSpace, a newly developed digital repository created to capture, distribute, and preserve the intellectual output of Massachusetts Institute of Technology.

PART I
Metadata in General

1

Metadata Basics

Simply put, metadata is data about data. It is the basis for numerous different domains. There is an old Chinese idiom that says that a 1,000-kilometer journey begins from where we're standing. Therefore, the first chapter of this book will discuss basic information about metadata, such as definitions, new implications, and functions of metadata.

1.1 METADATA DEFINITIONS

Though metadata has attracted more attention and research since the dramatically rapid increase in the number of networked information resources, the term is not new to the world. However, it is difficult to determine the definite date of the term's creation. One professional said that it first appeared in the U.S. National Aeronautics and Space Administration's (NASA) Directory of Interchange Format (1988) of the, while another said it was first used in the physics community and then borrowed by and extended into other areas. There is no universal definition of metadata.

However, no one can deny that the philosophy behind metadata has existed for a very long time. The bibliographic records for the documents carved on the clay tablets in the library of Assurbanipal in the seventh century B.C. are metadata. The simplest data about a digital object, such as size, format, and so forth, are also a kind of metadata. Needless to say, metadata is so paramount that it has been applied in many different areas and in many different ways.

1.1.1 Forms: Metadata, Meta Data, or Meta-data?

The prefix "meta-" is of Greek origin. It was defined as "between, with, after and akin to" in the *Webster's Revised Unabridged Dictionary* (1913). The Free On-line

Dictionary of Computing treats meta as a free-standing word rather than a prefix, and defines it as follows:

Meta

[Analytic philosophy] One level of description up. A {metasyntactic variable} (e.g. FOO) is a variable in notation used to describe syntax, and metalanguage is a language used to describe language (e.g. BNF). This is difficult to explain briefly, but much hacker humour turns on deliberate confusion between meta-levels (Imperial College 1993).

We accept the above definition of meta for our present purposes. Metadata can be spelled three different ways—metadata, meta-data, or meta data, and the three spellings share a single meaning. The first spelling is most popular in fields such as digital libraries, computers, and so forth, while the last one is especially common in the commercial and industrial fields.

1.1.2 Attribute: Singular or Plural?

The root of the term metadata, data, comes from Latin and is the plural of the word "datum." However, in English, the word "data" is sometimes treated as a singular word and other times as a plural. The Merriam-Webster Dictionary describes its usage as follows.

Data leads a life of its own quite independent of datum, of which it was originally the plural. It occurs in two constructions: as a plural noun (like earnings), taking a plural verb and plural modifiers (as these, many, a few) but not cardinal numbers, and serving as a referent for plural pronouns (as they, them); and as an abstract mass noun (like information), taking a singular verb and singular modifiers (as this, much, little), and being referred to by a singular pronoun (it). Both constructions are standard (Merriam-Webster, Inc. n.d.).

As shown above, the word "data" can be both singular and plural, but the first use is more common. In this book, metadata is used in its singular form, except when different kinds of metadata are discussed, when it will it be used in its plural form.

1.1.3 Definitions

Actually, metadata is not a mysterious concept at all. We often encounter metadata in our daily lives. The data on our identification cards is a simple example of metadata.

Almost every document discussing metadata provides a definition of the word. Each person has a unique perspective on metadata. Nevertheless, understandings of the term metadata could be roughly divided into two approaches.

The first approach defines the concept of metadata from the meaning and origin of the term itself. On one hand, more recent Latin and English usage employs meta to denote something transcendental or beyond nature. Metadata, then, can be thought of as data about data. This is the simplest and most common definition of metadata. The definition, "Metadata is the Internet-age term for structured data about data" (EU-NSF Working Group on Metadata n.d.), could be considered a refinement of the above definition. Therefore, metadata both originates from and functions as data. Nevertheless, this definition seems too concise to describe the characteristics of the concept clearly. On the other hand, when this definition is combined with the definition of the prefix *meta-* mentioned above, it could be said that metadata is data that describes the attributes of a resource.

The second approach is to define the concept from its implications, functions, relationships with others, and so forth. The following are several typical definitions of metadata that focus on the various aspects of the term:

- "Metadata is data associated with objects which relieves their potential users of having to have full advance knowledge of their existence or characteristics" (Dempsey and Lorcan 1997).

- "Metadata is a small summary of characteristics of each available resource" (Wood 1997).

- "Metadata as a kind of summary of information about the form and content of a resource" (Turner n.d.).

- "Metadata is machine understandable information about web resources or other things" (Berners-Lee 1997).

- "Metadata really is nothing more than data about data; a catalog record is metadata; so is a TEI header, or any other form of description. We could call it cataloging, but for some people that term carries excess baggage, like *Anglo-American Cataloging Rules* and USMARC. So to some extent this is a 'you call it corn, we call it maize' situation, but metadata is a good neutral term that covers all the bases" (Caplan 1995).

- "Metadata is 'information about data.' Metadata describes an Internet resource: what it is, what it is about, where it is, and so on" (Iannella and Waugh 1997).

- "Metadata is a succinct and systematic set of information that references, and can be used to efficiently and accurately retrieve, a larger set of information"(G. DeCandido1999).

- "Metadata is structured information that describes, explains, locates, or otherwise makes it easier to retrieve, use or manage an information resource. Metadata is often called data about data or information about information" (Hodge 2001).

- "Metadata is sometimes defined literally as 'data about data,' but the term is normally understood to mean structured data about resources that can be used to help support a wide range of operations. These might include, for example, resource description and discovery, the management of information resources and their long-term preservation" (Day 2001).

- "An item of metadata is a relationship that someone claims to exist between two entities" (Rust and Bide 2000).

In addition to definitions, some professionals even develop axioms in order to delineate the deeper implications of the concept. The following is a sample of axioms about metadata:

Metadata is data. That is to say, information about information is to be counted in all respects as information. There are various parts of this. One is that *metadata can be stored regarded as data*, it can be stored in a resource. So, one resource may contain information about itself or about another resource. The second part of the above axiom is: *Metadata can describe data.* That is, metadata itself may have attributes such as ownership and an expiry date, and so there is meta-metadata but we don't distinguish many levels, we just say that metadata is data and that from that it follows that it can have other data about itself. This gives the Web a certain consistency. (Berners-Lee n.d.)

Metadata takes the form of tags or markers that help identify all kinds of information. A metadata record consists of a set of attributes or elements necessary to describe the resource in question. For example, a common metadata system in libraries—the library catalog—contains a set of metadata records consisting of elements that describe books or other library items: author, title, date of creation or publication, subject coverage, and the call number specifying location of the item on the shelf (Hillmann 2001).

In practice, the basic metadata model is an "attribute type and value" model. Metadata is a set of facts about the resource (e.g., "title," "author") and each of those facts comprises an attribute or element. An attribute is composed of a type, which identifies the information contained in the attribute, and one or more values (the metadata itself). For example, the attribute "{Title} Tess of the d'Urbervilles" is a "Title" type and has the value "Tess of the d'Urbervilles."

1.2 NEW IMPLICATIONS OF METADATA

The way we work with and think about metadata is changing as metadata increasingly exists exclusively in distributed, heterogeneous networked information environments. So we have to deal with metadata differently.

As mentioned above, metadata is not a completely new concept. In China, when an old package contains something new, we say that the new drink is contained in an old bottle. However, when we apply this idiom to metadata, we might say that the old drink is contained in a new bottle. Though the philosophy of metadata comes from the remote past, with the development of technology and changes in society, something new has permeated the old concept.

Figure 1.1 contains two metadata samples that show the differences between records for different mediums.

Record 1 A bibliographic record of a traditional printed book

Title:	Future libraries : dreams, madness, & reality / Walt Crawford & Michael Gorman
Author:	Walt Crawford ; Michael Gorman *1941-*
Published:	Chicago [u.a.] : American Library Assoc., 1995
Extent:	VII, 198 S. ; 23 cm
Note:	Includes bibliographical references (p. 185–190) and index
ISBN:	0-8389-0647-8 *alk. paper
Subject heading:	*USA ; Bibliothek ; Automation *Libraries / United / Automation ; Libraries / United States
Subject:	06.54 Bibliotheksautomatisierung Z678.9.A4 025.00285
Decentral subject code:	AWD 600; ASR 350
Call number:	96 A 6727
Request info:	for loan presently lent ➤ Reserve

Figure 1.1 Two metadata samples.   (*Continued*)

Record 2 Metadata of the homepage of the Web site of MetaPhys: The Physics Meta Document Search Engine.

```
<meta http-equiv="Content-Type"

content="text/html; charset=iso-8859-1">

<meta name="keywords"

        content="physics, institute of physics, institute
    of physics publishing, electronic publishing, online
    products and services, electronic journals, scientific
    research, physical science, physics research journals,
    books and reference works, magazines, HyperCite, CoDAS
    Web, PhysicsWeb, PEERS, condensed matter, materials
    science, applied physics, engineering, mathematics,
    measurement science, plasma science, optics and optical
    science, atomic physics, molecular physics, high energy
    physics, particle physics, nuclear physics, physics
    education, computer science, astronomy and astrophysics,
    computational physics, neuroscience, medical physics,
    neural networks, neurobiology, psychology, sensors,
    optical systems, laser science and systems, fibre optics
    and fiber optics, geophysics, vacuum physics, quantum
    gravity, professional society, academic research,
    scientific computing, vacuum solutions, Physics Express
    Letters, physics news and information, conferences and
    exhibitions, jobs and employment, schools, colleges and
    universities, physicsnet, physics world, learned society
    Meta search Java Servlet MetaPhys MetaXChem engine
    crawler physics documents publisher publishers articles">

<meta name="owner" content="Peter Borrmann">

<meta name="contact"

        content="borrmann@uni-oldenburg.de,harting@uni-
    oldenburg.de">

<meta name="GENERATOR" content="Microsoft FrontPage Express
    2.0">

        <title>MetaPhys Physics Document Search Engine </title>
```

Figure 1.1 Two metadata samples. (Continued)

From the two metadata records we find some of the great differences in recording various mediums. The elements in Record 1, such as "Author," "Published," "Extent," "ISBN," and "Call number" are typical for printed books, a traditional medium. Comparatively, the second record is for a Web page, which is a product of the electronic age and relies on the latest medium, the network. Some new elements were born with networks, for example, "Content-Type" or "Generator." This example is just "a speck of a leopard": a tiny point demonstrating the new implications of metadata in the age of networks.

The following are the general innovations in current metadata:

- *New object*

  Metadata describes an object. Technological developments and societal changes result in changes in the types of objects described by metadata. The object might be a document carved on the mud board that was stored in the Alexander Library of Egypt several thousand years ago, while nowadays, it could be an electronic file transferred via the Internet. Paper has doubtlessly been the main medium for saving and transferring information in the past. Once societies enter the Internet age, paper, though still important, loses its dominant position and becomes replaceable. Academic conferences used to rely on proceedings in the form books or journal issues. However, some recent conferences, instead of providing paper proceedings, offered links to the papers on their websites. Furthermore, paper is not the most effective medium for saving and transferring some kinds of information, such as computing data of immense size.

- *New element*

  Obviously, different objects need to be described by different elements. The simpler the object, the fewer descriptive elements needed. For example, when describing a traditional print book, normally we just need elements such as title, author, edition, place of publication, year of publication, publisher, subject, page numbers, and so forth. However, with regard to electronic documents, some new elements, such as format, scheme, URL, and so on, might be necessary in addition to the traditional elements. Additionally, many traditional elements have new names. Previously, the element "Author" was used to describe the person who wrote a monograph. As a consequence of the increasingly complicated situation, this element is now entitled "Creator," a more adaptable term.

- *New context*

  Before the creation of the network, most metadata existed in niches. As networks increase in popularity, metadata has become part of the whole macroenvironment. The library catalog, the collection of bibliographic records that comprise one kind of metadata, is a good example of metadata developing in a niche. At first, every library had its own catalog that it did not share with other libraries; metadata existed in a niche. Eventually, in order to share resources efficiently, librarians invented the union catalog. Still, the union catalog was limited to certain subjects and physical locations. Finally, the ubiquitous use of computers and networks brought the catalog into a new era by overcoming temporal and spatial limitations. Currently, the metadata records of the online public access catalog (OPAC) can not only be used within the library for different processing procedures, but can also be accessed from all over the world for resource sharing. Relationships still exist among the different metadata records with respect to title, name, subject, and other clues. Furthermore, metadata can be connected directly with the object it describes via URL linkage. In addition, metadata and the object it describes existed separately beforehand. Nowadays it's possible either for metadata and object to be connected or for the metadata itself to exist within the object, such as in HTML documents.

- *New technology*

  In the course of its normal life cycle, metadata proceeds through five steps: creating, collecting, processing, organizing, and harvesting. Each one of these procedures has always depended heavily on technology. Advances in technology have greatly enhanced the availability of metadata and have made these procedures much easier than before. Manual work has been automated to a great degree. Technological advances, such as long-distance online communication, have even made previously impossible tasks easy. Before the existence of networks, if a researcher in China was interested in the size of a certain painting stored in the British Museum, it was quite difficult and time-consuming to learn such a detail. However, nowadays it takes a researcher mere seconds on the Internet to access the necessary metadata from the online catalog of the British Museum's collection.

- *New function*

  From its inception, the key function of metadata was to describe the profiles of the object and to facilitate locating the object. In library catalogs, a field such as the call number allows the reader to easily find the book's location. In the new information context, metadata has more functions than before. With the increasing use of HTML, metadata is increasingly used as a connection. In HTML, metadata is connected directly with the object it describes through hot links in the metadata. Furthermore, electronic files change so often that they are as unstable as paintings in the sand. Under these circumstances, archiving is very important for continuity and stability, factors in which metadata plays a critical role.

1.3 METADATA FUNCTIONS

In a large resource space, effective management of information resources increasingly relies on efficient management of metadata. The need for metadata services in the current information environment is clear. As the proportion of the intellectual record available through networks grows, appropriate metadata is a central component of a mature information, business, and technical environment. Effective metadata management will bring order to chaos, which will assist in the effective use of resources by humans and programs. "Metadata is knowledge which allows human and automated users [to] behave intelligently"(Dempsey and Rachel 1997).

The pyramid shown in Figure 1.2 illustrates the value of knowledge, with the least valuable data at its base. The ultimate purpose of knowledge creation and management

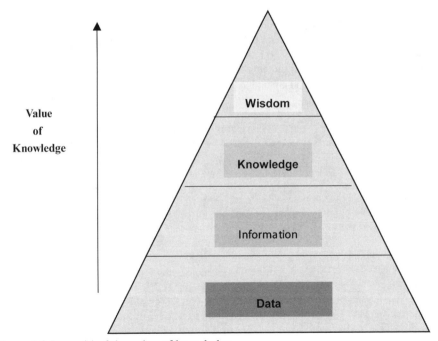

Figure 1.2 Pyramid of the value of knowledge.

is to sublimate data to wisdom through the procedure of data to information, information to knowledge, and finally knowledge to wisdom to knowledge, step-by-step. Data is the raw material for producing information that will lead to further advances. Metadata is essential for identifying and accessing the proper data for producing information and for properly managing data resources.

Iannella and Waugh (1997) argue that metadata has many functions that facilitate the use of electronic and nonelectronic resources on the Internet. Metadata makes it easier

- to summarize the meaning of the data (i.e., "What is the data about?");
- to allow users to search for the data;
- to allow users to determine if the data is what they want;
- to prevent some users (e.g., children) from accessing data;
- to retrieve and use a copy of the data (i.e., "Where do I go to get the data?");
- to instruct how to interpret the data (e.g., format, encoding, encryption);
- to help decide which instance of the data should be retrieved (if multiple formats are provided);
- to give information that affects the use of data, such as legal conditions on use, its size, or age;
- to give the history of data, such as the original source of the data and any subsequent transformations;
- to give contact information about the data, such as the owner;
- to indicate relationships with other resources (e.g., links to previous and subsequent versions, derived data sets, other data sets in a sequence, and other data or programs which should be used with the data); and
- to control the management of the data (e.g., archival requirements and destruction authority).

On the Web site of the Gateway to Educational Materials project, the main purposes of metadata are described as follows (Gateway to Educational Materials 2003):

- Creating metadata is important because metadata *facilitates the discovery of relevant information and resources*, digital and nondigital.
- Metadata *promotes interoperability* if accompanied by careful mapping of data elements and cross-walking standards.
- Metadata ensures that *resources will be accessible in the future.*
- Metadata can provide *persistent and unique digital identification* that assists in differentiating one object from another.
- Metadata also documents and tracks the layers of *rights and reproduction* that exist for digital objects and their multiple versions and the authenticity of version and provenance.
- Metadata *organizes information.*
- Problems with *polysemy* (words with multiple meaning, synonymy) can all be alleviated by the proper application of metadata, either manually or through selected harvesting.

Above all, the most important function of metadata is description. It's the basis for managing and organizing the information resources in a way that facilitates their retrieval. The wide-scale adoption of descriptive standards and practices for electronic resources will facilitate the retrieval of relevant resources from the "Internet commons"(Hillmann 2001). Thus, in addition to facilitating the capture and retrieval of structured information in research contexts, metadata can also "help organise electronic resources, foster their interoperability, verify their identification, and assure long-term preservation of them"(Turner n.d.).

Typically, metadata supports a number of functions, such as location, discovery, archiving, evaluation, selection, and so forth. These activities may be carried out by either human end users or their (human or automated) agents.

- *Description*

  Metadata may include descriptive information about the context, quality, and condition, or, characteristics of the data (Howe 1997). Metadata helps describe structured information in a uniform and stable way, and stores those descriptions on various supports. In doing so, metadata also plays a role in "providing context and allowing easy access and retrieval and understanding of the information over time and through changes in technology" (State Records Authority of New South Wales 2000). Weibel and Lagoze, two leaders in metadata development, once observed that "[metadata allows] access to the surrogate content that is distinct from access to the content of the resource itself"(Weibel and Lagoze 1997). As the Internet develops into a mixed information economy, deploying multiple application protocols and formats, the need for metadata will be all the greater.

In the above example, the metadata provides descriptive information about the poster, such as when it was created ("Created/published"), for what purpose it was created ("Summary"), to which subjects it relates ("Subjects"), on which medium it exists (the content of the element "Medium"), and so forth.

- *Location*

  Metadata provides information about the location of the object it describes. It enables searchers to find the information resource in a system and to see how it relates to other information resources. Traditional cataloging methods do not work for the Web; they are rendered insufficient by the proliferation of data. Metadata, described by Milstead and Feldman as "cataloging by any other name"(Milstead and Susan 1999), provides a way to organize Web information in a retrievable way. In Figure 1.3, the metadata element, "Call number," and its value, "POS—WPA—NY .01. C575, no. 1," indicates the location of the poster, allowing the searcher to find it. Another typical example is the metadata element, "URL," of a networked information resource, which indicates the location of the information resource in cyberspace.

- *Discovery*

  Metadata includes information about the object, such as title, creator, subject, location, and so on. Such information allows the searcher to not only navigate the information environment, but also to discover the exact information he or she really needs. Each element reflects a fact of the resource and provides access to the searcher. Metadata is not only essential to discovery, it will also be fundamental for the effective use of found resources (by establishing the technical or business frameworks in which they can be used) and to interoperability across protocol domains.

- *Archiving*

  Information about the edition of the information resource is sometimes a necessary part of its metadata. Such information is essential for archiving the information resource. Electronic files change editions so frequently that they are like "paintings on the sand." In addition, especially in the current networked age, the document occasionally changes location. Under the fluid

A bibliographic record describing a poster within the American Memory, the historical collections for the National Digital Library of the United States.

Community Center : Free - everybody welcome.
CREATED/PUBLISHED
N.Y.C. : Federal Art Project, [between 1936 and 1941]
SUMMARY
Poster promoting use of community centers for such activities as "athletic activities, cultural groups, arts and crafts, music and dancing, library and forum," as well as meeting rooms for club meetings, poster shows, musical instruments, tools, and sports equipment.
NOTES
Work Projects Administration Poster Collection (Library of Congress).
SUBJECTS
Community centers--New York (State)--New York--1930-1950.
Municipal services--New York (State)--New York--1930-1950.
Posters--1930-1950.
Screen prints--Color--1930-1950.
MEDIUM
1 print on board (poster) : silkscreen, color.
CALL NUMBER
POS - WPA - NY .01 .C575, no. 1
REPRODUCTION NUMBER
LC-USZC2-5316 DLC (color film copy slide)
REPOSITORY
Library of Congress Prints and Photographs Division
Washington, D.C. 20540 USA
DIGITAL ID
(color film copy slide) cph 3f05316
http://hdl.loc.gov/loc.pnp/cph.3f05316

Figure 1.3 A bibliographic record.

circumstances of the current electronic environment, metadata information is extremely important to the long-term preservation and discovery of information resources.

• *Evaluation and selection*

Metadata provides information that allows the user to identify appropriate resources without exploring the resources themselves. Metadata allows the user to evaluate an information resource's relative value or lack thereof. Once the available resources have been identified, the user may select the most useful information resource. Metadata allows the resource to be assessed in advance.

Additionally, it is said that metadata has other functions. For example, according to Milstead and Feldman, metadata elements resolve three specific language problems—polysemy, synonymy, and ambiguity—by providing consistent tagging with controlled vocabulary (Milstead and Feldman 1999).

As discussed above, metadata plays an important role in the retrieval, management, and use of information resources. However, many issues surrounding the effective support and deployment of metadata systems still need to be addressed.

REFERENCES

Berners-Lee, Tim. 1997. *Metadata Architecture.* Available at: http://www.w3.org/DesignIssues/ Metadata.html. Accessed 25 February 2003.

Caplan, Priscilla. 1995. "You Call It Corn, We Call It Syntax: Independent Metadata for Document-like Objects." *The Public-Access Computer Systems Review* 6(4). Available at: http://info. lib.uh.edu/pr/v6/n4/capl6n4.html. Accessed 25 February 2003.

Day, Michael. 2001. "Metadata in A Nutshell." *Information Europe* 6(2):11. Available at: http:// www.ukoln.ac.uk/metadata/publications/nutshell/. Accessed 11 April 2007.

DeCandido, GraceAnne A. 1999. *Metadata: Always More than You Think.* Available at: http:// www.ala.org/ala/pla/plapubs/technotes/metadata.htm. Accessed 11 April 2007.

DeCandido, Robert. 1999. "Metadata: What's It to You?" In *The Internet Searcher's Handbook.* 2nd ed., eds. Peter Morville, Louis B. Rosenfeld, and Joseph Janes, rev. by GraceAnn A. DeCandido, 37–49. New York: Neal Schuman.

Dempsey, Lorcan, and Rachel Heery. 1997. *DESIRE: Project Deliverable.* Available at: http:// www.ukoln.ac.uk/metadata/desire/overview/overview.rtf. Accessed 30 March 2003.

Dempsey, Lorcan, and Rachel Heery. 1998. "Metadata: A Current View of Practice and Issues." *Journal of Documentation* 54(2): 145–72.

EU-NSF Working Group on Metadata. n.d. *Metadata for Digital Libraries: A Research Agenda.* Available at: http://www.ercim.org/publication/ws-proceedings/EU-NSF/metadata.html. Accessed 23 June 2003.

Gateway to Educational Materials. 2003. *Why Should Metadata Be Created for Your Educational Resources?* Available at: http://www.geminfo.org/decision.html#1. Accessed 12 October 2003.

Hillmann, Diane. 2001. *Using Dublin Core.* Available at: http://www.dublincore.org/ documents/2001/04/12/usageguide/. Accessed 10 February 2003.

Hodge, Gail. 2001. *Metadata Made Simpler.* Available at: http://www.niso.org/news/Metadata_ simpler.pdf. Accessed 22 May 2003.

Howe, Denis. 1997. *Meta-data.* Available at http://foldoc.doc.ic.ac.uk/foldoc/foldoc.cgi?query = metadata. Accessed 14 May 2003.

Iannella, Renato, and Andrei Waugh. 1997. *Metadata: Enabling the Internet.* Available at: http:// archive.dstc.edu.au/RDU/reports/CAUSE97/. Accessed 14 May 2003.

Imperial College, Department of Computing. 1993. *FOLDOC: Free On-line Dictionary of Computing.* Available at: http://wombat.doc.ic.ac.uk/foldoc/. Accessed 22 April 2005.

Merriam-Webster, Inc. *Merriam-Webster Dictionary.* Available at: http://www.m-w.com/cgi-bin/ dictionary. Accessed 25 June 2003.

Milstead, Jessica, and Susan Feldman. 1999. "Metadata: Cataloging by Any Other Name." *Online* (January). Available at: http://www.onlinemag.net/OL1999/milstead1.html. Accessed 20 June 2003.

National Aeronautics and Space Administration. 1988. *Directory of Interchange Format Manual.* Version 1.0, July 13. NSSDC/WDC-A-R&S: 88–9.

Rust, Godfrey, and Mark Bide. 2000. *The <indecs> Metadata Framework: Principles, Model and Data Dictionary*. Available at: http://www.indecs.org/pdf/framework.pdf. Accessed 25 June 2003.

State Records Authority of New South Wales. 2000. *New South Wales Recordkeeping Metadata Standard*. Available at: http://www.records.nsw.gov.au/publicsector/rk/rib/rib18-en.pdf. Accessed 23 September 2003.

Turner, M. James. n.d. *What is Metadata?* Available at: http://mapageweb.umontreal.ca/turner/meta/english/metadata.html. Accessed 21 May 2003.

Weibel, Stuart, and Carl Lagoze. 1997. "An Element Set to Support Resource Discovery." *International Journal on Digital Libraries* 1: 176–86.

Wood, Andrew. 1997. *Metadata: The Ghosts of Data Past, Present, and Future*. Available at: http://archive.dstc.edu.au/RDU/reports/Sympos97/metafuture.html. Accessed 25 June 2003.

2

Metadata Types

A variety of metadata formats exist, and awareness of these formats is becoming more widespread. In fact, awareness of the focus, proper field, and even the advantages and disadvantages of the various formats allows one to choose the most appropriate format for a particular task.

Different repositories certainly have different requirements and priorities, which is the main reason so many different kinds of metadata are necessary. Some examples of different repositories are social science data archives, university Web sites, commercial publishers' collections of electronic journals, and archival finding lists. Objects on a university Web site may be briefly and simply described, while a data archive may need extensive documentation. In China we say that "it's not spring with just one flower." Only when hundreds of flowers bloom will the spring atmosphere fill the garden. Different kinds of metadata can coexist for long periods of time, and each of them has its own specific target.

2.1 GENERAL TYPOLOGY

Types of metadata develop in response to information management needs. Metadata functions are not limited to description. On a conceptual level, all metadata describes something. On the other hand, when we consider the functional use and intent of metadata, each type of metadata might have its own focus despite its most basic function of description. The typologies of metadata have developed in response to functional needs. For example, descriptive metadata is used for identification, discovery, and access, and can also help in evaluating resources. Record-keeping metadata, on the other hand, is used to order, validate, and archive an organization's resources, and, with the arrival of electronic information, is also a tool that can help ensure the significance, manageability, and longevity of records and the information they contain. Meanwhile, preservation metadata plays the specific role of contributing to the long-term conservation of digital resources. Whatever the particular uses of metadata, all types of metadata ensure short- and long-term access to resources through the physical and intellectual management of resources. Metadata schemes do not compete with one another, but instead coexist and indeed complement each other.

One of the most common typologies of metadata formats was advanced by Lorcan Dempsey and Rachel Heery. In Part II of the Development of a European Service for Information on Research and Education (DESIRE) project, the two professionals provide a thorough review of some major metadata formats (see Table 2.1). They suggest an approximate grouping along a metadata spectrum that becomes successively richer in terms of fullness and structure. For the purposes of analysis, they propose three bands within this spectrum, which allow them to sketch some shared characteristics across format groups. A format may not have all the characteristics of the band in which it is placed, but this grouping has proved beneficial in identifying the differences and similarities of formats.

An essential aspect of a format's richness is the extent of the content, both in terms of range and depth. The overall complexity of a format is dependent on the number of aspects of an object, such as designation or format rules for content, that are described.

With respect to the functional use and intent of metadata, Priscilla Caplan developed one of the simplest metadata typologies by classifying metadata into three groups: descriptive, administrative, and structural (2003, 3). Figure 2.1 is an example of the use of these three kinds of metadata from the Audio-Visual Prototyping Project of the U.S. Library of Congress (LC). The different focuses of various metadata can be seen very clearly from this example.

Table 2.2 is the present author's attempt to provide a slightly more in-depth and refined classification of metadata that is based on the experience of more senior colleagues.

In the following three sections, descriptive metadata, structural metadata, and administrative metadata (which includes preservation and technical metadata) will each be introduced briefly, and some representative examples will be given. It's quite difficult or even impossible to delineate every kind of metadata, so this chapter focuses only on the most common kinds of metadata in some fields. Furthermore, since this is not a thorough overview of metadata, the following sections mention only the most important or typical metadata schemes in each field.

Table 2.1 Typology of metadata formats created in the DESIRE project

	Band one	**Band two**	**Band three**
Record characteristics	Simple formats Proprietary Full text indexing	Structured formats Emerging standards Field structure	Rich formats International standards Elaborate tagging
Record formats	Lycos Altavista Yahoo, etc.	Dublin Core IAFA templates RFC 1807 SOIF LDIF	ICPSR CIMI EAD TEI MARC

Source: Dempsey and Heery 1997.

Descriptive metadata in the AV project
- For object as a whole
  - Often copy of descriptive data in LC central catalog
  - MODS XML schema (http://www.loc.gov/standards/mods/)
- Optional additional descriptive metadata for individual parts of object
  - Song titles, artists for disc sides, or cuts
  - Names of writers in manuscript file folder
  - MODS "related items"

Administrative metadata in the AV project
- Persistent identifier, ownership information
- Documentation of reformatting today and digital migration tomorrow
- About the source and actions taken to prepare items for digitization, for example, clean, bake
- About the digitizing process
- Rights data or at least categorization of objects for management of access

Structural metadata in the AV project
- Relationships between parts of objects
- Example: long-playing record album
  - Box, front
  - Three discs, two sides each (audio segments)
  - Disc label (images)
  - Booklet, cover, and 28 pages (images)

Figure 2.1 Three kinds of metadata included in the AV project.
Source: Fleischhauer 2003.

Table 2.2 Typology of metadata and their definitions

Type of metadata	Definition
Descriptive metadata	Metadata used to describe and identify the information resource.
Structural metadata	Metadata related to information about the structure of the information resource.
Administrative metadata	Metadata used in management of the information resource.
Preservation metadata	Metadata related to the preservation and archive of the information resource.
Technical metadata	Metadata dealing with technical details of the information resource in an information system.

2.2 DESCRIPTIVE METADATA

Descriptive metadata is metadata that describes and identifies information resources. Many standards have evolved for describing electronic resources. Nevertheless, most describe very specific resources and often rely upon complicated subject-specific schemes, which render the widespread adoption or easy accessibility of these records unlikely.

"Descriptive metadata is understood to serve the purposes of discovery (how one finds a resource), identification (how a resource can be distinguished from other, similar resources), and selection (how to determine that a resource fills a particular need, for example, for the DVD version of a video recording). Descriptive metadata may also be used for collocation (bringing together all versions of a work) and acquisition (obtaining a copy of the resource, or access to one)" (Caplan 2003, 3–4). The metadata in the following fields more or less serves these purposes. Metadata has been successfully developed in many domains. However, only typical examples in such areas have been chosen for the following parts of this section.

2.2.1 Library Cataloging Record

The library is said to be one of the earliest institutions to apply and practice the use of metadata. It has the longest tradition and most mature techniques in creating and using metadata, though these practices did not bear the name metadata until the networked age. When the library and information communities discuss metadata, the most commonly used analogy is the library catalog record. Priscilla Caplan, for example, once defined metadata as "a neutral term for cataloguing without the 'excess baggage' of the Anglo-American Cataloguing Rules or the MARC formats" (Caplan 1995). Therefore it isn't surprising that the library world is so involved in the current metadata research and applications. Even the most common metadata scheme, Dublin Core Elements Set, has absorbed many ideas from the library world and is described as the abridged edition of Machine-Readable Cataloging (MARC).

The term "cataloging record" means a bibliographic record, or the information traditionally shown on a catalog card. "The record includes (not necessarily in this order): (1) a description of the item, (2) main entry and added entries, (3) subject headings, and (4) the classification or call number" (Library of Congress 2003). The cataloging record serves as not only the description of the bibliographic information of the information resource but also the basis for other library procedures, such as acquisition, circulation, reference and system management.

International Standard Bibliographic Description (ISBD) and Anglo-American Cataloguing Rules (AACR) are the most important cataloging rules, and are commonly accepted all over the world. ISBD arose out of a resolution of the International Meeting of Cataloguing Experts, organized by the International Federation of Library Associations and Information Institutions (IFLA) Committee on Cataloguing in Copenhagen in 1969, to establish a standard for the form and content of bibliographic description. The ISBD for Monographic Publications was the first of the ISBDs developed pursuant to the 1969 mandate. As an international cataloging rule, ISBD has versions in different languages, and it was developed to be applicable to various cultural backgrounds. AACR is another important documentation system used in the library world for cataloging, access, and authority control. In September 2002, the *2002 Revision of Anglo-American Cataloguing Rules,* second edition, was published (American Library Association 2002). Furthermore, AACR3, the latest edition of AACR, will be published by the end of 2005 (American Library Association 2005). During the evolution of both the ISBD and AACR families, it's obvious that the compilers have kept in step with societal changes and technological developments.

Cataloging records have been increasingly created with computers since the 1960s. The MARC format was invented as a container for and as an exchangeable format of computerized bibliographic records. It is a format that defines elements set and the semantics of content designators, that is, the definitions of fields, subfields, indicators, and indicator values. Nevertheless, the content of the elements is defined by other standards, such as AACR2 or ISBD, mentioned above. In early 1999, the harmonized USMARC and CAN/MARC formats were issued under a new name, MARC 21. In August 2001, the British Library also decided to adopt MARC 21. In announcing its decision, the British Library indicated that it hoped "a major benefit would be in the future development of MARC to meet the challenge of new information sources, interoperability and interfacing with non-MARC metadata standards" (Pilling 2001). In general, MARC 21 has a more complex and specific set of data elements than other metadata schemes, such as Dublin Core. However, there are some data elements used frequently in other metadata schemes that MARC is unable to represent and which are of particular importance when describing online resources. For instance, MARC does not easily represent dates related to the creation, modification, and validity of online resources. A discussion paper, "Types of Dates for Electronic Resources in MARC 21 Formats," (Discussion Paper 2001-DP03) examines how these dates may be handled in MARC 21. MARC 21 has also added a new field, 887, to contain information from other metadata schemes that cannot be mapped to an existing MARC 21 field (Proposal No.: 2001–11; Kiorgaard and Whiting 2001). The Network Development and MARC Standards Office and a number of other organizations have also devised crosswalks or mappings between different metadata schemes and MARC. These metadata schemes that are MARC-compatible include Dublin Core, ONIX, Digital Geospatial Metadata, and the Government Information Locator Service (GILS). Converters are also available.

As its name suggests, a MARC record is a machine-readable cataloging record. The term "machine-readable" means that one particular type of machine, a computer, can read and interpret the data in the cataloging record. The invention of MARC led to both technical and organizational reforms in the library environment. It renders the sharing of bibliographic records through the library network possible. In Priscilla Caplan's words,

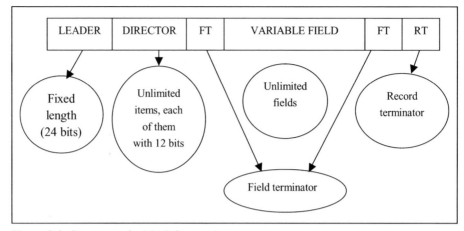

Figure 2.2 Structure of a MARC record.

"Shared cataloguing and similar library systems in turn reinforced a library culture of communication, cooperation, and respect for standards" (2003, 12).

With regard to the influence of MARC, it is important to remember that MARC itself is not a metadata scheme, but is a framework for traditional library cataloging. When people talk about MARC, they are referring to two things: a structure for machine-readable records and a set of very detailed and complicated encoding rules documented in the MARC 21 Format for Bibliographic Data and other LC publications. Because of its dual nature, MARC will be discussed in both chapter 2 and chapter 3.

A MARC record consists mainly of leader, directory, controlled, and variable fields. Figure 2.2 displays the simplest structure of a MARC record.

"The investigations into extending MARC and AACR2 to better accommodate the description of and access to the networked information resources began in 1991" (Guenther 2002, 41). The most remarkable addition to MARC, field 856 (Electronic Location and Access), allows the user to link from the bibliographic record to the resource itself. The addition of fields 720 (Added Entry—Uncontrolled Name) and 856$q (Electronic Format Type), which allowed cross walking between Dublin Core and MARC, were further changes to accommodate Dublin Core–type descriptions (see Figure 2.3). Undoubtedly, catalogers have made great efforts to meet the new requirements of the electronic age. The longevity of MARC shows its ability to evolve over time.

Michael Gorman, a world-famous library expert and theorist, believes that paper will continue to be used for the foreseeable future. He believes "'metadata', as presently conceived, will evolve toward standardization of elements and content and will be indistinguishable from real cataloguing in a relatively short time" (Gorman 2002, 181). Library cataloging will be further developed as an efficient method for recording worthwhile information resources in the near future. As resource creators have learned how to exploit the opportunities presented by information resources in general, and electronic resources in particular, these resources have developed rapidly. In parallel, each of the library standards—the ISBD, AACR2, and MARC—has shown a continuing ability to adapt and change.

```
Leader *****nam##*******#a
001 2521854
005 19950215082838.3
008 950215s1994####enk######b#####||||#eng##
040 ##$aDLC $cDLC $dDLC
050 00$aHA29$b.A5828 1993
082 00$a300/.1/5195 $220
245 00 $aAnalyzing qualitative data /$cedited by Alan Bryman and Robert G. Burgess.
260 ##$aLondon ;$aNew York :$bRoutledge,$c1994.
300 ##$axii, 232 p. :$bill. ;$c24 cm.
504 ##$aIncludes bibliographic references and index.
020 ##$a0415060621
020 ##$a041506063X (pbk.)
650 #0$aSocial sciences $xStatistical methods.
650 #0$aSocial sciences $xResearch $xmethodology.
700 10$aBryman, Alan.
700 10$aBurgess, Robert G.
856 4#$3Table of contents $uhttp://www.loc.gov/catdir/toc/93-3471.html
```

Figure 2.3 A MARC record with 856 link.

2.2.2 Archival Description Record

"Archives, by providing evidence of human actions and transactions, underlie the rights of individuals and states, and are fundamental to democracy and good governance. They are also central to defining the cultural identity of nations" (European Archive Network 2002). Archive materials, though they share some of the attributes of books, are by definition unique, and their arrangement and description is necessarily complex. Archival description implies that the documentation of both provenance and original order is of the most importance. Archives are normally registered as an aggregation or a series, which is an interrelated document collection rather than discrete objects.

Like the library world, the archive community also has a long tradition of description. According to the definition of the Society of the American Archivists (SAA), "Archival description is the process of capturing, collating, analyzing, and organizing any information that serves to identify, manage, locate, and interpret the holdings of archival institutions and explain the contexts and records systems from which those holdings were selected" (Society of American Archivists 1999). An archival catalog may be only one part of a more complex institutional descriptive system, which may include several other types of finding aids (e.g., registers, inventories, calendars, indexes, and shelf and container lists). "In such a system, a catalog record created according to these rules is usually a summary or abstract of information contained in other finding aids, which in turn contain summaries, abstracts, or lists based on information found in the archival materials themselves" (Hensen 1989). *Archives, Personal Papers, and Manuscripts* (APPM) makes it very clear that "cataloging is only one of a whole range of interrelated activities that comprise an archival descriptive program" (Hensen 1989).

Emerging archival metadata standards, such as International Standard for Archival Description (General) (ISAD[G]), International Standard Archival Authority Record for Corporate Bodies, Persons, and Families (ISAAR[CPM]), and Encoded Archival Description (EAD), refer primarily to the area of intellectual control—archival description for purposes of access to and retrieval of records—even if ISAD is somewhat broader and includes some standards for administrative and physical control (see Figure 2.4). Basically, "the standards reflect the complexity of archival description, paying full attention to the records context, content and structure" (Horsman 2000). ISAD (G) to archival description is the same as ISBD to bibliographical description. EAD deals with encoding archival description and will be discussed in the next chapter.

The very close relationship between the archive and library cataloging communities is evident. This relationship is further demonstrated by the following three points.

- It was a librarian working at the Library of Congress who published APPM in 1983. APPM is a standard manual of rules for archival description and cataloging, and has become the fundamental standard for cataloging archives and manuscripts. APPM was created on the basis and adopted the structural system of ISBD. Clearly, the compilation of APPM relied heavily on the experience gained from the library world.

- *The USMARC Format for Archives and Manuscripts Control (AMC)* was developed by the National Information Systems Task Force, a group formed by the SAA. As indicated by the title of the document, its origins lie in the USMARC format. Archivists and manuscript curators use APPM as the content standard for creating AMC records. "Most online catalogs are web-enabled and using the MARC 21 856 field (and soon 555 field) repositories that create catalog records for their archival materials and can link the MARC record directly to its corresponding finding aids for a given collection" (Kiesling 2002, 69)

- In addition to playing an important role in research libraries, the Research Libraries Information Network (RLIN), the catalog and cataloging system of the Research Libraries Group (RLG) in the United States, has become one of the main online union catalogs of archives and manuscript collections in the United Sates. As Ms. Kiesling comments, "Long as a supporter of archival cataloging, Research Libraries Group of the United States has created a search utility that simultaneously searches indexes built from the MARC records in the AMC file of its international RLIN database and from finding aids, in either EAD or HTML, submitted to the service" (Kiesling 2002, 69).

One important discrepancy between bibliographic description and archival description is that the finding aid is crucial during archival description. APPM has prescribed that the chief source of information for archival materials is the finding aid prepared for those materials. Finding aids describe archival materials, which can comprise anything from letters and diaries to photographs, sound recordings, and electronic data files. The relationship between EAD and finding aids is the same as that between MARC and catalog records, that is, the relationship between a communication format and data structure standard.

Title and Physical Description
Odessa State Archives fonds. -- 1799-1828. -- 11 microfilm reels, 16mm
Administrative History
The Odessa Region State Archives (SAOR) was established in 1920 as Odesa Historical Archive. Its main activities were to preserve, keep safe, conduct research and publish based on the archival documents of the territory of Odessa and the surrounding provinces of Odessa. The archives originated with 22 fonds and collections obtained from various organizations, agencies, and churches which ceased their activities after the Revolution. Since 1920, the main regional institutions have been systematically transferring their valuable records to SAOR for permanent keeping under protection of the State. By 1940, over 44,000 fonds were held by the SAOR. ...
Scope & Content
The fonds consist of The series consists of microfilms from fond 6, inventory 1 of the Board of Guardians held in the Odessa State Archives. Arranged chronologically by file number.
Source of Supplied Title
Title based on the contents of the fonds.
Source of Acquisition
Gift by Tim Janzen
Access Restrictions
None
Finding Aids
See Files Inventory & Film Contents Inventory
Online Resources:
www.scarch.kiev.ua/Eng/Odessa.php
Accruals
Expected
Notes
Accession 2002.024, 2002.025
Language - Russian and German
Last updated 28 Jul 2003 - Judith Rempel
Films Inventory
Accession2002.24
1 - Fond 6 (Board of Guardians) - Inventory 1 - Files 6-48
2 - Fond 6 (Board of Guardians) - Inventory 1 - Files 49-124
3 - Fond 6 (Board of Guardians) - Inventory 1 - Files 129-201
4 - Fond 6 (Board of Guardians) - Inventory 1 - Files 208-679
5 - Fond 6 (Board of Guardians) - Inventory 1 - Files 688-850
6 - Fond 6 (Board of Guardians) - Inventory 1 - Files 852-973
7 - Fond 6 (Board of Guardians) - Inventory 1 - Files 1018-1236
Accession2002.25
8 - Fond 6 (Board of Guardians) - Inventory 1 - Files 866-1750
9 - Fond 6 (Board of Guardians) - Inventory 1 - Files 1752-2407
10 - Fond 6 (Board of Guardians) - Inventory 1 - Files 2410-2600
11 - Fond 6 (Board of Guardians) - Inventory 1 - Files 2612-3055
Film Contents Inventory (Selected)
Film No. 6
File 858 - The business manager of the settlements, College Adviser Lifanov, made a suggestion to the Guardianship Office to send him information about the sowing and harvest of spring crops in the colonies supervised by the Guardianship Office in 1814 (91 pages) - 1813.
File 861 - The Chortitza Colony community wished to send two deputies, Jacob Enns and Gerhard Willems, to St. Petersburg to obtain Emperor Alexander the I's approval of the Charter of Privileges that had been given by Emperor Paul the I on September 6, 1800. The Chortitza Village Governments reported to the Guardianship Office about this (15 pages) - 1813.
File 867 - The Ekaterinoslav City Police wrote two official letters to the Guardianship Office regarding the necessity to bring the "prohibition against housing people without written residence permits" to the notice of the colonists. The first letter contains a demand to take the Mennonite Johann Brandt to the police and the second letter contains a demand to take the colonist Martha Brimer to the police as she had housed a woman who did not have a written residence permit (13 pages) - 1813.
(microfilm record sheet indicates: *File 870 (23 pages) - 1813*, but no documents were filmed for this.
File 872 - The Melitopol District Court sent a court decision to Inspector Sieber regarding a case concerning the Mennonite Gerhard Wiebe about the clandestine making of wine and other matters. Inspector Sieber reported to the Guardianship Office about this (60 pages) - 1813.
File 879 - Information about the arrest of the Mennonite Joseph Nowitzky by the Ekaterinoslav city police for not having a written residence permit. This was reported to the Guardianship Office (9 pages) - 1813.
File 880 - File concerning an incident in which the Mennonite Peter Boris? saw his horse with a man from the Caucasus, Anderm Scheneev, and had brought an action against him. The Melitopol District Court delivered a verdict stating that Anderm Scheneev was not guilty and that obliged Peter Boris? to pay legal costs of 15 rubles (21 pages) - 1813.

Figure 2.4 A MHSA archival description record structure of a MARC record.
Source: MHSA, Mennonite Historical Society of Alberta.

> ✓   High-level description of provenance
> ✓   Biographic sketch
> ✓   Corporate history
> ✓   Organizational profile
>   • Scope and content of the body of materials
> ✓   Description of individual groupings of materials
> ✓   Description of files
> ✓   Individual items

Figure 2.5 Components of a finding aid.

In practice, a finding aid does not necessarily include all the components mentioned in Figure 2.5. It will include more or less of them, depending on the individual case.

2.2.3 Metadata for Governmental Resources

The government and its various agents produce, collect, disseminate, and maintain large amounts of information, either in paper or electronic format. Organizing these information resources and providing access to them is very important for both the public and the government itself. These information resources inform the public about the services provided by the government and provide the framework for interaction between the state and its citizens. The government uses information resources to both inform the public of its work and assist its agencies in providing more effective and efficient services, especially in areas of Information Resource Management and public access to information.

"The European Commission estimates the value of public sector information at 68 billion Euro per year" (Government of Ireland 2002), and has recognized the potential of exploiting this information to boost economic activity and job creation. The use of metadata is essential if this potential is to be realized. It is widely accepted that use of metadata, in general, has considerable advantages. In addition to them, the application of metadata in current Electronic Government, or eGovernment can further (European Committee for Standardization 2003):

- enable public authorities to catalog their resources;
- provide citizens and businesses with access to nonelectronic resources;
- allow public authorities to publish governmental resources via the Internet to anyone in the world;
- contribute to the integration of public services online through the improved means of retrieval resulting from standardized data entry and description; and
- facilitate information sharing across public authorities and their systems.

So far, a number of European Union (EU) member states have done considerable work towards establishing national standards on the use of metadata for describing governmental resources. These include the United Kingdom, Ireland, Iceland, Finland, and Denmark. A lot of countries outside the EU have also established metadata application profiles for governmental resources. Some of these countries include the United States, Canada, Australia, and New Zealand. As it is said in the "Government On-Line Metadata Standard," "Establishing a metadata standard will ensure that, across domains and clusters and business functions, the effort that goes into assigning metadata is coordinated, cost effective and client-service focused. Adopting a metadata standard as the core which can be extended or mapped to for specific subject domains or purposes preserves high level consistency and interoperability" (Treasury Board of Canada Secretariat 2003, 2 [Purpose]).

It is readily apparent that Dublin Core has been widely adopted as the metadata standard for the government resources being implemented in various countries. The United States is a notable exception to this point. There, the metadata standard is the American Government Information Locator Service (GILS) system, which also serves as a kind of common model for official government information service systems all over the world, the official definition of which is "a decentralized collection of locators and associated information services used by the public either directly or through intermediaries to find public information throughout the U.S. Federal government" (National Institute of Standards and Technology. Department of Commerce n.d.). The Australian Government Locator Service (AGLS) metadata standard is one of the pioneers and an outstandingly successful example in this domain.

The AGLS metadata standard was developed between 1997 and 1998, in response to Recommendation 6 of the Information Management Steering Committee report, "The Management of Government Information as a National Strategic Resource." The National Archives of Australia is an agency that maintains this standard, which has been mandated for use by Commonwealth government agencies. "The AGLS metadata standard is a set of 19 descriptive elements which government departments and agencies can use to improve the visibility and accessibility of their services and information over the Internet" (Australian Government n.d.). It is based upon the 15 descriptors of the Dublin Core Metadata Elements Set (DCMES). Nevertheless, AGLS is a more complex element set than the Dublin Core standard, containing a number of element qualifiers that enable it to describe more categories of resources and allow it to provide a richer description of resources. Despite this, AGLS is entirely compatible and interoperable with the DCMES. AGLS is not intended to displace any other metadata standard. It is envisaged that AGLS will coexist with other metadata standards based on different semantics. Table 2.3 shows the AGLS metadata elements. In addition, AGLS metadata standard specifies some qualifiers that are additions to and extensions of the metadata elements. The qualifiers provide information about how the semantics (meaning) of an element have been refined, or about how the value (specific content) of an element should be interpreted.

An American GILS record is provided below (Figure 2.6) to illustrate the possible content of a GILS record. There are three types of information resources included in the American GILS system: locators for information dissemination products, automated information systems, and Privacy Act systems of records. Figure 2.6 is an automated information system.

Table 2.3 AGLS metadata elements

Obligation	Element name
Mandatory obligation	Creator Date Title
Conditional obligation	Availability Function Identifier Publisher Subject
Optional obligation	Audience Contributor Coverage Description Format Language Mandate Relation Rights Source Type

GILS records identify public information resources within the Federal Government, describe the information available in these resources, and assist in obtaining the information. Descriptive data about agency information resources in the form of structured metadata became a centerpiece of the evolving GILS concept. The GILS core metadata elements are shown in Figure 2.7.

The GILS application profile allows mapping between GILS and USMARC, since more agency users were thought to be familiar with USMARC. The mapping form has been recorded in the Appendix file. The Library of Congress Network Development and MARC Standards Office also built a mapping relationship between the 15 unqualified Dublin Core elements and GILS elements (see http://www.loc.gov/marc/dccross.html).

In fact, the American GILS system has had a worldwide effect on government information services. In Canada, the GILS record locator is also used as the identification mechanism for government information resources. GILS has become a critical component of the government's digital information delivery infrastructure. GILS has been proposed as a Global Information Locator within the G7 Global Information Society initiative. In February 1995, the G-7 Ministerial Conference participants approved a project for Environment and Natural Resources Management that incorporates a Global Information Locator, using GILS as a model. In Australia, the Environmental Resources Information Network has also experimented with the inclusion of GILS records on its Web server.

Title: Retained Records Database
Acronym: RET
Originator:
Department/Agency Name: National Archives and Records Administration
Name of Unit: Office of Records Administration
Local Subject Index:
Local Subject Term: US Federal GILS
Abstract: RET contains descriptions of unscheduled records as well as scheduled records that other Federal agencies have not transferred to the National Archives. Information contained in the database also includes the conditions under which the records are maintained, where they are located, the contact person, a tickler date indicating when the records should be re-evaluated, and scheduling data. The History File contains records previously listed in RET that have now been transferred to the National Archives or a Federal Records Center. The Oral History File contains descriptions of oral history projects through 1992. Routine updates and additions to the system occur semi-annually.
Begin Date: 1990
Purpose: The Retained Records Database was created to provide a centralized source of information about older series of permanent or potentially permanent records maintained in agency custody so that these records can be tracked and eventually transferred to the National Archives.
Agency Program: 44 U.S.C. 29 authorizes the Archivist of the United States to undertake certain records management functions.
Time Period of Content: 1755–
Availability:
Distributor:
Name: Office of Records Administration
Organization: National Archives and Records Administration
Street Address: 8601 Adelphi Road
City: College Park
State: MD
ZIP Code: 20740
Country: USA
Telephone: 301-713- 6677
Fax: 301-713-6850
Order Process: Currently, there is no on-line access to the system outside of the Office of Records Administration. Printouts from the system may be requested by calling or writing the Office. The first 100 pages are free; additional pages cost $.20 per page. Fees may be paid in cash, by check, or money order payable to the National Archives Trust Fund and must be paid in advance.
Technical Prerequisites: Connection to ICASS, IBM- PC compatible microcomputer
Sources of Data: The data come from physical inspections by National Archives staff.

Access Constraints: A password is required to make changes to the system.
Documentation: Technical Documentation manual; User Guide manual

Use Constraints: None.

Point of Contact:
Name: RET System Administrator
Organization: Office of Records Administration, NARA
Street Address: 8601 Adelphi Road
City: College Park
State: MD
ZIP Code: 20740
Country: USA
Network Address: kathleen.meman@arch2.nara.gov
Hours of Service: 8:00 A.M.–4:30 P.M.
Telephone: 301-713-6677
FAX: 301-713-6850
Supplemental Information:
Schedule Number: Scheduled: N1-64-93-3
Control Identifier: NARA0004

Record Source:
Department/Agency Name: National Archives and Records Administration
Name of Unit: Policy and IRM Services

Date of Last Modification: 19941215

Figure 2.6 A GILS record.

1. Title
2. Originator
3. Contributor
4. Date of publication
5. Place of publication
6. Language of resource
7. Abstract
8. Controlled subject index
9. Subject terms uncontrolled
10. Spatial domain
11. Time period
12 Availability
13. Sources of data
14. Methodology
15. Access constraints
16. Use constraints
17. Point of contact
18. Supplemental information
19. Purpose
20. Agency program
21. Cross reference
22. Schedule number
23. Control identifier
24. Original control identifier
25. Language of record
26. Date of last modification
27. Record review date

Figure 2.7 GILS core metadata elements.

2.2.4 Metadata for Art and Architecture Works

Art and architecture collections include audio, visual, and multimedia materials. These materials require the development of special kinds of metadata for information discovery and retrieval.

Libraries, academic institutions, archives, museums, historical societies, architectural domains, local/state governments, and private industries are increasingly converting documents and images and engaging in preservation projects, resulting in the creation of digital images depicting textual, visual, and artifactual collections. However, the metadata accompanying these images is very inconsistent. Activities have focused on descriptive or intellectual metadata, but relatively few efforts have addressed the types of information, sometimes categorized as structural and administrative metadata, that describe aspects of the capture process and certain technical characteristics of the digital images. The consistent recording of such information, whether in file headers or in separate associated files, will be critical to ensure that image files are and remain usable, and will require the development of specialized standards. It has been observed that "there is indeed a need for image specific metadata—as well as metadata at higher levels such as metadata that described the image production process, metadata that described the object, and metadata that described the project of which the image was a part, etc." (Bearman 2003).

"*Categories for the Description of Works of Art* (CDWA) is a product of the Art Information Task Force (AITF), which encouraged dialogue between art historians, art information professionals, and information providers so that together they could develop guidelines for describing works of art, architecture, groups of objects, and visual and textual surrogates" (Baca and Harpring n.d.). CDWA describes the content of art databases and articulates a conceptual framework for describing and accessing information about objects and images. The fields of CDWA Version 2.0 appear in Table 2.4.

VRA Core Categories is another important metadata standard for visual materials. "The Visual Resources Association (VRA) is an international organization of image media professionals. It is a multi-disciplinary community of image management professionals working in educational and cultural heritage environments" (Schwab 2003). "The VRA Core Categories, Version 3.0 consists of a single element set that can be applied as many times as necessary to create records to describe *works* of visual culture as well as the *images* that document them" (Visual Resources

Table 2.4 List of CDWA fields

Object, Architecture, or Gr

1.	Object/Work ♦	2.	Classification ♦
	Catalog Level		Term ♦
	Quantity		Remarks
	Type ♦		Citations
	Components		
	• Quantity		
	• Type ♦		
	Remarks		
	Citations		
3.	Orientation/Arrangement	4.	Titles or Names ♦
	Description		Text ♦
	Remarks		Type
	Citations		Date
			Remarks
			Citations
5.	State	6.	Edition
	Identification		Number or Name
	Remarks		Impression Number
	Citations		Size
			Remarks
			Citations

(Continued)

Table 2.4 Continued

Object, Architecture, or Group

7. Measurements ◆
    Dimensions ◆
    - Extent
    - Type
    - Value
    - Unit
    - Qualifier
    - Date
    Shape
    Size
    Scale
    Format
    Remarks
    Citations

8. Materials and Techniques ◆
    Description ◆
    Extent
    rocesses or Techniques
    - Name
    - Implement
    Materials
    - Role
    - Name
    - Color
    - Source
    - Marks
        - Date
    Actions
    Remarks
    Citations

9. Facture
    Description
    Remarks
    Citations

10. Physical Description
    Physical Appearance
    - Indexing Terms
    Remarks
    Citations

11. Inscriptions/Marks
    Transcription Or Description
    Type
    Author
    Location
    Typeface/Letterform
    Date
    Remarks
    Citations

12. Condition/Examination History
    Description
    Type
    Agent
    Date
    Place
    Remarks
    Citations

(Continued)

13. Conservation/Treatment History
    Description
    Type
    Agent
    Date
    Place
    Remarks
    Citations

14. Creation ♦
    Creator ♦
      • Extent
      • Qualifier
      • Identity ♦
      • Role ♦
      • Statement
    Date ♦
      • Earliest Date
      • Latest Date
    Place/Original Location
    Commission
      • Commissioner
          • Type
      • Date
      • Place
      • Cost
    Numbers
    Remarks
    Citations

15. Ownership/Collecting History
    Description
    Transfer Mode
    Cost or Value
    Legal Status
    Owner
      • Role
    Place
    Dates
    Owner's Numbers
    Credit Line
    Remarks
    Citations

16. Copyright/Restrictions
    Holder Name
    Place
    Date
    Statement
    Citations

(Continued)

31

Table 2.4 Continued

Object, Architecture, or Group

17. Styles/Periods/Groups/Movements
    Description
    Indexing Terms
    Remarks
    Citations

18. Subject Matter ♦
    Description
    • Indexing Terms ♦
    Identification
    • Indexing Terms ♦
    Interpretation
    • Indexing Terms ♦
    Interpretive History
    Remarks
    Citations

19. Context
    Historical/Cultural
    • Event Type
    • Event Name
    • Date
    • Place
    • Agent
      • Identity
      • Role
    • Cost Or Value
    Architectural
    • Building/Site
      • Name
      • Part
      • Type
      • Place
    • Placement
    • Date
    Archaeological
    • Excavation Place
      • Site
      • Site Part
      • Site Part Date
    • Excavator
    • Excavation Date
    Remarks
    Citations

20. Exhibition/Loan History
    Title or Name
    Curator
    Organizer
    Sponsor
    Venue
    • Name
    • Place
    • Type
    • Dates
    Object Number
    Remarks
    Citations

(Continued)

21. Related Works
Relationship Type
Relationship Number
Identification
- Creator
- Qualifier
  - Identity
  - Role
- Titles Or Names
- Creation Date
  - Earliest Date
  - Latest Date
- Repository Name
- Geographic Location
- Repository Numbers
- Object/Work Type
Remarks
Citations

22. Related Visual Documentation
Relationship Type
Image Type
Image Measurements
- Value
- Unit
Image Format
Image Date
Image Color
Image View
- Indexing Terms
- View Subject
- View Date
Image Ownership
- Owner's Name
- Owner's Numbers
Image Source
- Name
- Number
Copyright/Restrictions
Remarks
Citations

23. Related Textual References
Identification
Type
Work Cited
Work Illustrated
Object/Work Number
Remarks

24. Critical Responses
Comment
Document Type
Author
Date
Circumstance
Remarks
Citations

25. Cataloging History
Cataloger Name
Cataloger Institution
Date
Remarks

26. Current Location ◆
Repository Name ◆
Geographic Location ◆
Repository Numbers ◆
Remarks
Citations

27. Descriptive Note
Text
Remarks
Citations

◆ = indicates core category.
Source: J. Paul Getty Trust.

Association 2002). The following is a list of the elements included in the VRA Core Categories, Version 3.0.

- Record type
- Type
- Title
- Measurements
- Material
- Technique
- Creator
- Date
- Location
- ID Number
- Style/Period
- Culture
- Subject
- Relation
- Description
- Source
- Rights

Audio materials are the focus of the Library of Congress Audio-Visual Prototyping Project's current work. Between 1999 and 2004, it explored aspects of digital preservation for audio and video. The project developed approaches for reformatting recorded sound and moving image collections, and studied issues related to so-called born-digital audio-visual content. One key emphasis was the packaging or "wrapping" of digital content with a focus on metadata. "The project is an activity of the Motion Picture, Broadcasting, and Recorded Sound Division, joined by the American Folklife Center and other Library units. The prototyping effort is contributing to the planning for the new National Audio-Visual Conservation Center in Culpeper, Virginia, scheduled to open in 2005. The activity is coordinating its work with Library of Congress planning efforts concerned with the digital content life cycle and the design of repository systems to store, maintain, and deliver digital content" (Library of Congress 2003). The metadata of the project was first captured in a relational database and subsequently output as an Extensible Markup Language (XML) document. The prototyping project used the Metadata Encoding and Transmission Standard (METS) for a variety of extension schemas. METS metadata might provide core elements for a future archival information package.

Meanwhile, efforts in the field of metadata for multimedia have also been made in Europe. For example, the first CEN (i.e., the European Committee for Standardization)/ Information Society Standardization System (ISSS) workshop on Metadata for Multimedia Information (MMI) was held in Brussels on February 24th and 25th, 1998. In September 1999, CEN issued the "Model for Metadata for Multimedia Information," which set up a model of metadata for multimedia information. The model divides metadata for multimedia information into the following classes (European Committee for Standardization 1999):

- General
- Life cycle
- Meta-metadata
- Technical
- Use dependent
- Rights management
- Relation
- Annotation
- Security

The above classification of the model's metadata elements is based on the categories identified by the Institute of Electrical and Electronics Engineers, Inc. (IEEE) Learning Object Metadata Working Group.

2.2.5 Metadata for Educational Materials

Because of the information age's unprecedented increased rate and speed of change, learning continues throughout one's lifetime, instead of ending when one finishes school. Therefore, educational materials occupy a more important status in society. Learning throughout life is motivation for both the research and practice. As Pete Johnston observes, "e-Learning is big business, and likely to get bigger. Globally, the report estimates e-Learning to be worth $365 Billion by 2003" (Moe 2000). Educational resources, such as lesson plans, distance education curricula, and curriculum standards documentation, are increasingly accessed electronically through the digital libraries of educational institutions and online catalogs.

Metadata for educational materials is a description of learning objects, such as courses, subjects, learning materials, and so forth. "Educational metadata is necessary more or less for four points, which are information retrieval, content, access and modelling" (Gateway to Educational Materials 2003). "The stakeholder (suppliers and users) needs for metadata has now been extended to reuse, repackaging, preservation, context of use-associated features (annotations, grade & comments)" (Coleman 2002). In order to describe and manage educational materials more efficiently and to increase the possibility of discovering these materials, institutions have been increasingly involved in activities related to metadata for learning materials.

- *Learning Object Metadata (LOM)*

   The IEEE Learning Technology Standards Committee (LTSC) has provided support for the development and maintenance of the LOM standard since 1997. This process has been and continues to be "an international effort with the active participation on the LOM Working Group by members representing more than 15 countries" (Institute of Electrical and Electronics Engineers, Inc. 2002b). The LOM standards focus on the minimal set of attributes needed for the management, location, and evaluation of the learning objects. The standards facilitate the local extension of the basic fields and entity types, and allow the fields to be given the status of obligatory (must be present) or optional (may be absent). The learning objects' relevant attributes described by LOM include type of object, author, owner, terms of distribution, and format. Where applicable, LOM may also include pedagogical attributes, such as teaching or interaction style, grade level, mastery level, and prerequisites. It is possible for any given learning object to have more than one set of LOM. The elements of the metadata that are regarded as the "key educational or pedagogic characteristics" of a learning object in the IEEE LOM standard are (Institute of Electrical and Electronics Engineers, Inc. 2002a):

- Interactivity type—for example, Active, Expositive, Mixed, Undefined
- Learning resource type—for example, Exercise, Simulation, Questionnaire, Diagram, Graph, Self-Assessment
- Interactivity level—for example, very low, low, medium, high, very high
- Semantic density—for example, very low, low, medium, high, very high
- Intended end user role—for example, Teacher, Author, Learner, Manager
- Context—for example, Primary Education, Higher Education, University First Cycle, Continuous Formation, Vocational Training
- Typical age range—for example, 7–9, 0–5, 15, 18-
- Difficulty—for example, very easy, easy, medium, difficult, very difficult
- Typical learning time
- Description
- Language

The increasing popularity of the use of educational metadata with Dublin Core is a trend in learning technologies. "IEEE & DCMI have created a joint MOU (Memorandum of Understanding) to develop the education categories. In addition, the Centre for Educational Technology Interoperability Standards (CETIS) has been developing Metadata for Learning Resources standard (International Organization of Standardization [ISO] SC36) which is essentially about semantic interoperability" (The Centre for Educational Technology Interoperability Standards 2004). Since the inception of the Centre's work, its professionals have made an effort to create metadata that is compatible with LOM.

- *Metadata for Education Group (MEG)*

In an effort to reduce duplication, share experiences, and place the needs of the learner firmly at the fore, "public and private sector organizations responsible for creating, storing, using and delivering educational resources have come together in forming the Metadata for Education Group (MEG)" (Miller n.d.). Formed following a meeting of key UK stakeholders, "the *Metadata for Education Group* (MEG) serves as an open forum for debating the description and provision of educational resources at all educational levels across the United Kingdom. One of MEG's aims is to become the United Kingdom's forum for exchange of best practices and policy in the arena of learning resource metadata" (Miller 2002). The focus of MEG's work is explicitly *not* the creation of whole new standards for educational metadata. Rather, members focus upon developing a consensus as to the best approaches to a range of problems within the framework of existing standards and specifications. When new or revised standards are required, the recommendations are passed from MEG to the relevant national and international committees for action.

Table 2.5 GEM 2.0 metadata elements

Element name	Qualifier name
Audience	
	Mediator
	Beneficiary
	Level
	Age
	Prerequisites
Cataloging	
	Role
Contributor	
	Role
Coverage	
	Spatial
	Temporal
Creator	
	Role
Date	
	Created
	Valid
	Available
	Issued
	Modified
	PlacedOnline
	RecordCreated
Description	
	Table of Contents
	Abstract
Duration	
Essential Resources	
Format	
	Extent
	Medium
	Platform
Identifier	
	PublicID
	SID
	SDN

(*Continued*)

Table 2.5 (Continued)

Element name	Qualifier name
Language	
Pedagogy	
	Grouping
	TeachingMethod
	Assessment
Publisher	
	Role
Quality [Deprecated]	
	Authority [Deprecated]
	Criteria [Deprecated]
	Scale [Deprecated]
	Category [Deprecated]
Relation	
	conformsTo
	isVersionOf
	hasVersion
	isReplacedBy
	replaces
	isRequiredBy
	requires
	isPartOf
	hasPart
	isReferencedBy
	references
	isFormatOf
	hasFormat
	isParentOf
	isChildOf
	isSiblingOf
	isDerivedFrom
	hasBibliographicInfo
	isRevisionHistory
	isCriticalReview
	isOverview
	isContentRating
	isDataFor
	isSourceOf
	isSponsoredBy
	isStandardsMapping [Deprecated]

	isQualityScore
	isPeerReview
	isSiteCriteria
	isAgencyReview
	isOrderInfo
	isUserReview
Rights	
	PriceCode
Source	
Standard	
	Correlator
Subject	
	Keyword
Title	
	Alternative
Type	

Source: Gateway to Educational Materials 2003.

- *Gateway to Educational Materials (GEM) metadata*

"The Gateway to Educational Materials (GEM), a project of the U.S. Department of Education, is located at the Information Institute of Syracuse at Syracuse University. It is a consortium of more than 400 organizations and individuals who support the goals and mission of the GEM Project. Its metadata standards and technical mechanisms provide efficient, simple access to educational materials" (Gateway to Educational Materials n. d.) GEM metadata is based on a widely implemented and formally endorsed standard, the 15 Dublin Core elements. Currently there are 21 easy to use GEM metadata elements. GEM provides a metadata creation and editing tool (GEMCat). GEM metadata can also be generated from database collections. Table 2.5 shows the metadata elements of GEM Version 2.0. "GEM 2.0 fully integrates the Dublin Core qualifier decisions and recommendations of the Dublin Core Education Working Group" (Gateway to Educational Materials 2003).

2.2.6 Metadata for Geographic Resources

Internationalization and globalization have increased the need for geographic information for the purposes of local and distant cooperation, management, traveling, antiterrorism, and so forth. Metadata for geographic resources is a basic description of geographic information resources. According to the statement of the Federal Geographic Data Committee (FGDC) of the United States:

The major uses of such metadata are:

- to maintain an organization's internal investment in geospatial data,

- to provide information about an organization's data holdings to data catalogues, clearinghouses, and brokerages, and

- to provide information needed to process and interpret data to be received through a transfer from an external source (Federal Geographic Data Committee 1998).

The FGDC began work in the field of geographic metadata in early 1992. The Content Standard for Digital Geospatial Metadata (CSDGM) is one of the earliest geographic metadata standards. The first version of CSDGM was issued in 1994 by the FGDC. Executive Order 12906, "Coordinating Geographic Data Acquisition and Access: The National Spatial Data Infrastructure," was signed on April 11, 1994, by President William Clinton. Section 3, Development of a National Geospatial Data Clearinghouse, paragraph (b) states: "Standardized Documentation of Data...each agency shall document all new geospatial data it collects or produces, either directly or indirectly, using the standard under development by the FGDC, and make that standardized documentation electronically accessible to the Clearinghouse network" (Federal Geographic Data Committee 2003).

The objective of CSDGM is to provide a common set of terminologies and definitions for the documentation of digital geospatial data. "The standard establishes the names of data elements and compound elements (groups of data elements) to be used for these purposes, the definitions of these compound elements and data elements, and information about the values that are to be provided for the data elements" (Federal Geographic Data Committee 2003). A hierarchy of data elements and compound elements document a set of digital geospatial data by defining the information content for metadata. The starting point is the compound element "metadata" (section 0), which is composed of other compound elements representing different concepts about the data set. Each of these compound elements is part of a numbered section in the standard. The following 10 sections comprise the CSDGM standard (Federal Geographic Data Committee 1998):

- Identification information
- Data quality information
- Spatial data organization information
- Spatial reference information
- Entity and attribute information
- Distribution information
- Metadata reference information
- Citation information
- Time period information
- Contact information

Figure 2.8 clearly shows a portion of the metadata elements list of the section Identification information.

A key feature of the CSDGM Version 2 is that it allows geospatial data communities to develop customized profiles from the base standard. These communities extend the base standard profile by adding metadata elements that meet their specific metadata

1.1 Citation—information to be used to reference the data set.
Type: compound
Short Name: citation

1.2 Description—a characterization of the data set, including its intended use and limitations.
Type: compound
Short Name: descript

  1.2.1 Abstract—a brief narrative summary of the data set.
  Type: text
  Domain: free text
  Short Name: abstract

  1.2.2 Purpose—a summary of the intentions with which the data set was developed.
  Type: text
  Domain: free text
  Short Name: purpose

  1.2.3 Supplemental Information—other descriptive information about the data set.
  Type: text
  Domain: free text
  Short Name: supplinf

1.3 Time Period of Content—time period(s) for which the data set corresponds to the currentness reference.
Type: compound
Short Name: timeperd

  1.3.1 Currentness Reference—the basis on which the time period of content information is determined.
  Type: text
  Domain: "ground condition" "publication date" free text
  Short Name: current

Figure 2.8 A piece of the metadata elements list of the identification information section of CSDGM.
Source: Federal Geographic Data Committee 1998.

requirements. Another widely used metadata standard for geographic resources was developed by the Australian New Zealand Land Information Council (ANZLIC). "ANZLIC, the Spatial Information Council, is the peak inter-governmental council responsible for the coordination of spatial information management in Australia and New Zealand. It provides focus and leadership for the spatial information community" (ANZLIC Metadata Working Group 2001). ANZLIC has developed a metadata standard that sets out the minimum requirements for metadata to be included in the Australian Spatial Data Directory (ASDD). "The 'ANZLIC Metadata Guidelines' (version 2) were designed for use by data custodians to assist them to create, store and distribute core metadata elements and have been widely adopted" (ANZLIC Metadata Working Group 2001). All of the ANZLIC core metadata elements are displayed in Table 2.6.

ANZLIC has historically delivered metadata standards and profiles based on international best practices. The International Standards Organization (ISO) Technical Committee for Geographic Information/Geomatics (ISO/TC 211) worked on a standard for metadata known as ISO 19115:2003 ("Geographic Information: Metadata"). This international standard was published on May 8, 2003. Australia provided extensive input during the development of this standard, and as a result, ISO 19115 incorporates several ANZLIC core metadata elements.

With regard to ISO 19115:2003, the Digital Geographic Information Working Group (DGIWG) took a leading role in the project teams created to establish the second part of the standard ("Geographic Information: Metadata. Part 2, Metadata for Imagery and Gridded Data"); these teams also worked a lot on ISO 19139: 2003 ("Geographic Information: Metadata Implementation Specification"). Like CSDGM, ISO 19115:2003 also focuses on the digital geographic data. It defines the schema required for describing geographic information and services. It provides information about the identification, the extent, the quality, the spatial and temporal schema, spatial reference, and distribution of digital geographic data. ISO 19115:2003 standard defines (International Standards Organization n.d.):

- mandatory and conditional metadata sections, metadata entities, and metadata elements,
- the minimum set of metadata required to serve the full range of metadata applications (data discovery, determining data fitness for use, data access, data transfer, and use of digital data),
- optional metadata elements—to allow for a more extensive standard description of geographic data, if required, and
- a method for extending metadata to fit specialized needs.

Though ISO 19115:2003 is applicable to digital data, its principles can be extended to many other forms of geographic data, such as maps, charts, and textual documents, as well as nongeographic data.

Europe is home to one project related to metadata for geographic resources that should not be neglected. The project is entitled Infrastructure for Spatial Information in Europe (INSPIRE), and is a recent initiative launched by the European Commission and developed in collaboration with member states and accession countries. Its goal is to make available relevant, harmonized, and good quality geographic information to support the formulation, implementation, monitoring, and evaluation of community policies with a territorial dimension or impact. The INSPIRE initiative is not directly related to the use of metadata in eGovernment, but rather to the issue of sharing geographic information across Europe. "The approach followed by INSPIRE in the domain of geographic information paves the way for similar initiatives in other relevant domains such as the use of metadata in eGovernment" (European Committee for Standardization 2003). INSPIRE has been implemented in steps, beginning with the exploitation of the existing spatial data and spatial data infrastructures, then gradually harmonizing data and information services, and eventually allowing the seamless integration of systems and data sets at different levels into a coherent European spatial data infrastructure. The

Table 2.6 ANZLIC core metadata elements

Category	Element	Definition of Element	Obin	Max Occ	Field
Data set	ANZLIC Identifier	The unique identifier given of the dataset by ANZLIC.	M	1	Text(15)
	Title	The ordinary name of the dataset.	M	1	Text(160)
Custodian	Custodian	The business name of the custodial organisation or responsible party associated with the dataset.	M	1	Text(120)
	Jurisdiction	The state or country in which the Custodian of the dataset is domiciled.	M	1	Text(30)
Description	Abstract	A brief narrative summery of the content of the dataset.	M	1	Text(2000)
	Search Word	Words likely to be used by a non-expert to find the dataset.	M	N	Text(60)
	Geographic Extent Name	The ordinary name of one or more pre-defined, known geographic objects that reasonably show the extent of geographic coverage of the dataset. This element is usually implemented as three discrete elements as listed below	O	N	
	Gen Category	Category to which the Geographic Extent Name belongs including map series, local government area, and drainage divisions and major river basins.	C	11	Text(80)

(Continued)

Table 2.6 (Continue)

Category	Element	Definition of Element	Obin	Max Occ	Field
	GEN Custodial Jurisdiction	Country, state or territory that is responsible for maintaining the detail of the geographic object	C	11	Text(30)
	GEN Name	Name of the geographic object.	C	11	Text(80)
	Geographic Extent Polygon	Boundary enclosing the dataset expressed as a closed set of geographic coordinate (latitude, longitude) of the polygon referenced of describing geographic extent of the dataset if no pre-defined area is satisfactory.	O	N	Text(1000)
	Geographic Bounding Box	A rectangle defining the minimum and maximum coordinate of the entire data. This element is implemented as four discrete elements as listed below.	M	1	
	North Bounding Latitude	Northern-most coordinate of the limit of the dataset expressed in latitude, in decimal degrees.	M	1	Signed Real Number
	South Bounding Latitude	Southern-most coordinate of the limit of the dataset expressed in latitude, in decimal degrees.	M	1	Signed Real Number
	East Bounding Longitude	Eastern-most coordinate of the limit of the dataset expressed in longitude, in decimal degrees.	M	1	Signed Real Number
	West Bounding Longitude	Western-most coordinate of the limit of the dataset expressed in longitude, in decimal degrees	M	1	Signed Real Number

Category	Field	Description			Type
Data Currency	Beginning data	Earliest date at which the phenomena in the dataset actually occurred.	M	1	Text(10)
	Ending date	Latest date at which the phenomena in the dataset actually occurred.	M	1	Text(10)
Dataset Status	Progress	The status of the process of creation of the dataset.	M	1	Text(20)
	Maintenance and Update Frequency	Frequency of changes or additions that are made to the dataset after its initial completion.	M	1	Text(20)
Access	Stored Data Format	The format in which the dataset is stored by the custodian.	M	1	Text(500)
	Available Format Type	The format in which the dataset is available.	O	N	Text(240)
	Access Constraint	Any restrictions or legal prerequisites that may apply to the access and use of the dataset including licensing, liability and copyright.	M	1	Text(500)
Data Quality	Lineage	A brief history of the source and processing steps used to produce the dataset.	M	1	Text(4000)
	Positional Accuracy	A brief assessment of the closeness of the location of spatial objects in the dataset in relation to their true position on the Earth.	M	1	Text(4000)
	Attribute Accuracy	A brief assessment of the reliability assigned to features in the dataset in relation to their real world values.	M	1	Text(4000)

(Continued)

45

Table 2.6 (Continued)

Category	Element	Definition of Element	Obin	Max Occ	Field
	Logical Consistency	A brief assessment of the degree of adherence of logical rules of data structure, attribution and relationships. Data structure can be conceptual, logical or physical.	M	1	Text(4000)
	Completeness	A brief assessment of the extent and range in regard to completeness of coverage, completeness of coverage, completeness of classification and completeness of verification.	M	1	Text(4000)
Contact Information	Contact Organisation	Name of the organisation from which the dataset may be obtained.	M	12	Text(120)
	Contact Position	The position in the Contact Organisation that will answer questions about the dataset.	M	12	Text(40)
	Mail Address	Postal address or delivery point of the Contact Position.	M	22	Text(40)
	Locality	Locality associated with the Mail Address.	M	12	Text(60)
	State	Aust: State associated with the Mail Address. NZ: Optional extension for Locality.	M	12	Text(40)
	Country	Country associated with the Mail Address.	M	12	Text(40)
	Postcode	Aust: Postcode associated the Mail Address. NZ: Optional postcode for mail sorting.	M	12	Text(10)

46

Telephone	Telephone number of the Contact Position.	O	12	Text(25)
Facsimile	Facsimile number of the Contact Position	O	12	Text(25)
Electronic Mail Address	Electronic Mail Address of the Contact Position.	O	12	Text(80)
Metadata Date	Date on which the metadata record was created or modified.	M	1	Text(10)
Additional Metadata	Any additional metadata the supports documentation of the dataset including a reference to another directory or report.	O	1	Text(4000)

[1] Dependent upon the repeatability of the parent element.

[2] Number of occurrences associated with each contact—a data set may have many contacts.

Source: ANZLIC Metadata Working Group 2001.

first step focused on harmonizing the documentation of existing data sets (metadata) and on the necessary tools to make this documentation accessible.

2.2.7 Dublin Core Metadata Elements Set

All of the metadata schemas mentioned above do not focus on networked resources. This section introduces the Dublin Core Metadata Elements Set (DCMES, Dublin Core, for short, or simply DC), which is used to describe a wide range of networked resources from their creation. Due to the expanding range of its applications, the types of objects described by Dublin Core have extended greatly. It has become a kind of metadata standard, and has been used or referenced in more areas and disciplines than any other metadata scheme. "Dublin Core may have a role as a minimal metadata set in order to allow for interoperability between other, more complex, metadata formats. ... It is possible that if Dublin Core metadata is attached to or embedded in a large number of Web documents, a new generation of Web robots or harvesters could collect this metadata and make it available through improved search services" (Day 1997).

The DCMES was created to address the difficulty in finding items of interest on the Internet. Automatically indexing all information resources on the Internet is problematic. Searching very large collections may yield large result sets. If the collection contains resources from different fields of study, the differences in jargon may cause additional problems. For instance, the term "period" is used quite differently in mathematics than it is in geology. Furthermore, "Resources may not have a description at all except a filename, which may not describe its contents" (Weibel, Godby, and Miller 1995). Each of the formats mentioned above was developed to operate within a narrowly defined field of work, and is poorly suited to the description of a wide range of resources. Many of these existing metadata schemes are also extremely complex, and "have not been developed for use by the general public, but were instead developed to be created by experts and interpreted by computers" (Miller 1996). The Dublin Core Metadata Initiative (DCMI) intends to create a set of common terms that are accessible to the widest possible audience, thereby maximizing the compatibility and sharing of metadata across various fields. As Stuart L. Weibel outlined in his presentation at the IFLA Satellite Meeting held in the summer of 2003 at the Goettingen State and University Library:

DCMI has played the following unique roles (three "I"s):

International

  20+ languages in the DCMI metadata registry

  Participants from 50 countries

Independent

  Not bound to country, institution or industry: accountable to its stakeholders

Open (Influenceable)

  Governance and decision-making based on open participation and public process (Weibel 2003).

The primary goal of DCMES, defined during the first Metadata Workshop (the Online Computer Library Center/National Center for Supercomputing Applications

(OCLC/NCSA) Metadata Workshop) held in Dublin, Ohio in 1995, is to facilitate resource discovery regardless of the subject or the complexity of the information resource. DCMES discovers and describes document-like objects (DLOs). The mission of the first Metadata Workshop was to define a single sheet of guidelines that could be distributed to the widest possible audience. To complete this mission, "The core element set had to be short, the data elements had to be reasonably easy to understand and to provide, and the elements had to apply broadly to most of the resources under consideration" (Caplan 1995). The principles of intrinsicality, extensibility, syntax independence, optionality, repeatability, and modifiability were followed during the development of the DC elements (Weibel 1995).

The DCMES is a method of organizing and accessing information on the Web. The challenge is not only to create a universally agreed upon set of elements, but also to foster widespread use of those elements. Presently, there are a total of 15 elements in the DCMES. These elements and their labels are displayed below in Table 2.7. The DCMES was presented as the minimum number of metadata elements required to facilitate the discovery of DLOs in a network environment such as the Internet.

Unlike a more formal description method such as MARC, the DCMES is not bound by strict rules. All elements are optional and may be repeated without any constraint. The syntax of the elements is simply the name—or Identifier—and the value of the element. The value may consist of free text, or it may be taken from a standardized resource. The description may reside in a separate file, or it may be a part of the information resource itself. While no formal syntax rules have been developed, several

Table 2.7 The DCMES elements

Element name	Label
Title	Title
Creator	Creator
Subject	Subject and key words
Description	Description
Publisher	Publisher
Contributor	Contributor
Date	Date
Type	Resource type
Format	Format
Identifier	Resource identifier
Source	Source
Language	Language
Relation	Relation
Coverage	Coverage
Rights	Rights management

Source: Dublin Core Metadata Initiative 2003.

syntax recommendations have been created for generic text files, such as HTML and the Resource Description Framework (RDF).

The DCMES is a simple resource description format. "It has attracted considerable attention recently, partly because of the eloquence and consensus-building activity of it principal proponent, but importantly because it has situated itself as a potential solution for some pressing requirements" (Weibel 1995). The DCMES is targeted to provide the foundation for semantic interoperability between domains where metadata is richer than Dublin Core. The core set of data of a richer record format might be mapped onto Dublin Core to provide a common set of elements for discovery purposes in various service and technical environments; for example, there was discussion about creating a Dublin Core–based attribute set for Z39.50. The creators and developers of almost all the above-described metadata schemas have established mapping relationships between their schemas and Dublin Core. In some areas, the metadata developers even directly import elements of the DCMES and base their own application profiles directly on the Dublin Core. Much attention has also been paid to the converse mapping. The document, "CWA 14856: Guidance Material for Mapping between Dublin Core and ISO in the Geographic Information Domain," is one such outstanding effort. The results reported in the document are important in facilitating wider exploitation of the Dublin Core technique in conjunction with geographic information. A new standard on geographic metadata was ratified by ISO in 2003 (e.g., ISO 19115:2003), making the issue of interoperability of geographic metadata particularly timely. Furthermore, the DCMI also continues broadening its adoptability by creating various application profiles that satisfy the requirements of different areas and disciplines. Evidently, the Dublin Core is a kind of metadata that has been most commonly used in a wide range of areas. For example, the Dublin Core Spatial Application Profile exists for geographic resource description and discovery, while the Dublin Core eGovernment Application Profiles are used for the metadata in governments' electronic domain. To summarize, the Dublin Core is indisputably the most widely used and referenced metadata standard to date.

Nevertheless, the Dublin Core is not omnipotent. While the Dublin Core metadata supports the four user tasks set forth in "Functional Requirements for Bibliographic Records: Final Report" (IFLA Study Group on the Functional Requirements for Bibliographic Records 1998) to varying degrees, Dublin Core lacks established rules and procedures to govern the content of data elements, which makes its elements less reliable than cataloged data. "The explicit simplicity of the element set and the fact that all elements are optional also undermines the reliability of Dublin Core metadata" (American Library Association 1998). Although some initially hoped that the Dublin Core would eventually replace all other metadata schemes, it is now clear that this will not come to pass. Table 2.8 shows a general conclusion about DCMES, which is the result of an objective evaluation.

Two points must be taken into consideration when employing DCMES metadata. First, that DCMES metadata was originally created to describe the resources available on the Internet and was then applied to a wider range of subjects. The second point is that the Dublin Core was initially designed to describe only DLOs. Fortunately, researchers have recognized that the experience gained from describing DLOs could be used to extend the DCMES to describe other more complicated materials. According to the DESIRE project's report, "The DCMES could be extended in two ways. Firstly, it could be extended to accommodate elements which contain other types of metadata: terms and conditions, archival responsibility, administrative metadata and so on. Secondly,

Table 2.8 A general conclusion about the DCMES

Dublin Core *is not*	Dublin Core *is*
○ a replacement for existing detailed metadata schemes.	• a useful means by which discrete data types and sets may be described in a comparable fashion.
○ they still have an (important) role to play.	• small enough to remain manageable, yet extensible enough to (hopefully) be suitably descriptive.
○ a means for describing data sets, concepts, or subject issues in great detail.	• a fascinating example of interdisciplinary and international cooperation.
○ the answer to all our problems (!).	• (if used in conjunction with the concepts of the Warwick Framework) an extremely powerful means of drawing complex metadata and data together, facilitating access and reuse.
○ Many of the problems encountered by workshops were not with Dublin Core itself, but were related to more generic data description and cataloging issues.	
○ In many cases, workshops began by confusing their external issues with those integral to Dublin Core.	

Source: Miller 1999.

it could be designed for resource description of different levels of fullness and within different communities" (Dempsey and Rachel 1997).

Since the field of social work has so many subdivisions, a comprehensive metadata scheme for this field is impractical. No single metadata scheme could fulfill the diverse requirements of social work and all its divisions. The varied problems in social work metadata require a variety of solutions. The most practical solution is to develop metadata schemes that complement each other or are compatible with at least one of the most popular metadata schemes in the field. The relationship between MARC and the DCMES in OPAC is a good example. Priscilla Caplan thought that "librarians need to see the DCMI as a complementary, not a competitive, effort that needs the librarians' participation to succeed. This is an area full of tradeoffs, and he didn't believe the librarians had yet found the appropriate balance between effort and utility" (Caplan 1995). As Lorcan Dempsey argued, "Dublin Core metadata descriptions exist between the crude metadata currently employed by search engines and the complex mass of information encoded within records such as those for MARC or the Federal Geographic Data Committee" (Dempsey 1996).

2.3 STRUCTURAL METADATA

"Structural metadata is metadata that describes the types, versions, relationships and other characteristics of digital materials" (Arms, Blanchi, and Overly 1997). It is data that defines the logical components of complex or compound objects and how to access these components. A simple example is a table of contents for a text document. A more complex example is the definition of the different source files, subroutines, and data definitions in a software suite.

Structural metadata describes the internal organization of a resource. In a digital environment, information resources often comprise multiple physical files. For instance, the official Web site of METS is composed of a series of Web pages. Figure 2.9 shows METS's home page, which consists of 10 sections (e.g., "News and Announcements," etc.), and each section includes several links. Each link leads to a particular Web page. Here, structural metadata describes the hierarchical system and indicates the section in which each Web page belongs. For example, the "METS Opening Day Now Open for Registration (August 5, 2003)" Web page is included in the section "News and Announcements" rather than in "Upcoming Events." In addition, structural metadata also either links the user directly to the specific document, or returns the user to the original Web page.

Structural metadata displays and navigates a particular object for a user and includes information about the internal organization of that object. For example, "A given diary has three volumes: volume one is comprised of two sections called *dated entries* and *accounts* respectively; the entry section has two-hundred entries; entry twenty is dated August 4th, 1890 and starts on page fifty of volume one" (Library of Congress 1998a). Structural metadata exists in various levels of complexity. The diary example above is a rich structure that may be created for an important work and would include a transcription of the digitized handwritten pages. The structure of the diary could be encoded in this transcription, and the structural metadata could be extracted from the same. At the other extreme, structural metadata might be as simple as a diary with only enough structural metadata to turn the pages.

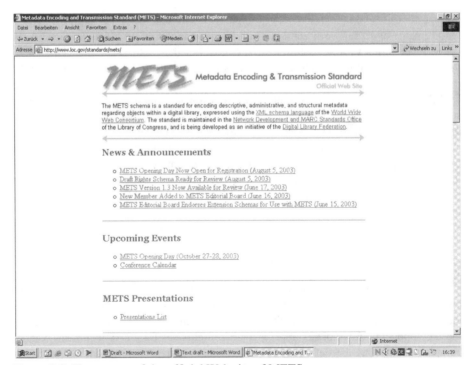

Figure 2.9 Home page of the official Web site of METS.

Table 2.9 is a practical example that illustrates how various structural metadata attributes are used to represent information related to digitized items stored in the LC digital repository.

Structural metadata also has other functions in the situation illustrated by Table 2.9.

- For digital objects with multiple versions, structural metadata includes metadata specific to the particular version being described. The structural metadata might include fields for description, owner, handler of metaobject, data size, data type (e.g., "jpg"), version number, description, date deposited, use (e.g., "thumbnail"), and the date of the last revision.

- For the metaobject, "Structural metadata is the metadata that applies to the original photograph and to all of its versions. It includes a description, the owner, the number of versions, the date deposited, the use ("meta-object"), and the date of last revision. If bibliographic information were to be included, it would be added to this part of the meta-object" (Arms, Blanchi, and Overly 1997).

- Structural metadata is used for the creation and maintenance of information warehouses, and fully describes the structure and content of the information warehouse. Structural metadata's basic foundation is composed of descriptions of its data entities, their characteristics, and how they relate to one another. "Structural metadata identifies the system of record for all information warehouse data entities. It also fully describes the integration and transformation logic for moving each information warehouse entity from its system of record to the information warehouse. In addition, structural metadata defines the refreshment schedule and archive requirements for every data entity" (Perkins 2004).

Table 2.9 Structural metadata of the numbered 10-page article

Image	Contains	Data element relationship (Rel)		Page information (PI)	
		Rel type	Rel value	PI type	PI value
First	Text	00002	001:010	0003	1
Second	Text	00002	002:010	0003	2
Third	Text	00002	003:010	0003	3
Fourth	Text	00002	004:010	0003	4
Fifth	Text	00002	005:010	0003	5
Sixth	Text	00002	006:010	0003	6
Seventh	Text	00002	007:010	0003	7
Eighth	Text	00002	008:010	0003	8
Ninth	Text	00002	009:010	0003	9
Tenth	Text	00002	010:010	0003	10

Data Element Relationship Type 00002 = Presentation Sequence.
Page Information Type   0003 = Printed Page Number.
Source: Library of Congress 1998b.

Table 2.10 Structural metadata for one digital object

Attribute	Field name	Required	Repeatable
Handle	Handle	Yes	No
Description	Description	Yes	Yes
Original content type	Orig_content_type	Yes	No
Rights and permissions	Rights_and_permissions	Yes	Yes
Owner of digital object	DO_Owner	Yes	No
Number of data elements	Num_data_elements	Yes	No
Number of instances	Num_instances	No	No
Parent object information	Parent_object_info *Not yet fully defined*	No	Yes

Deposit information
  Date deposited
  Time deposited
	Deposit_info
	  Date_deposited
	  Time_deposited
		Yes	No

Digital object use	DO_use	Yes	No
Special function	DO_special_function	No	No

Last revision
  Date last revised
  Time last revised
	Last_revision
	  Date_last_revision
	  Time_last_revision
		Yes	No

Data element	See the table at URL: http://lcweb.loc.gov:8081/ ndlint/repository/de-attribs	Yes	Yes

Source: National Digital Library Program 1998.

Table 2.10 below lists the structural metadata of the LC Digital Objects used in the Digital Repository Development Project, implemented by the National Digital Library Program of the US Library of Congress. This structural metadata supports static visual material (e.g., photographs, images of text document pages), Standard Generalized Markup Language (SGML) encoded documents, sound recordings, and dynamic visual material (e.g., video tape, motion pictures). This list was intended to be comprehensive, and includes recommendations for the full set of possible structural metadata attributes for the digital object.

2.4 ADMINISTRATIVE METADATA

Administrative metadata is metadata used for the management of information resources. Some administrative metadata manages the information resource throughout its life cycle, while other metadata only manages the resource during specific periods of its life cycle. Administrative metadata includes information about certain technical factors (e.g., the device or device setting used in digitizing the items), information about rights or restrictions, and other information of value to those who manage the digital resource. This section will discuss not only general administrative metadata, but also preservation metadata, technical metadata, and rights metadata, which are crucial to the administration of information resources and are applied to particular aspects of information resource management.

2.4.1 Administrative Metadata

In fact, there is no clear distinction between descriptive and administrative metadata schemes. Some data elements can be used in both descriptive and administrative contexts. For example, DCMES is mainly a descriptive metadata scheme, but it also includes some elements that have administrative functions, such as "rights," "relation," and so forth. Furthermore, some metadata elements may be both structural and administrative, and may be used for similar purposes in those two areas. For example, "content type" is a structural metadata element used to present available file formats to a service, while "file format" is an administrative metadata element that informs system administrators of a particular file's format. Nevertheless, most schemes tend to focus on one aspect of metadata. For the purposes of the present, administrative metadata means metadata whose primary function is administrative.

Administrative metadata contains the information object's management information, such as its creation date, the file format of its content (JPEG, JTIP, etc.), rights information, and so forth. The administrative metadata in the following example contains the elements required for managing a Web site. This sample solution was put forward during the Institutional Web Management Workshop sponsored by UKOLN (UK Office for Library and Information Networking 1998):

- **Author** or **Creator:** the person (or organization) responsible for the intellectual content of the resource.
- **Maintainer:** the person (or organization) responsible for maintaining the resource.
- **Review-by:** a date after which the resource should be (manually) reviewed by the maintainer.
- **Delete-by:** a date after which the resource should be (automatically) deleted or moved to an archive area.
- **Creation-date:** the date on which the intellectual content of the resource was originally created.
- **Web-creation-date:** the date on which the resource was originally made available in its current (online) format.
- **No-index:** indicates that the resource should not be indexed by robots or local indexing software.

Administrative metadata consists of the information that allows the repository to manage its digital collection. The information includes:

- Data related to the creation of the digital image (date of scan, resolution, etc.);
- Data that can identify an instantiation (version/edition) of the image and help determine what is needed to view or use it (storage or delivery file format, compression scheme, filename/location, etc.) and;
- Ownership, rights, and reproduction information (Library of Congress 1998a).

Administrative metadata is especially critical for long-term file management. Without well-designed administrative metadata, image files may be as unrecognizable and unreadable a decade from now as Wordstar or VisiCalc files are today. Administrative metadata should help future administrators determine a file's format, when it was created, original from which it was created, the methods or personnel that might have introduced artifacts into the image, and the location of different parts of this or related digital objects. It is hoped that administrative metadata will eventually help objects take care of their own long-term management.

Certain administrative metadata elements (such as file formats) have always been contained in file headers, while others have been housed in accompanying databases, and this situation is not expected to change greatly. Nevertheless, increasing amounts of administrative metadata is being stored in the file header so that the metadata can be updated more easily and quickly.

Table 2.11 is an example of administrative metadata attributes. The example focuses on a small set of attributes describing a collection-level description (CLD) record, using

Table 2.11 Administrative metadata attributes

Attribute label	RDF property	Definition
Date CLD created	dcterms:created	The date (in W3C-DTF format) on which the content of the CLD was created.
Creator of CLD	dc:creator	The name of the agent who created the content of the CLD.
Date CLD last modified	dcterms:modified	The date (in W3C-DTF format) on which the content of the CLD was last modified.
Modifier of CLD	dc:contributor	The name of the agent who modified the content of the CLD.
Publisher of CLD	dc:publisher	The name of the agent who published the CLD, e.g., the organization or project making this CLD available.
Language of CLD	dc:language	The language (in the form of a value from the RFC 3066 scheme) of the CLD.
Source	dc:source	The identifier (URI) of another metadata record from which this CLD is derived. For example, if this CLD is derived from a richer record, such as an Encoded Archival Description (EAD) finding aid, then this would be the identifier of that finding aid.
Rights	dc:rights	A statement about rights held in or over the CLD and/or any restrictions on the use of the CLD.
Audience for CLD	dcterms:audience	A class of entity for whom the CLD is intended or useful.

Source: Johnston 2002.

properties taken from the DCMES. All attributes are optional. The prefixes in the XML-qualified names are assumed to be associated with XML namespace names as follows:

dc: http://purl.org/dc/elements/1.1/

dcterms: http://purl.org/dc/terms/

2.4.1.1 A-Core

Normally, the organizations responsible for maintaining information resources have their own internal systems for handling their resources with application-specific metadata schemes. It is rare that any one administrative metadata scheme is adopted by a wide range of applications. In practice, this situation means that the interoperability of administrative metadata records among different applications is inevitable. Accordingly, the DCMI established a working group on this issue. The DCMI Administrative Metadata Working Group was constituted on October 6, 2000, with the goal of proposing an element set for the management of metadata, based on the Admin Core - Administrative Container Metadata (A-Core).

"A-Core, metadata about metadata, is useful to designate information about the provenance, management or administration of other sets of descriptive metadata. The objective of A-Core is to provide simple verification of the integrity, ownership, and authorship of metadata retrieved from networked resources. The A-Core elements are utilised to associate the instruments (who, what) with the events (when) of the process of metadata management" (Iannella and Campbell 2000). Administrative Dublin Core (A-Core) is indeed a kind of administrative metadata scheme. However, it focuses on the management of the information resource's metadata rather than on the resource itself. That's why A-Core is considered meta-metadata.

There are four main categories of A-Core elements:

- Who, what, when
- Validity dates
- Metadata location
- Rights ownership

Iannella and Campbell define the A-Core as following:

Metadata about metadata—referred to as the A-Core—is useful to designate information about the provenance, management or administration of other sets of descriptive metadata. The objective of A-Core is to provide simple verification of the integrity, ownership, and authorship of metadata retrieved from networked resources. The A-Core elements are utilised to associate the instruments (who, what) with the events (when) of the process of metadata management. (Iannella and Campbell 1999)

Each A-Core element is formally described using a set of nine attributes from the ISO 11179 standard. These include:

- Name—The label assigned to the data element

- Identifier—The unique identifier assigned to the data element
- Version—The version of the data element
- Language—The language in which the data element is specified
- Definition—A statement that clearly represents the concept and essential nature of the data element
- Obligation—Indicates if the data element is required to always or sometimes be present (contain a value)
- Datatype—Indicates the type of data that can be represented in the Value of the data element
- Maximum Occurrence—Indicates any limit to the repeatability of the data element
- Comment—A remark concerning the application of the data element (Iannella and Campbell 2000).

It is important to recognize that A-Core is a so-called accessory metadata element set, as opposed to a content metadata element set. It was created to be used by systems and users to determine the currency and integrity of content metadata and to provide details on how to contact entities involved in the management of content metadata.

During the DC-8 held in Ottawa in the year 2000 and the DC-9 workshop held in Tokyo in the year 2001, the proposed A-Core element was discussed and drew much attention. Nevertheless, the A-Core discussed here is not limited to DCMES, but is intended to apply to as many metadata schemes as possible.

The following is an example of A-Core metadata elements using the HTML META syntax (Iannella and Campbell 2000):

```
<head>
  <link rel  = "schema.DC"
    href   = "http://purl.org/DC/elements/1.0/">
  <link rel  = "schema.AC"

    href   = "http://metadata.net/ac/2.0/">

<META NAME="DC.Title" CONTENT="Saving the Forests">
<META NAME="DC.Creator" CONTENT="Nicola Corks">
<META NAME="DC.Type" CONTENT="Article">
<META NAME="DC.Contributor" CONTENT="Maddie J (photographer)">
<META NAME="DC.Date.Modified" CONTENT="1999-03-09">

<META NAME="AC.name" CONTENT="Crystal, Jacky">
<META NAME="AC.email" CONTENT="jacky@tree-online.com">
<META NAME="AC.contact" CONTENT="Phone 555 11111">
<META NAME="AC.activity" CONTENT="created">
<META NAME="AC.date" CONTENT="1999-01-01">

<META NAME="AC.name" CONTENT="Oldman, Sam">
<META NAME="AC.email" CONTENT="sam@tree-online.com">
<META NAME="AC.contact" CONTENT="Phone 555 22222">
<META NAME="AC.activity" CONTENT="modified">
<META NAME="AC.date" CONTENT="1999-03-10">
```

```
<META NAME="AC.dateRange" CONTENT="1999-01-01/1999-12-31">
<META NAME="AC.rights" CONTENT="Copyright Trees Journal 1999">
</head>

Note: The HTML META encoding does not provide any element
grouping mechanism. It is assumed that the order of the
elements will be preserved.
```

2.4.2 Technical Metadata

Technical metadata records the technical details in an information system, such as the functions of the information systems or the behaviors of metadata. It documents the creation and technical characteristics of the object, and its components vary greatly in different applications.

One of the most commonly mentioned examples of the effort to standardize technical metadata is the National Information Standards Organization (NISO)'s NISO Technical Metadata for Digital Still Images Standards. Technical metadata, which describes various aspects of image characteristics and the capture process, is increasingly perceived as an essential component of any digitization initiative. Technical metadata is required not only to support the quality assessment, enhancement, and processing of images, but is also crucial for the long-term collection management necessary to ensure the longevity of digital collections. The goal of the NISO Technical Metadata for Digital Still Images Standards initiative is to "develop a generalized technical metadata standard applicable to all images regardless of their method of creation" (Elkington 2001). The *Data Dictionary for Technical Metadata for Digital Still Images* (National Information Standards Organization and AIIM International 2002) presents a comprehensive list of the technical data elements required to manage digital image collections. Version 1.0 of the working draft of the standard was released on July 5, 2000, and trial use was valid until December 31, 2003. The technical metadata elements were grouped into four categories: basic parameters, image creation, performance assessment, and change history. Basic parameters include format information, such as Multipurpose Internet Mail Extensions (MIME) type and compression, and file information, such as file size, checksum, and orientation. Image creation elements record detailed information about whether the image was captured with a digital camera or was scanned from an analog source. The performance assessment elements are designed to "serve as metrics to assess the accuracy of output (today's use), and to assess the accuracy of preservation techniques, particularly migration (future use). These include spatial metrics, such as image length and width, and non-spatial metrics, such as the number of color components per pixel. Change history elements are designed to document any editing operations performed on the image, including the responsible party, the date and time, and the software used" (Caplan 2003, 153).

Table 2.12 is extracted from the Digital Repository Service (DRS) system of the Harvard University Library and is a concrete example of technical metadata. In the first section, it lists the image metadata required for digital still images by the DRS system. As shown in Table 2.12, the system applies a total of 11 image metadata elements to digital images. The values of these data elements are constructed to facilitate parsing and reporting. Data in the mandatory fields (1–3, 6) and mandatory-if-applicable fields

Table 2.12 Technical metadata for the digital still image

Number	Name	Definition
1	bitspersample	The number of bits per component for each pixel. This field provides N values, depending upon the number of components (or channels) in the image.
2	compression	Designates the compression scheme used to store the image data.
3	photointerp	Designates photometric interpretation, the color space of the decompressed image data.
4	xres	Designates the number of pixels per *resunit* in the image width.
5	yres	Designates the number of pixels per *resunit* in the image length.
6	resunit	Designates the intended placement of pixels in the *xres* and *yres* dimensions of the printed image.
7	qualitylayers	Number of quality layers to which each JPEG2000 image tile has been decomposed. Useful in determining the number of lower quality images that can be extracted from the JPEG2000 image.
8	reslevels	Number of resolution levels to which each JPEG2000 image tile has been decomposed. Useful in determining the size of the smallest subresolution thumbnail image available in the JPEG2000 image.
7	imagewidth	Designates the number of columns per image, i.e., the total number of pixels in the horizontal or X dimension.
8	imageheight	Designates the number of rows per image, i.e., the total number of pixels in thevertical or Y dimension.
9	orientation	Designates the orientation of the image, with respect to the placement of its columns (imagewidth) and rows (image-height), as it was saved to disk..
10	targetnotes	Designates the name of the "internal" target(s) scanned in-frame with the source item.
11	history	Designates the image change history.

Source: Harvard University Library 2002.

(4–8) are used to process image files in order to produce new deliverables or to migrate master files. Optional data (fields 9–13) is collected to support image processing in some cases, and to generate summary collection assessment reports for data managers and object owners. The definitions in Table 2.12 indicate each element's function.

2.4.3 Preservation Metadata

"Preservation metadata is metadata related to the preservation of the information resource. Metadata could be used as a means of recording migration and emulation strategies, ensuring the authenticity of digital objects, noting rights management and collection management issues and will also be used for resource description and discovery" (Day n.d.). Preservation metadata is the information infrastructure that supports the processes of digital preservation. More specifically, it is the information necessary to maintain the long-term *viability*, *renderability*, and *understandability* of digital resources. It can serve as "input to preservation processes, and also record the output of these same processes" (OCLC/RLG Working Group on Preservation Metadata 2002).

There is a growing awareness that metadata has an important role in preserving information resources. "Metadata does have an acknowledged role in the organisation of and access to networked information, but it could additionally be important in the general area of digital preservation" (Day 1997). Preservation metadata is integral to an information system that ensures the long-term preservation of resources. The creation and deployment of preservation metadata is likely to be a key component of most digital preservation strategies. "Rapid changes in the means of recording information, in formats for storage, in operating systems, and in application technologies threaten to make the life of information in the digital age 'nasty, brutish, and short'" (Waters 1998). The need for preservation metadata has become increasingly dire, especially for so-called born-digital material which is increasingly popular but is generally fragile and transient. More than any other type of media, digital information resources require detailed metadata to ensure that they persist through various transformations, thereby ensuring their preservation and accessibility for future generations. "Preservation metadata may, have a useful role in helping ensure that digital information will be available to future generations" (Day 1997).

It is now widely accepted that identifying and recording appropriate metadata is a crucial part of any strategy for preserving digital information objects. "If one ignores the technology preservation option, there are currently two main proposed strategies for long-term digital preservation: first the emulation of original hardware, operating systems and software; and secondly the periodic migration of digital information from one generation of computer technology to a subsequent one" (Ross 1997). The emulation approach requires the development of an annotation scheme that can save a human-readable form of the data, along with metadata that provides the historical, evidential, and administrative context for preserving digital documents. As Michael Day suggested, "Successful migration strategies will, depend upon metadata being created to record the migration history of a digital object and to record contextual information, so that future users can either reconstruct or—at the very least—begin to understand the technological environment in which a particular digital object was created" (Day 1999). Regardless of whether emulation- or migration-based preservation strategies are adopted—and it is likely that both will have some role—the long-term preservation of digital information will involve the creation and maintenance of metadata. Clifford Lynch once described metadata as follows:

Within an archive, metadata accompanies and makes reference to each digital object and provides associated descriptive, structural, administrative, rights management, and other kinds of information. This metadata will also be maintained and will be migrated from format to format and standard to standard, independently of the base object it describes (1999).

Lynch's comments indicate that preservation metadata must be able to do more than simply support the implementation of a particular preservation strategy. Michael Day has suggested, for example, that "metadata could be used to help ensure the authenticity of digital objects, to manage user access based on intellectual property rights information as well as for more traditional metadata applications like resource description and discovery" (Day 2001). In practice, preservation metadata, by supporting the management of digital objects in an archival setting, also fulfills an administrative function. Preservation metadata can also serve a structural function, by handling the relationships between multiple objects in an archival repository. For example, several archived objects might collectively represent a single complex object. Metadata could bind the constituent components together.

A research project at the University of Pittsburgh School of Library and Information Science has been investigating "Functional Requirements for Recordkeeping," and has identified and specified the fundamental properties of records. The project identified the functional requirements for recordkeeping as follows: records must be comprehensive, identifiable, complete, authorized, preserved, removable, exportable, accessible, and redactable. The project suggested that records (or "Business Acceptable Communications") should have metadata structured in six layers, which would contain not only a "Handle Layer" (including a unique identifier and resource discovery metadata), but also very detailed information on terms and conditions of use, data structure, provenance, content, and the use of the record after its creation. The metadata is intended to carry all the information necessary for the use of the record—even when the "individuals, computer systems and even information standards under which it was created have ceased to be" (Bearman and Sochats 2004).

Preservation metadata has been developed to support and facilitate the long-term retention of digital information. It is crucial to preserve the integrity and ensure the persistence of such information.

In detail preservation metadata may be used to:

- store technical information supporting preservation decisions and actions
- document preservation actions taken, such as migration or emulation policies
- record the effects of preservation strategies
- ensure the authenticity of digital resources over time
- note information about collection management and the management of rights (OCLC/RLG Working Group on Preservation Metadata 2001).

One of the most important problems cultural heritage professions face in the early twenty-first century is the long-term preservation of information in digital form. Hedstrom defines digital preservation as "the planning, resource allocation, and application of preservation methods and technologies necessary to ensure the digital information of continuing value remains accessible and usable" (Hedstrom 1998, 190). One of the widespread approaches to preservation metadata for digital resources emerged in 1997. In May 1997, the RLG constituted the Working Group on the Preservation Issues of Metadata. The goal of this working group is to ensure that the information essential to the continued use of digital resources is captured and preserved in an accessible form. A preliminary report provided the semantic framework for the 16 preservation metadata elements it identified, which are listed below:

1. Date
2. Transcriber

3. Producer

4. Capture device

5. Capture details

6. Change history

7. Validation key

8. Encryption

9. Watermark

10. Resolution

11. Compression

12. Source

13. Color

14. Color management

15. Color bar/Grayscale bar

16. Control targets (Research Libraries Group 1998).

As a further step, in March 2000, OCLC and RLG sponsored the creation of a working group to build a consensus on preservation metadata. The group began its work by publishing a white paper entitled, "Preservation Metadata for Digital Objects: A Review of the State of the Art," which "defined and discussed the concept of preservation metadata, reviewed current thinking and practice in the use of preservation metadata, and identified starting points for consensus-building activity in this area" (OCLC/RLG Working Group on Preservation Metadata 2001). The most valuable work and the main focus of the working group is the collaborative development of a framework for preservation metadata. This comprehensive preservation metadata framework describes the set of essential preservation metadata elements needed to support the framework, examines implementation issues associated with preservation metadata, and creates testbed/pilot applications.

There is a tendency in digital preservation metadata—at least among the library projects—to use the terminology defined by the Open Archival Information System (OAIS) model as a basis for discussion. Michael Day reached a similar conclusion after a review of the recent developments in digital preservation metadata. "The OAIS model is important for digital preservation standards and strategies because it defines the functions and requirements for a digital archive by providing terminology, conceptual data models, and functional modes for interoperable open archives" (Day 2000). The model was defined as an organization of people and systems taking responsibility for preserving information and making it available for a designated community. The OAIS model has proliferated rapidly through the digital preservation community, and has been explicitly adopted by, or has at least informed, many prominent digital preservation initiatives. Because of the rapid diffusion and great influence of the OAIS model, the working group sponsored by OCLC and RLG selected the OAIS model to organize the preservation metadata framework. The OAIS information model is illustrated in Figure 2.10.

The OAIS reference model lays much of the foundation necessary to achieve the working group's objectives. In particular, it describes a conceptual framework for a complete, generic archival system, along with a complementary information model. Indeed,

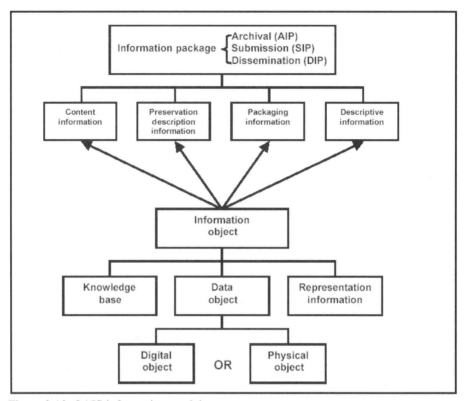

Figure 2.10 OAIS information model.
Source: OCLC/RLG Working Group on Preservation Metadata 2001.

"Several ongoing digital preservation initiatives (e.g., the CEDARS and NEDLIB proj-ects) have explicitly adopted the OAIS framework. In this regard, the OAIS could rep-resent common ground, in the form of shared terminology and concepts, linking the variety of institutional backgrounds and initiatives represented in the Working Group membership"(OCLC/RLG Working Group on Preservation Metadata 2001).

Another international project, PREservation Metadata: Implementation Strategies (PREMIS)—also sponsored by the OCLC Office of Research, OCLC Member Services, and RLG—is forthcoming. The working group's goal is to develop recommendations and best practices for implementing preservation metadata. The project began in June 2003 and ended one year later. Using the metadata framework as a conceptual founda-tion and starting point for its work, the PREMIS working group continued the activities of the first working group. The PREMIS group is focused on the practical aspects of implementing preservation metadata in digital preservation systems.

2.4.4 Rights Metadata

Ownership is a concept that has been rooted in the human mind almost from the inception of human society. From the time intellectual labor was identified as some-thing to be respected, intellectual property rights (IPR), an extension of the concept of ownership, have begun to be protected and at the same time somewhat restricted. However, the birth of digital media has made it increasingly difficult to cope with IPR because of the extreme ease of copying, modifying, or delivering digital objects. Table 2.13 is a comparison of the effect of various different information carriers on intellectual rights.

Copyright law, developed for a world dominated by printed material, has had to be enriched significantly to adapt to the current situation. Rights management in the digital environment is a new challenge. New solutions are required to address the issues raised by the more complicated context. As before, to give permission or enforce restrictions for using, modifying, or broadcasting an information object, it is necessary to have separate documents attached to the information object. When this statement is taken at face value, it describes rights metadata.

Rights metadata is metadata primarily designed to enable rights management when dealing with information resources. Chris Rusbridge commented that "rights metadata is necessary for coping with use for learning and teaching (E-reserve, on demand publishing, etc.), scholarly monograph crisis, Disney-dominance and lead times" (Rusbridge 1999). As Renato Iannella observed, "It's concerned with digital management of rights rather than management of digital rights" (Iannella 2001).

Rights enforcement is complicated. Rights are bestowed by law, and national copyright laws grant different rights depending on the material being protected. In the United Kingdom, for example, "The rights conferred on an author of a literary work are to authorise or prevent copying the work; issuing copies of the work to the public; performing the work in public; broadcasting the work or including it in a cable programme service; and to make an adaptation of the work or do any of the above in relation to an adaptation, in most cases for the duration of their lifetime plus seventy years"

Table 2.13 Impacts of carrier

Physical carrier	Digital carrier
Books, journals, magazines, recordings, videos, etc.	Data sets, e-journals, e-books, etc.
Terms and conditions from copyright law – Complex but consistently applicable – Includes educational exceptions (e.g., fair use)	Licences based on copyright law – Varied terms and conditions – Restriction or loss of educational exceptions (e.g., fair use)

Information access through
– ownership (purchase: allows royalties)
   o term: indefinite
– borrowing (public lending right)
– copying (CLA licences, etc.)
	Information access through
	– licenses (even CD-based objects)
	– often remotely hosted (implies continuing cost)
	   o term: while you pay
	– no borrowing
	– no copying

Source: Rusbridge 1999.

(United Kingdom, Stationery Office Limited 1988). The duration of copyright and interpretations of the term "copy," for instance, vary for different materials. "The rights which might be dealt with could be divided into the following categories" (Martin and Pearson 2001):

- Transport

    Governs the creation and movement of persistent copies of a work under the control of trusted repositories.

    - COPY—create a new copy of a work
    - TRANSFER—an existing authorized copy moves to another repository
    - LOAN—loan a copy for a period of time

- Render

    Governs the creation of representations of a digital work outside of the control of trusted systems.

    - PLAY—make an ephemeral copy available for use
    - PRINT—make permanent copies to external media
    - EXPORT—makes a digital source copy available outside of trusted system control

- Derivative work

    Governs the reuse of a digital work, in whole or part, to create a new composite work. Not intended to cover all possible forms of reuse; rather automate the simple case where the rights owner can predetermine fees and repository-testable conditions on a work.

    - Extract, Edit, and Embed

- File management

    Governs access to directory and file information in operations when two repositories are connected, for example, when exercising rights that engage multiple repositories, such as TRANSFER or LOAN. Also, controls the making and restoring of backup copies.

    - FOLDER, DIRECTORY, DELETE, VERIFY, BACKUP

- Configuration

    Governs the adding and removing of system software from secure repositories.

    - INSTALL, UNINSTALL

Rights metadata makes the above-listed rights as clear as possible. Rights metadata should involve the following:

- Restrictions on use
- Permission statements
- Subscriber/licensing/pay-per-use fees
- Acknowledgements
- Copyright notice
- Retention schedules

- Use disclaimers
- And so forth

Rights metadata fall into three distinct categories, which can be described as follows (Rust 1998):

- Requests—the specified use to which a party wishes to put a creation
- Offers—the terms under which a creation may be put to specified uses
- Agreements—the terms of a completed transaction

As shown in Figure 2.11, rights metadata is key to the management of both the digital repository itself and its utilization. In practice, rights metadata prescribes the kind of user authorized to retrieve or access each resource. In other words, the audience is described by rights metadata. Furthermore, some rights metadata clarifies the kind of processes that can be applied to the digital resource. In the present context, rights metadata exists between the stakeholder and user, two groups with different rights to the content of the digital resource. To the content provider and administrator, rights metadata allows them to add new records, delete unsuitable or obsolete records, modify existing records, and so on. To the user, rights metadata grants permission or restricts rights to search and access records. Rights metadata is necessary for content providers and administrators of different levels. The rights of stakeholders and administrators to upload, reinforce, or modify, and so forth, the digital repository differ based on the levels of those stakeholders

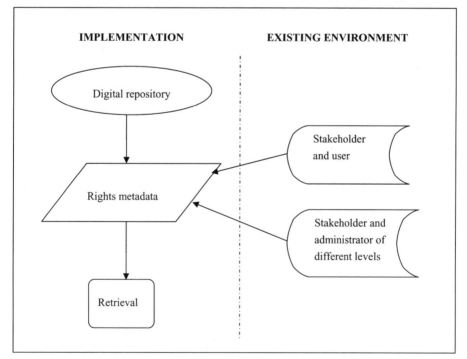

Figure 2.11 A rights metadata model.

and administrators, with higher level content providers and administrators detaining more rights to the digital content.

Rights specifications must be formally expressed in a machine-readable form, so that permissions, restrictions, and conditions can be unambiguously determined. Accordingly, a number of attempts have been made to model the seemingly endless number of permutations of rights expressions. These models are expressed in Digital Rights Expression Languages (DRELs). There are currently two main DREL players: eXtensible Rights Markup Language (XrML) and Open Digital Rights Language (ODRL).

According to one announcement, "The METS community has developed an interim solution for rights metadata until other larger standards can be hashed out" (Metadata Encoding and Transmission Standard 2003). The Rights MEtadata for Open archiving (RoMEO) Project is a very good example of a project directly related to rights metadata.

"The RoMEO Project launching at the Loughborough University was funded by Joint Information Systems Committee of the United Kingdom for one year (1 August 2002–31 July 2003). It's aimed at investigating the rights issues surrounding the 'self-archiving' of research in the UK academic community under the Open Archive Initiative's Protocol for Metadata Harvesting (OAI-PMH)" (Project RoMEO n.d.). The project developed some simple rights metadata to protect the e-print papers in an open-access environment. It also tried to "investigate the issues relating to the IPR protection of metadata disclosed by Data Providers and harvested by Service Providers, with a view to developing a means by which the rights of such freely-available metadata might be protected under the OAI-PMH" (Project RoMEO n.d). After weighing the advantages and disadvantages of several kinds of rights expressions, the project decided to align RoMEO's work with the Creative Commons (CC) Initiative. One of the key benefits of the CC is that "it provides not just rights metadata, but a whole rights system with human readable statements for end users, legal licences for lawyers, and rights metadata for machines!" (Gadd, Oppenheim, and Probets n.d.). However, because CC licenses don't set strict limitations in terms of reproduction and noncommercial sale of a work that the RoMEO project wants, it decided to write Open Digital Rights Language (ODRL) versions of the CC licenses which would conform to the ODRL XML schema.

The <indecs> project is a successful rights management project that uses rights metadata in the commercial world. "The <indecs> project, and its successor the not-for-profit Indecs Framework Ltd, was created to address the need, in the digital environment, to put different creation identifiers and their supporting metadata into a framework where they could operate side by side, especially to support the management of intellectual property rights" (Rust 2000). The project developed a metadata framework or reference model.

REFERENCES

American Library Association. Association for Library Collections & Technical Services. 2002. *Announcements and reports.* Available at: http://www.libraries.psu.edu/tas/jca/ccda/ann0210.html. Accessed 16 May 2007.

American Library Association. Association for Library Collections & Technical Services. 2005. *AACR3: The Next Big Thing in Cataloging.* Available at: http://www.ala.org/ala/alcts/alctsconted/alctsceevents/alctsannual/AACR3prog.htm. Accessed 16 May 2007.

ANZLIC Metadata Working Group. 2001. *ANZLIC Metadata Guidelines: Core Metadata Elements for Geographic Data in Australia and New Zealand.* Version 2. Available at: http://www.anzlic.org.au/download.html?oid=2358011755. Accessed 17 December 2003.

Arms, William Y, Christophe Blanchi, and Edward A. Overly. 1997. "An Architecture for Information in Digital Libraries," *D-Lib Magazine* (February). Available at: http://www.dlib. org/dlib/february97/cnri/02arms1.html. Accessed 10 October 2003.

Australian Government. National Archives of Australia. n.d. *AGLS*. Available at: http://www.naa. gov.au/recordkeeping/gov_online/agls/summary.html. Accessed 18 June 2004.

Baca, Murtha, and Patricia Harpring, eds. n.d. *Introduction*. Available at: http://www.getty.edu/ research/conducting_research/standards/cdwa/index.html. Accessed 10 October 2003.

Bearman, David. 2003. *NISO/CLIR/RLG Technical Metadata for Images Workshop, April 18–19, 1999*. Available at: http://www.niso.org/news/events_workshops/imagerpt.html. Accessed 9 October 2003.

Bearman, David, and Ken Sochats. 2004. *Metadata Requirements for Evidence*. Available at: http://www.archimuse.com/papers/nhprc/BACartic.html. Accessed 28 January 2004.

Caplan, Priscilla. 1995. "You Call It Corn, We Call It Syntax: Independent Metadata for Document-like Objects." *The Public-Access Computer Systems Review* 6 (4). Available at: http://info. lib.uh.edu/pr/v6/n4/capl6n4.html. Accessed 25 February 2003.

Caplan, Priscilla. 2003. *Metadata Fundamentals for All Librarians*. Chicago, Ill.: The American Library Association.

Centre for Educational Technology Interoperability Standards. 2004. *ISO SC36 'Metadata for Learning Resources' Working Group Approved*. Available at: http://www.cetis.ac.uk/ content/20030204163914. Accessed 12 October 2003.

Coleman, Anita. 2002. *Metadata Standards*. Available at: http://www.asu.edu/ecure/2002/ coleman/coleman.ppt. Accessed 11 October 2003.

Day, Michael. 1997. *Extending Metadata for Digital Preservation*. Available at: http://www. ariadne.ac.uk/issue9/metadata/. Accessed 12 October 2003.

Day, Michael. 1999. "Metadata for Digital Preservation: An Update," *Ariadne* 22 (December 21). Available at: http://www.ariadne.ac.uk/issue22/metadata/#1. Accessed 28 June 2004.

Day, Michael. 2000. "LC 21: A Digital Strategy for the Library of Congress" Washington, DC: The National Academies Press. Quoted in Calanag, Maria Luisa, and Shigeo Sugimoto, Koichi Tabata. 2001. "A Metadata Approach to Digital Preservation." In *DC-200:1 Proceedings of the International Conference on Dublin Core and Metadata Applications 2001*, National Institute of Informatics, 143–150. Tokyo, Japan: Nihon Printing Co. Available at http://www.nii.ac.jp/dc2001/proceedings/product/paper-24.pdf. Accessed 28 January 2004.

Day, Michael. 2001. "Metadata for Digital Preservation: A Review of Recent Developments." In *Research and Advanced Technology for Digital Libraries: 5th European Conference on the Digital Libraries, September 2–49, 2001, Darmstadat, Germany*, eds. P. Constantopoulos and I. T. Solvberg, 161–172. Berlin, Germany: Springer-Verlag. Availble at: http://www.ukoln.ac.uk/metadata/presentations/ecdl2001-day/paper.html. Accessed 14 April 2007.

Day, Michael. n. d. *CEDARS: Digital Preservation and Metadata*. Available at: http://www.ercim. org/publication/ws-proceedings/DELOS6/cedars.rtf. Accessed 16 January 2004.

Dempsey, Lorcan. 1996. "ROADS to Desire: Some UK and Other European Metadata and Resource Discovery Projects," *D-Lib Magazine* (July/August). Available at: http://www.dlib. org/dlib/july96/07dempsey.html. Accessed 18 December 2003.

Dempsey, Lorcan, and Rachel Heery. 1997. *DESIRE: Project Deliverable*. Available at: http:// www.ukoln.ac.uk/metadata/desire/overview/overview.rtf. Accessed 30 March 2003.

Dublin Core Metadata Initiative. 2003. *Dublin Core Metadata Element Set, Version 1.1: Reference Description*. Available at: http://dublincore.org/documents/dces/. Accessed 19 December 2003.

Elkington, Nancy. 2001. *NISO Technical Metadata for Digital Still Images*. Available at: http:// jodi.ecs.soton.ac.uk/noticeboard/nisoimage.html. Accessed 16 January 2004.

European Archive Network. 2002. *European Archive Network Project: Final Report*. Available at: http://www.euan.org/euan_final.doc#_Toc23207967. Accessed 14 November 2003.

European Committee for Standardization. 1999. *Model for Metadata for Multimedia Information.* Available at: ftp://cenftp1.cenorm.be/PUBLIC/CWAs/e-Europe/MMI-DC/cwa13699–00–1999-Sep.pdf. Accessed 21 June 2004.

European Committee for Standardization. 2003. *Guidance on the Use of Metadata in eGovernment.* English version. Available at: ftp://ftp.cenorm.be/PUBLIC/CWAs/e-Europe/MMI-DC/cwa14859–00–2003-Nov.pdf. Accessed 15 June 2004.

Federal Geographic Data Committee. Metadata Ad Hoc Working Group. 1998. *FGDC-STD-001–1998, Content Standard for Digital Geospatial Metadata.* Available at: http://www.fgdc.gov/standards/documents/standards/metadata/v2_0698.pdf. Accessed 16 December 2003.

Federal Geographic Data Committee. 2003. *Content Standard for Digital Geospatial Metadata (CSDGM).* Available at: http://www.fgdc.gov/metadata/contstan.html. Accessed 16 December 2003.

Fleischhauer, Carl. 2003. *Audio-Visual Prototyping Project.* Available at: http://lcweb.loc.gov/rr/mopic/avprot/SoundSavings03.ppt. Accessed 10 October 2003.

Gateway to Educational Materials. 2003. *GEM 2.0 Element Set and Semantics.* Available at: http://www.geminfo.org/Workbench/GEM2_elements.html. Accessed 12 October 2003.

Gadd, Elizabeth, Charles Oppenheim, and Steve Probets. n.d. *RoMEO Studies 6: Rights Metadata for Open Archiving.* Available at: http://www.lboro.ac.uk/departments/ls/disresearch/romeo/Romeo%20Studies%206.pdf. Accessed 26 January 2004.

Gateway to Educational Materials. 2003. *Why Should Metadata Be Created for Your Educational Resources?* Available at: http://www.geminfo.org/decision.html. Accessed 12 October 2003.

Gateway to Educational Materials. n.d. *The Gateway to Educational Materials (GEM) is. . .* Available at: http://www.geminfo.org/index.html. Accessed 12 October 2003.

Government of Ireland. 2002. *The Irish Public Service Metadata Standard: User Guide.* Available at: http://www.gov.ie/webstandards/metastandards/index.html. Accessed 19 October 2004.

Guenther, Rebecca.. 2002. "MARC 21 as a Metadata Standard: A Practical and Strategic Look at Current Practices and Future Opportunities." In *Cataloging the Web: Metadata, AACR, and MARC 21*, eds. Wayne Jones, Jodith R. Ahronheim, and Joesephine Crawford, transc. Jina Choi Wakimoto, 41. Lanha, Md., and London: The Scarecrow Press, Inc.

Harvard University Library. Digital Repository Service. 2002. *DRS Documentation: Administrative Metadata for Digital Still Images.* Available at: http://preserve.harvard.edu/resources/imagemetadata.pdf. Accessed 19 January 2004.

Hedstrom, Margaret. 1998. "Digital Preservation: A Time Bomb for Digital Libraries," *Computers and the Humanities* 32: 189–202.

Heery, Rachel, Robina Clayphan, Michael Day, Lorcan Dempsey, and David Martin. 1996. *BIBLINK-LB 4034: D1.1 Metadata Formats.* Available at: http://hosted.ukoln.ac.uk/biblink/wp1/d1.1.rtf. Accessed 25 February 2003.

Hensen, Steven L. 1989. *Archives, Personal Papers, and Manuscripts: A Cataloging Manual for Archival Repositories, Historical Societies, and Manuscript Libraries.* 2nd ed. Washington, D.C.: Society of American Archivists.

Horsman, Peter. 2000. *Metadata and Archival Description. Version 1.1.* Available at: http://www.euan.org/euan_meta.html. Accessed 14 November 2003.

Iannella, Renato. 2001. "Digital Rights Management (DRM) Architectures," *D-Lib Magazine* 7 (6). Available at: http://www.dlib.org/dlib/june01/iannella/06iannella.html. Accessed 28 January 2004.

Iannella, Renato, and Debbie Campbell. 2000. *The A-Core: Metadata about Content Metadata.* Available at: http://dublincore.org/archives/2001/02/purl-dc-website/documents/notes/acore-20000719.htm. Accessed 14 January 2004.

IFLA Study Group on the Functional Requirements for Bibliographic Records; approved by the Standing Committee of the IFLA Section on Cataloguing. 1998. *Functional Requirements for Bibliographic Records: Final Report.* Muenchen, Germany: Saur. Available at http://www.ifla.org/VII/s13/frbr/frbr.pdf. Accessed 14 April 2007.

Institute of Electrical and Electronics Engineers, Inc. Learning Technology Standards Committee. 2002a. *Draft Standard for Learning Object Metadata*. Available at: http://www. learninglab.de/elan/kb3/lexikon/metadaten-standards/docs/LOM_1484_12_1_v1_Final_ Draft.pdf. Accessed 15 December 2003.

Institute of Electrical and Electronics Engineers, Inc. Learning Technology Standards Committee. 2002b. *Position Statement on 1484.12.1—2002 Learning Object Metadata (LOM) Standard Maintenance/Revision*. Available at: http://ltsc.ieee.org/news/20021210-LOM.html. Accessed 12 October 2003.

International Standards Organization. n.d. *Geographic Information—Metadata*. Available at: http://www.iso.org/iso/en/CatalogueDetailPage.CatalogueDetail?CSNUMBER=26020&ICS1=35&ICS2=240&ICS3=70. Accessed 17 December 2003.

J. Paul Getty Trust. n.d. *Categories for the Description of Works of Art*. Available at: http://www. getty.edu/research/conducting_research/standards/cdwa/2_overview/index.html. Accessed 10 October 2003.

Johnston, Pete. 2002. *Administrative Metadata for Collection-level Description Records*. Available at: http://www.ukoln.ac.uk/cd-focus/guides/gp3/. Accessed 14 January 2004.

Kiesling, Kris. 2002. "Archival Finding Aids as Metadata: Encoded Archival Description." In *Cataloging the Web: Metadata, AACR, and MARC 21*, eds. Wayne Jones, Jodith R. Ahronheim, and Joesephine Crawford, 69. Lanha, Md., and London: The Scarecrow Press, Inc.

Kiorgaard, Deirdre and Whiting, Julie. 2001. *Describing and Managing Digital Collections*. Available at: http://www.nla.gov.au/nla/staffpaper/2001/dkiorgaard1.html. Accessed 16 May 2007.

Library of Congress. 1998a. *The Making of America II Testbed Project White Paper. Version 2.0*. Available at: http://sunsite.berkeley.edu/moa2/wp-v2.html. Accessed 10 October 2003.

Library of Congress. 1998b. *How to Use Structural Metadata Attributes: Digital Element Relationship Information and Page Information*. Available at: http://memory.loc.gov/ammem/ techdocs/repository/rep-examples/example-1a.html#top. Accessed 12 January 2004.

Library of Congress. 2003. *Digital Audio-Visual Preservation Prototyping Project*. Available at: http://lcweb.loc.gov/rr/mopic/avprot/avprhome.html. Accessed 10 October 2003.

Lynch, Clifford. 1999. "Canonicalization: A Fundamental Tool to Facilitate Preservation and Management of Digital Information," *D-Lib Magazine* 5 (9). Available at: http://www.dlib. org/dlib/september99/09lynch.html. Accessed 28 June 2004.

Martin, Mairéad, and Doug Pearson. 2001. *Rights Metadata: XrML and ODRL for Digital Video*. Available at: www.vide.net/conferences/mdvc2001/DRM5.ppt. Accessed 26 January 2004.

Metadata Encoding and Transmission Standard. 2003. *METS News and Announcements: Draft Rights Declaration Schema is Ready for Review*. Available at: http://www.loc.gov/ standards/mets/news080503.html. Accessed 28 January 2004.

Miller, Paul. 1996. *Metadata for the Masses*. Available at: http://www.ariadne.ac.uk/issue5/ metadata-masses/. Accessed 7 December 2003

Miller, Paul. 1999. *Lessons from An Examination of Dublin Core*. Available at: http://www. ukoln.ac.uk/interop-focus/presentations/metalib/ahds/iap-html/sld001.htm. Accessed 29 April 2003.

Miller, Paul. 2002. *The MEG Concord*. Available at: http://www.ukoln.ac.uk/metadata/education/documents/concord.html. Accessed 12 October 2003.

Miller, Paul. n.d. *The UK's Metadata for Education Group*. Available at: http://www.ukoln.ac.uk/ metadata/education/. Accessed 12 October 2003.

Moe, M. T. 2000. *The Knowledge Web*. New York: Merrill Lynch & Co. Available at: http:// internettime.com/itimegroup/MOE1.PDF. Accessed 13 April 2007.National Digital Library Program. Digital Repository Development Project. 1998. *Structural Metadata List*.

Version 1.04b. Available at: http://lcweb.loc.gov:8081/ndlint/repository/attlist.html. Accessed 13 January 2004.

National Information Standards Organization and AIIM International, developed. 2002. *Data Dictionary: Technical Metadata for Digital Still Images*. Available at: http://www.niso.org/standards/resources/Z39_87_trial_use.pdf. Accessed on 14 April 2007.

National Institute of Standards and Technology. Department of Commerce. n.d. *Approval of Federal Information Processing Standards Publication 192, Application Profile for the Government Information Locator Service (GILS)*. Available at: http://www.dtic.mil/gils/documents/naradoc/fip192.html. Accessed 3 October 2003.

OCLC/RLG Working Group on Preservation Metadata. 2001. Preservation Metadata for Digital Objects: A Review of the State of the Art . Available at: http://www.oclc.org/research/pmwg/presmeta_wp.pdf. Accessed 6 June 2003.

OCLC/RLG Working Group on Preservation Metadata. 2002. *A Metadata Framework to Support the Preservation of Digital Objects: Preservation Metadata and the OAIS Information Model*. Available at: http://www.oclc.org/research/pmwg/. Accessed 20 January 2004.

Perkins, Alan. 2004. *Developing a Data Warehouse: The Enterprise Engineering Approach*. Available at: http://members.ozemail.com.au/~ieinfo/dw.htm. Accessed 12 January 2004.

Pilling, Dennis. 2001. Quoted in McCallum, Sally H. "MARC harmonization report" *MARC listserv:* MARC@listserv.loc.gov.

Project RoMEO. n.d. *Final Report*. Available at: http://www.lboro.ac.uk/departments/ls/disresearch/romeo/. Accessed 28 January 2004.

Research Libraries Group. Working Group on Preservation Issues of Metadata. 1998. *Final Report*. Available at: http://www.rlg.org/preserv/presmeta.html. Accessed 19 January 2004.

Ross, Seamus. 1997. "Consensus, Communication and Collaboration: Fostering Multidisciplinary Co-operation in Electronic Records." In *Proceedings of the DLM-Forum on Electronic Records, Brussels, 18–20 December 1996*, INSAR: European Archives News, Supplement II, 330–336. Luxembourg: Office for Official Publications of the European Communities.

Rusbridge, Chris. 1999. *Rights Metadata: Why and Why Now? Models 10*. Available at: www.ukoln.ac.uk/dlis/models/models10/cr-mod10.ppt. Accessed 26 January 2004.

Rust, Godfrey. 1998. "Metadata: The Right Approach: An integrated Model for Descriptive and Rights Metadata in e-Commerce." *D-Lib Magazine* (July/August). Available at: http://www.dlib.org/dlib/july98/rust/07rust.html. Accessed 4 November 2003.

Rust, Godfrey, and Mark Bide. 2000. *The <indecs>Metadata Framework: Principles, Model and Data Dictionary*. Available at: http://www.indecs.org/pdf/framework.pdf. Accessed 25 June 2003.

Schwab, Eric. 2003. *Visual Resources Association*. Available at: http://vraweb.org/index.html. Accessed 10 October 2003.

Society of American Archivists. 1999. *Standards for Archival Description: A Handbook*. Available at: http://www.archivists.org/catalog/stds99/index.html. Accessed 14 November 2003.

Treasury Board of Canada Secretariat. 2003. *TBITS 39: Treasury Board Information Management Standard. Part1: Government On-Line Metadata Standard*. Available at: http://www.tbs-sct.gc.ca/its-nit/standards/tbits39/crit391_e.asp. Accessed 17 June 2004.

UK Office for Library and Information Networking. 1998. *Administrative Metadata: Sample Solutions*. Available at: http://www.ukoln.ac.uk/web-focus/metadata/seminar-materials/exercises/admin-metadata/admin-metadata-solution.pdf. Accessed 14 January 2004.

United Kingdom. Stationery Office Limited. 1988. Copyright, Designs and Patents Act, c. 48. Available at: http://www.opsi.gov.uk/acts/acts1988/Ukpga_19880048_en_1.htm. Accessed 14 April 2007.

Visual Resources Association. 2002. *VRA Core Categories. Version 3.0*. Available at: http://www.vraweb.org/vracore3.htm. Accessed 10 October 2003.

Waters, Donald. 1998. *Current Issues in Digital Preservation: A Perspective from the Digital Library Federation*. Available at: http://ssdoo.gsfc.nasa.gov/nost/isoas/dads/presentations/Waters/sld001.htm. Accessed 23 January 2004.

Weibel, Stuart. 1995. "Metadata: The Foundations of Resource Description." *D-Lib Magazine* (July). Available at: http://www.dlib.org/dlib/July95/07weibel.html. Accessed 18 December 2003.

Weibel, Stuart. 2003. *State of the Dublin Core Metadata Initiative*. Available at: http://post-ifla.sub.uni-goettingen.de/agenda/weibel1.ppt. Accessed 24 June 2004.

Weibel, Stuart, Jean Godby, and Eric Miller. 1995. *OCLC/NCSA Metadata Workshop Report*. Available at: http://www.oasis-open.org/cover/metadata.html. Accessed 15 September 2005.

3

Metadata Encoding Standards

In the business world, attention has usually been focused on improving computer hardware and software, while encoding standards and data formats are seldom addressed. In fact, developments in encoding standards and data formats have no less impact on the processing, management, and usage of information than improvements in hardware and software. The encoding standards and data formats adopted must guarantee the appropriate preservation of all the information over the long term and its access and transmission in the most efficient way, especially when organizing a large sum of public information, such as a digital library.

Metadata is a kind of structured information about information. It is necessary to encode metadata because only encoded metadata can be processed with machines and then provided to the user. Metadata provides a description that is primarily technical, with the goal of instructing future users and computer systems on how to extract and render a document. In order to be read, searched, and exchanged by computer systems across different applications, metadata must be expressed in a standard way or encoded in an appropriate standard. Management, migration, and transportation of digital objects require a standard encoding method for the metadata of digital objects. For instance, the California Digital Library has adopted an XML Document Type Definition (DTD) as the standard for encoding complex objects, and requires that all metadata submitted with a collection be encoded in this format. This XML encoding keeps track of which files represent master, viewing, and thumbnail images, as well as the administrative metadata that relates to these different file groups, the object's internal organization encoded as a structural map, and so forth (California Digital Library 2001).

An encoding is a physical representation of a document, equivalent to a file on a computer. A document may have several encodings, for example, a report may be represented as a Word file, a Portable Document Format (PDF) file, and a Rich Text Format (RTF) file. Many types of documents can be represented in a lot of different formats.

For example, a color picture could be saved in at least the following formats: Photoshop PSD, Amiga IFF, BMP, Photoshop EPS, FlashPix, JPEG, PCX, Photoshop PDF, PICT, Pixar, PNG, Raw, Scitex, Targa, and TIFF, though not all of these would be suitable long-term preservation formats. There are some discipline-specific ways to encode metadata, but metadata can generally be expressed in the standard encodings listed below:

- MARC
- METS
- Standard Generalized Markup Language (SGML), HyperText Markup Language (HTML), XML, Extensible HyperText Markup Language (XHTML)
- Text Encoding Initiative (TEI) header
- Encoded Archival Description (EAD)

Before introducing the above metadata encoding standards, the concept of DTD must be clear, since it will often be dealt with during the coming introduction to the above standards.

Three descriptions about DTD are provided below:

- "n SGML or XML, a formal description of the components of a specific document or class of documents. DTDs provide a formal grammar used for machine processing (parsing) of documents expressed in SGML or XML. A DTD description includes (User Guide Committee 2001):
  - The containers or elements that make up the document; e.g., paragraphs, headings, list items, figures, tables, etc.
  - The logical structure of the document; e.g., chapters containing sections, etc.
  - Additional information associated with elements (known as attributes); e.g., identifiers, date stamps, etc."
- One of the most important sections of an *SGML* document is the section that defines the tag set and composition rules which will be used in the document. This "grammar" is typically located in another file and is included at the top of the document in much the same way that LᴬTEX-macro packages would be included in LᴬTEX documents. This grammar section is called the DTD (Associated Universities Inc. 1999).
- DTD is a formal, machine-readable expression of the *XML* structure and syntax rules to which a document instance of a specific document type must conform; the schema type used in XML 1.0 to validate conformance of a document instance to its declared document type. The same markup model may be expressed by a variety of DTDs (World Wide Web Consortium 1999).

The above definitions of DTD demonstrate that DTD is so flexible, it can be expressed with different kinds of markup language. A DTD is a specification that accompanies a document and identifies the funny little codes or markups that separate paragraphs, identify topic headings, and so forth, and indicates how each is to be processed. If a DTD is included with a document, any location that has a DTD "reader" will be able to process the document and display or print it as intended. Thus, a single standard SGML compiler, for example, can serve many different kinds of documents that use a range of different markup codes and related meanings. The compiler reads the DTD and then prints or displays the document accordingly.

DTD defines the structure of a particular document type. It prescribes

- the elements that might be part of a particular document type,
- the names of the elements and whether they are repeatable,
- the order for arranging the elements,
- the content of the elements,
- the markup types that could be neglected,
- the characteristics and default values of identifiers, and
- the name of the suitable body.

In certain applications, a DTD is used to describe the metadata element set and its structure. "DTDs serve the same purpose as schemas, but are more limited. Most new metadata applications now use schemas, not DTDs" (Canadian Heritage Information Network 2002).

Previously, various DTDs were formed and used commonly, the most well known of which are:

- MARC DTD—DTD for encoding MARC records,
- HTML DTD—DTD for encoding Web pages,
- TEI DTD—DTD for encoding literary texts, AND
- EAD DTD—DTD for encoding file-finding aids.

It should be mentioned that, rather than providing a thorough introduction to the metadata standards themselves, this chapter only deals with encoding metadata to the corresponding standard.

3.1 MARC

As mentioned in the first section of chapter 2, the MARC format can function as both a structure for machine-readable records defined in American National Standards Institute/National Information Standards Organization (ANSI/NISO) Standard Z39.2 and, where MARC 21 is considered a representative of the MARC format, a set of encoding rules documented in the MARC 21 Format for Bibliographic Data and other LC publications. This section will focus on MARC as a metadata encoding standard.

A MARC record consists of three main sections: the leader, the directory, and the variable fields. Fields are marked with three-character tags, and some fields are further defined by indicators. According to ANSI Z39.2, the tag must consist of alphabetic or numeric ASCII graphic characters, that is, decimal integers 0 through 9 or letters A through Z (either upper or lowercase). MARC 21 formats use only numeric tags. The tag is stored in the directory entry for the field, not in the field itself. Variable fields are grouped into blocks according to the first character of the tag that identifies the function of the data within a record, for example, main entry, added entry, or subject entry. The type of information in the field, for example, personal name, corporate name, or title, is identified by the remainder of the tag. MARC 21's tags for the bibliographic format blocks of MARC 21 are the following:

```
0XX = Control information, numbers, codes
```

```
1XX = Main entry

2XX = Titles, edition, imprint

3XX = Physical description, and so forth

4XX = Series statements

5XX = Notes

6XX = Subject access fields

7XX = Name, and so forth; added entries or series; linking

8XX = Series-added entries; holdings and locations

9XX = Reserved for local implementation
```

It should be noted that MARC records are only standardized at a certain level. ISO 2709 standardizes physical encoding for records. However, each national or other format determines the format of the data content by defining its own set of designators and rules. Several national formats have made changes to accommodate electronic resources. It is likely that conversion into and out of MARC will always be a problem, and, in some contexts, service providers may even have to address the issue (Dempsey and Heery 1997).

Figure 3.1 is a sample local system record encoded with MARC 21 that illustrates the appearance of the data entry screen when uploading a record into a library automation system. The descriptors in the left-hand column are not stored in a MARC record, but are part of the software program's screen display. Most systems are designed so that records can be edited to add additional fields containing local information.

In the mid-1990s, the Network Development and MARC Standards Office of the U.S. Library of Congress developed two SGML DTDs capable of converting cataloging data between the MARC data structure and SGML without the loss of data. As technology develops and changes, SGML DTDs are increasingly converted to XML DTDs. These XML DTDs differ from the MARC XML schema by specifying each MARC data element as an XML element. This approach results in very large DTDs.

Meanwhile, XML is increasingly deployed in computer applications, particularly on the Web, as a richer, more flexible alternative to HTML. Many have expressed the need to switch to XML for metadata in libraries and other cultural institutions. Investigations into the development of an XML version of MARC are appropriate since MARC is perhaps the oldest metadata standard designed for use in computers (Guenther and McCallum 2003, 12). Therefore, the Library of Congress's Network Development and MARC Standards Office, in consultation with interested experts, developed Metadata Object and Description Schema (MODS), a MARC-compatible XML schema for encoding descriptive data to satisfy the expressed need for an abbreviated XML version of MARC 21. Though MARC is recognized as the most suitable existing metadata encoding format in the library world, complaints about the number of its data elements and their complexity are not new. There has even been talk of replacing this format with DCMES. However, DCMES addresses a much wider range of purposes and communities than MARC and, furthermore, cannot perform all of the same functions as MARC. Concern about MARC's limitations is one of the reasons the Library of Congress developed MODS. MODS is an XML schema with language-based tags that includes a subset of data elements derived from MARC 21. It is intended to carry selected data from MARC 21 records, as well as to enable the creation of original resource description records.

Leader	01041cam 2200265 a 4500
Control No.	001 ###89048230
Control No. ID	003 DLC
DTLT	005 19911106082810.9
Fixed Data	008 891101s1990 maua j 001 0 eng
LCCN	010 ## $a ###89048230
ISBN	020 ## $a 0316107514 :
	$c $12.95
ISBN	020 ## $a 0316107506 (pbk.) :
	$c $5.95 ($6.95 Can.)
Cat. Source	040 ## $a DLC
	$c DLC
	$d DLC
LC Call No.	050 00 $a GV943.25
	$b .B74 1990
Dewey No.	082 00 $a 796.334/2
	$2 20
ME:Pers Name	100 1# $a Brenner, Richard J.,
	$d 1941-
Title	245 10 $a Make the team.
	$p Soccer :
	$b a heads up guide to super soccer! /
	$c Richard J. Brenner.
Variant Title	246 30 $a Heads up guide to super soccer
Edition	250 ## $a 1st ed.
Publication	260 ## $a Boston :
	$b Little, Brown,
	$c c1990.
Phys Desc	300 ## $a 127 p. :
	$b ill. ;
	$c 19 cm.
Note: General	500 ## $a "A Sports illustrated for kids book."
Note:Summary	520 ## $a Instructions for improving soccer skills. Discusses dribbling, heading, playmaking, defense, conditioning, mental attitude, how to handle problems with coaches, parents, and other players, and the history of soccer.
Subj: Topical	650 #0 $a Soccer
	$v Juvenile literature.
Subj: Topical	650 #1$a Soccer.

Figure 3.1 A sample bibliographic record encoded with MARC 21.

3.2 METS

The METS schema is a standard for encoding descriptive, administrative, and structural metadata about objects in a digital library that uses the World Wide Web Consortium's (W3C) XML schema language. The standard is maintained in the Network Development and MARC Standards Office of the Library of Congress, and is being developed as an initiative of the Digital Library Federation (Library of Congress 2003b). METS is essential to a digital material repository and to the interchange of digital objects for viewing and use by other systems.

The work of METS began in May 2001, and is in fact a continuation of work undertaken as part of the Making of America II (MOA2) testbed project, which was itself a follow-up to a collaboration between the University of Michigan and Cornell University, the MOA digital library initiative. METS's objective was to create a digital library object standard by providing an encoding format for descriptive, administrative, and structural metadata for both text- and image-based items. This standard was a response to the need for metadata about digital objects that reflected the vital roles of structural metadata in understanding the organization of digital items and technical metadata in understanding the accuracy of a digital surrogate's reflection of the original. "The MOA2 project attempted to address these issues by offering a DTD that defined the digital object's elements and encoding, in doing so promoting interoperability, scalability and digital preservation" (Napier 2001). Depending on the case, a METS document could be used in the role of Submission Information Package (SIP), Archival Information Package (AIP), or Dissemination Information Package (DIP) within the Open Archival Information System (OAIS) Reference Model.

METS packs into an XML document, the metadata associated with a digital resource—the descriptive, administrative, structural, rights, and other data—needed for retrieving, preserving, and serving up digital resources. The following seven major sections (see also Figure 3.2) might be included in a METS document (Library of Congress 2003b):

- *METS header*

  The METS header contains metadata describing the METS document itself, including such information as creator, editor, and so forth.

- *Descriptive metadata*

  This section may point to descriptive metadata external to the METS document (e.g., a MARC record in an OPAC, or an EAD finding aid maintained on a World Wide Web server), or contain internally embedded descriptive metadata, or both. Multiple instances of both external and internal descriptive metadata may be included in the descriptive metadata section.

- *Administrative metadata*

  The administrative metadata section provides information regarding how the files were created and stored, intellectual property rights, metadata regarding the original source object from which the digital library object derives, and information regarding the provenance of the files comprising the digital library object (i.e., master/derivative file relationships and migration/transformation information). As with descriptive metadata, administrative metadata may be either external to the METS document or encoded internally.

- *File section*

  The file section lists all files containing content which comprise the electronic versions of the digital object. <file> elements may be grouped within <fileGrp> elements to provide for subdividing the files by object version.

- *Structural map*

  The structural map is the heart of a METS document. It outlines a hierarchical structure for the digital library object, and links the elements of that structure to content files and metadata that pertain to each element.

- *Structural links*

  The structural links section of METS allows METS creators to record the existence of hyperlinks between nodes in the hierarchy outlined in the structural map. This is of particular value in using METS to archive Web sites.

- *Behavior*

  A behavior section can be used to associate executable behaviors with content in the METS object. Each behavior within a behavior section has an interface definition element that represents an abstract definition of the set of behaviors represented by a particular behavior section. Each behavior also has a mechanism element which identifies a module of executable code that implements and runs the behaviors defined abstractly by the interface definition.

The above sections are all optional except for the header and structural map, which are needed for basic access to the digital resource. The descriptive metadata, administrative metadata, and behavior sections may reside either in the METS document or externally. Therefore, descriptive and administrative metadata may be handled in two ways:

- Embedded directly within the METS file in a <mdWrap> element (with any namespace)
- Held in an external file and referenced from the METS file through an <mdRef> element

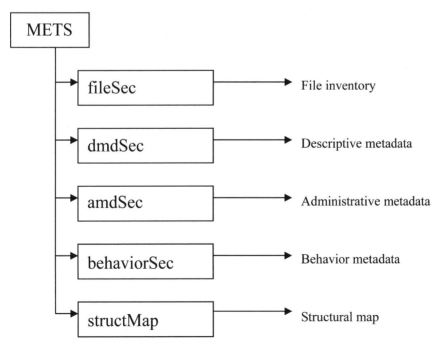

Figure 3.2 Structure of a METS file.

Although METS does not prescribe the content (particularly the descriptive metadata) that it contains, the METS board does recommend some schemas (Gartner 2003):

- Descriptive metadata:
  - Dublin Core
  - MODS
  - MARCXML MARC 21 schema
- Administrative metadata:
  - Schema for Technical Metadata for Text (New York University)
  - Library of Congress Audio-Visual Prototyping Project
  - NISO Technical Metadata for Digital Still Images
  - Schema for Rights Declaration

Simply put, a METS file has the following features (Gartner 2003):

- All metadata (descriptive, administrative, and structural) are encoded in single document.
- Each type of metadata is held in a separate section, linked by identifiers.
- All metadata and external data (e.g., images, text, video) are either referenced from METS files or can be held internally.

Yet to some extent, METS's purpose is to deal with the multiplication of metadata types in recent years, especially metadata types dealing with nonpaper materials, more particularly, audio-visual sources and their digital representations. "METS was developed for a purpose. It is an integral part of the Open Archival Information System (OAIS) reference model and serves to facilitate the exchange of digital objects from one repository to another" (Seadle 2002, 256).

METS is an open standard, and its structure is highly flexible and relatively simple. International organizations, such as the ISO, have considered recognizing METS as a formal standard.

To a large extent, the metadata marketplace will reveal if METS is really needed. The metadata market has changed significantly in the last decade. MARC remains dominant among libraries, DCMES has acquired a substantial following, EAD has attracted interest outside archives, and TEI is widespread among text-encoding projects. The degree of change suggests that METS has a chance, and it certainly has some powerful backers, including the Library of Congress. But the metadata market may also be saturated.

3.3 SGML, HTML, XML, AND XHTML

The section title might suggest that all the encoding standards discussed in this section are markup languages. Markup makes explicit the distinctions desired when processing a string of bytes. It is a way of naming and characterizing the parts of a text in a formalized way (Burnard 2004). Markup could be broadly defined as "any means of making explicit an interpretation of a text" (Sperberg-McQueen and Burnard 1994) and a markup language may be no more than a loose set of markup conventions used together for encoding text. "A markup language must specify what markup is allowed, what markup is required, how markup is to be distinguished from text, and what the markup means"

(Burnard n.d.). For instance, SGML provides the tools for completing the first three tasks of a markup language, as mentioned above, and documentation is required for the last. Both SGML and XML are parent languages, and a lineage has been traced from SGML to HTML, XML, and XHTML. SGML is the earliest of these four encoding standards. Each of these standards has been used to encode metadata, particularly XML and HTML, since interest began shifting toward these standards in the 1990s (see Table 3.1).

SGML is an international standard for the description of marked-up electronic text. More precisely, SGML is a metalanguage, a formal means of describing a language—describing a markup language in this case (Sperberg-McQueen and Burnard n.d.). The first working draft of the SGML standard was published in 1980. It developed out of the Generalized Markup Language (GML), which was invented by Charles Goldfarb and his colleagues in 1969. By 1986, SGML was adopted as an international standard (ISO 8879:1986) (Goldfarb n.d.). There are three characteristics of SGML that distinguish it from other markup languages: its emphasis on descriptive rather than procedural markup, its document-type concept, and its independence from any one system for representing the script in which a text is written (Sperberg-McQueen and Burnard n.d.).

Conceived theoretically between the 1960s and 1970s, SGML gave birth to a profile/subset called XML in 1996, which was published as a W3C recommendation in 1998 (OASIS 2004). On February 4, 2004, the third edition of XML was published as a W3C recommendation. XML describes a class of data objects called XML documents, and partially describes the behavior of the computer programs that process them.

The following 10 points, compiled by W3C, are an introduction to XML (Bos 2001):

- XML is for structuring data.
- XML looks a bit like HTML.
- XML is text, but isn't meant to be read.
- XML is verbose by design.
- XML is a family of technologies.

Table 3.1 Simplest comparison of SGML, XML, HTML, and XHTML

Encoding standards	SGML	HTML	XML	XHTML
Full name	Standard Generalized Markup Language	HyperText Markup Language	eXtensible Markup Language	eXtensible HyperText Markup Language
First publishing year	1980	1992	1996	1998
Inventor	Charles Goldfarb and colleagues	Tim Berners-Lee	W3C	W3C
Origin	GML (Generalized Markup Language)	SGML	SGML	XML and HTML

- XML is new, but not that new.

- XML leads HTML to XHTML.

- XML is modular.

- XML is the basis for RDF and the Semantic Web.

- XML is license free, platform independent, and well supported.

As shown in Figure 3.3, an XML document is comprised of storage units called *entities,* which contain either parsed or unparsed data. Parsed data is made up of *characters*, some of which form the *character data* in the document, and some of which form *markup.* Markup encodes a description of the document's storage layout and logical structure. XML imposes constraints on the storage layout and logical structure. "A software module called an *XML processor* is used to read XML documents and provide access to their content and structure. It is assumed that an XML processor is doing its work on behalf of another module, called the *application.* This specification describes the required behavior of an XML processor in terms of how it must read XML data and the information it must provide to the application" (Bray et al. 2004).

The advent of SGML and digital resources has changed the appearance of metadata. The demands created by the rapid proliferation of digital resources are met by XML's new versatile structure for tagging and packaging metadata that allows the rapid production of descriptive data and the encoding of more types of metadata. Two emerging standards harness these developments for library needs. The first is MODS, a MARC-compatible XML schema for packaging descriptive and various other important types of metadata necessary for the use and preservation of digital resources (Guenther and McCallum 2003). Many metadata schemes have XML versions, with XML offering the following important features (Gartner 2003):

- An ISO standard, not dependent on any given application

- Interchangeability with other applications

- Handles structural metadata easily

- Easy to integrate cataloging information with text transcription, images, and so forth

The following is a simple DC record in XML extracted from "Guidelines for Implementing Dublin Core in XML," prepared by Andy Powell and Pete Johnston (2003).

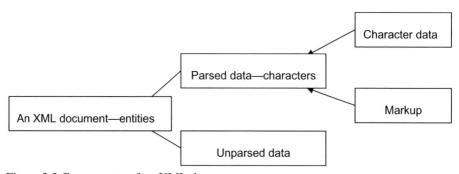

Figure 3.3 Components of an XML document.

```
<?xml version="1.0"?>

<metadata

xmlns="http://example.org/myapp/"

xmlns:xsi="http://www.w3.org/2001/XMLSchema-instance"

xsi:schemaLocation="http://example.org/myapp/ http://example.org/myapp/schema.xsd"

xmlns:dc="http://purl.org/dc/elements/1.1/">

<dc:title>

 UKOLN

</dc:title>

<dc:description>

 UKOLN is a national focus of expertise in digital information
management. It provides policy, research, and awareness
services to the UK library information and cultural heritage
communities. UKOLN is based out of the University of Bath.

</dc:description>

<dc:publisher>

 UKOLN, University of Bath

</dc:publisher>

<dc:identifier>

 http://www.ukoln.ac.uk/

</dc:identifier>

</metadata>
```

XML is an application profile or restricted form of SGML. The structure of XML doc-uments is in conformity with SGML documents. "Compared with XML, SGML is more customizable (thus flexible and more 'powerful') at the expense of being (much) more expensive to implement"[1] (Cover 2002). Since July 2002, relatively few enterprise-level projects have begun as SGML applications, but many SGML applications implemented before 1999 still run productively. In some cases, particular business requirements using features that have been eliminated in XML necessitate the use of SGML. Both SGML and XML are so-called metalanguages because they are used for defining markup languages. "A markup language defined using SGML or XML has a specific vocabulary (labels for elements and attributes) and a declared syntax (grammar defining the hierarchy and other features)" (OASIS n.d.). The designers of XML, guided by experience with HTML, sim-ply took the best aspects of SGML and produced something as powerful as SGML, but

---

1. An overview of comparisons of SGML and XML can be found here: James Clark, *Comparison of SGML and XML: World Wide Web Consortium Note 15-December-1997*, http://www.w3.org/TR/NOTE-sgml-xml.html (accessed 8 February 2004).

vastly more regular and simple to use. Some evolutions, however, are hard to distinguish from revolutions. While SGML is used mostly for technical documentation and much less for other kinds of data, XML is the exact opposite.

However, XML is most frequently compared with HTML, the markup language in which Web pages had always been written until XML began to replace it. Some of XML's important defining characteristics are listed below (Text Encoding Initiative 2002):

- XML is extensible; it does not contain a fixed set of tags.

- XML documents must be well formed according to a defined syntax, and may be formally validated.

- XML focuses on the meaning of data, not its presentation.

HTML was originally developed by Tim Berners-Lee, who worked at CERN (European Organization for Nuclear Research), where the World Wide Web was born, and popularized by the Mosaic browser developed at National Computer Security Association (NCSA). It blossomed with the explosive growth of the Web during the 1990s. Over the years, HTML has been extended in a number of ways. HTML 4.0 was first released as a W3C Recommendation on December 18, 1997. A second release, with changes limited to editorial corrections, was issued on April 24, 1998. This edition has now been superseded by HTML 4.01, published in December 1999.

"HTML is the *lingua franca* for publishing hypertext on the World Wide Web. It is a non-proprietary format based upon SGML, and can be created and processed by a wide range of tools, from simple plain text editors—you type it in from scratch- to sophisticated WYSIWYG authoring tools" (World Wide Web Consortium 2004).

HTML is a method for marking up text and graphics in a way that can be interpreted by most popular Web browsers. It consists of a set of markup tags with specific meanings. Moreover, HTML is a very basic type of SGML markup that is easy to learn and easy for computer applications to generate. But the simplicity of HTML is both its virtue and its weakness. Because of HTML's limitations, Web users and programmers have had to extend and enhance it by a series of customizations and revisions that still fall short of accommodating current, to say nothing of future, needs.

HTML, like XML, is a syntax format in which metadata can be expressed and, if permitted, embedded in the described resource. The META tag of HTML is designed to encode a named metadata element. Simple metadata can easily be expressed in HTML. Each element describes a given aspect of a document or other information resource. The following are two simple examples of DC element encoded with HTML tags:

```
<meta name = "DC.Title"

   lang = "de"

   content = "Das Wohltemperierte Klavier, Teil I">

<meta name = „DC.Subject"

   content = „Vietnam War">

<meta name = „DC.Subject"

   scheme = „LCSH"

   content = „Vietnamese Conflict, 1961-1975">
```

When embedded in the HEAD part of an HTML file, a sequence of LINK and META tags describes the information in the surrounding HTML file itself. Here is a complete HTML file with its own embedded description:

```
<html>

<head>

<title> A Dirge </title>

<link rel = "schema.DC"

   href = "http://purl.org/DC/elements/1.0/">

<meta name = "DC.Title"

   content = "A Dirge">

<meta name = "DC.Creator"

   content = "Shelley, Percy Bysshe">

<meta name = "DC.Type"

   content = "poem">

<meta name = "DC.Date"

   content = "1820">

<meta name = "DC.Format"

   content = "text/html">

<meta name = "DC.Language"

   content = "en">

</head>

<body><pre>

   Rough wind, that moanest loud

    Grief too sad for song;

   Wild wind, when sullen cloud

    Knells all the night long;

   Sad storm, whose tears are vain,

   Bare woods, whose branches strain,

   Deep caves and dreary main, -

    Wail, for the world's wrong!

     </pre></body>

</html>
```

HTML is not only well suited for expressing simple metadata, but can also be used to a limited extent to express more complex metadata, such as qualified Dublin Core.

In spite of HTML's limited ability to express complex metadata, it cannot clearly express the relationships between various metadata elements, with the result that complex metadata encoded in HTML is often semantically ambiguous. XML has been used more successfully as a binding for highly structured, complex metadata. Consequently, W3C developed an XML application called the Resource Description Framework (RDF), which enables the encoding of structured metadata in a semantically unambiguous way. RDF/XML is often used to express qualified Dublin Core and other structured, complex metadata.

Obviously, HTML is closely related to both SGML and XML. HTML is an example of a markup language defined in SGML, which is an international standard that describes how markup languages are defined. SGML does not contain particular tags or rules for their usage. XML is an intelligent improvement on HTML, and XML compatibility is already being built into most popular Web browsers. XML is not a new markup language designed to compete with HTML, nor is it designed to create conversion headaches for people with numerous HTML documents. "XML is intended to alleviate compatibility problems with browser software; it's a new, easier version of the standard rules that govern the markup itself, or, in other words, a new version of SGML" (Walsh and Muellner 2002). XML's rules are designed to facilitate the writing of applications that both interpret and generate its type of markup.

W3C developed XHTML in response to the challenges faced by HTML at the end of the twentieth century, such as the prevalence of sloppy markup practices, new kinds of browsers, pressure to either subset HTML for simple clients or extend HTML for richer, more complex clients, and so forth. Reformulated in XML, XHTML is a family of current and future document types and modules that reproduces, subsets, and extends HTML. "XHTML family document types are all XML-based, and ultimately are designed to work in conjunction with XML-based user agents. XHTML is the successor of HTML, and a series of specifications has been developed for XHTML" (World Wide Web Consortium 2004). In 1999, HTML 4 was recast in XML, and the resulting XHTML 1.0 became a W3C Recommendation in January 2000. During 2000 and 2001, work continued on modularizing XHTML, producing XHTML profiles, and planning for the future. XHTML 1.0 brings the Web of the future to content authors today. It is a reformulation of HTML 4 in XML, brings the rigor of XML to HTML, and can be put to immediate use with existing browsers by following a few simple guidelines. W3C's work with XHTML helps create standards that provide richer Web pages on an ever-increasing range of browser platforms, including cell phones, televisions, cars, wallet-sized wireless communicators, kiosks, and desktops. "XHTML is intended to be used in conjunction with tag sets from other XML vocabularies, so that in principle, you can say, XHTML tags with SVG graphics tags or XML tags from any other XML vocabulary" (World Wide Web Consortium 2003).

XHTML can be used to encode more complex metadata or metadata for more complicated resources than HTML. As in an HTML document, metadata should be embedded into the <head> section of an XHTML Web page using the <meta> and <link> elements. A qualified DC metadata record for the document, "Expressing Dublin Core in HTML/XHTML Meta and Link Elements," by Andy Powell is shown below.

```
<head profile="http://dublincore.org/documents/dcq-html/">

<title>Expressing Dublin Core in HTML/XHTML Meta and Link
  Elements</title>
```

```
<link rel="schema.DC" href="http://purl.org/dc/elements/1.1/" />

<link rel="schema.DCTERMS" href="http://purl.org/dc/terms/" />

<meta name="DC.title" lang="en" content="Expressing Dublin Core

in HTML/XHTML Meta and Link Elements" />

<meta name="DC.creator" content="Andy Powell, UKOLN, University

of Bath" />

<meta name="DCTERMS.issued" scheme="DCTERMS.W3CDTF" con-

tent="2003-11-01" />

<meta name="DC.identifier" scheme="DCTERMS.URI"

content="http://dublincore.org/documents/dcq-html/" />

<link rel="DCTERMS.replaces" hreflang="en"

href="http://dublincore.org/documents/2000/08/15/dcq-html/" />

<meta name="DCTERMS.abstract" content="This document describes how

qualified Dublin Core metadata can be encoded

in HTML/XHTML &lt;meta&gt; elements" />

<meta name="DC.format" scheme="DCTERMS.IMT" content="text/html" />

<meta name="DC.type" scheme="DCTERMS.DCMIType" content="Text" />

</head>
```

It is clear from the present discussion of the development of markup languages that the more recent the markup language, the more complicated the metadata it is capable of expressing.

3.4 TEI

Initially launched in 1987, the TEI, named for the Text Encoding Initiative, is an international and interdisciplinary standard that helps libraries, museums, publishers, and individual scholars represent all kinds of literary and linguistic texts for online research and teaching, using an encoding scheme that is maximally expressive and minimally obsolescent (Text Encoding Initiative 2001). It is an encoding standard for describing the physical and logical structure of textual material for the purposes of research analysis and data interchange. One evaluation of the TEI is that it is "the most systematic effort so far to create standards for scholarly memory in an evolving digital culture" (Mueller n.d.).

The TEI grew out of a planning conference sponsored by the Association for Computers and the Humanities (ACH) and funded by the U.S. National Endowment for the Humanities (NEH), held at Vassar College in November 1987. At this conference, some 30 representatives of text archives, scholarly societies, and research projects met to discuss the feasibility of a standard encoding scheme and to make recommendations for its scope, structure, content, and drafting. During the conference, the Association for Computational Linguistics and the Association for Literary and Linguistic Computing agreed to join ACH as sponsors of a project to develop the TEI Guidelines (Sperberg-McQueen and Burnard 2003). TEI P4 is the current version of the Guidelines that appeared in print in June 2002. Work on the next full revision of the Guidelines, TEI P5, has been ongoing since early 2002, and will hopefully conclude sometime in 2004.

The TEI addresses many of the needs of the "language technology community which is amassing substantial multi-lingual, multi-modal corpora of spoken and written texts and lexicons in order to advance research in human language, understanding, production, and translation" (MIT Libraries 2004b). It defines a general purpose scheme that makes it possible to encode different textual views. The primary goals of the TEI can be summarized as follows:

- Better interchange and integration of scholarly data
- Support for all texts, in all languages, from all periods
- Guidance for the perplexed: what to encode—hence, a user-driven codification of existing best practice
- Assistance for the specialist: how to encode—hence, a loose framework into which unpredictable extensions can be fitted

These apparently incompatible goals result in a highly flexible modular environment for DTD customization. The TEI was created to provide an environment into which documents of scholarly interest can be encoded in such a way that the documents' properties are represented in their transcribed form and that the resultant transcription is independent of any particular programming environment and capable of surviving technological change.

William Fietzer described the TEI as a subset of SGML, designed specifically to plumb the content and structure of textual documents in new and original ways. Like HTML, TEI documents have a header-body structure, but unlike HTML, TEI elements are not prescribed. That is, the encoder in the header uses a DTD to define the encoding rules to be followed in the body of the document (Fietzer 2002). Generally, a TEI document has two main sections: a TEI header section containing descriptive and administrative metadata and a text section containing the bulk of the text itself and divided into front matter, body, and back matter. There are a wide variety of tags within these two document sections, very few of which are required.

Text that conforms to TEI carries a set of descriptions prefixed to and encoded in it. The description set is known as the TEI header, tagged <teiHeader>, which includes the document's descriptive and administrative metadata. It is comprised of the following four principal components (Sperberg-McQueen and Burnard 2003a):

- <fileDesc> contains a full bibliographic description of an electronic file. In this part , descriptive metadata may be included.
- <encodingDesc> documents the relationship between an electronic text and the source or sources from which it is derived. Administrative and technical metadata might be included in this section.
- <profileDesc> provides a detailed description of nonbibliographic aspects of a text, specifically the languages and sublanguages used, the situation in which it was produced, the participants, and their setting. Both administrative and descriptive metadata may be included in this section.

- <revisionDesc> summarizes the revision history for a file. This section includes some administrative metadata.

The body of a TEI document contains tags that clearly define its structure.

Of the above components, only the <fileDesc> element is required in all TEI headers. The full form of a TEI header is as follows:

```
<teiHeader>

 <fileDesc> <!-- ... --> </fileDesc>

 <encodingDesc> <!-- ... --> </encodingDesc>

 <profileDesc> <!-- ... --> </profileDesc>

 <revisionDesc> <!-- ... --> </revisionDesc>

</teiHeader>
```

A minimal header takes the following form:

```
<teiHeader>

 <fileDesc> <!-- ... --> </fileDesc>

</teiHeader>
```

Carole E. Mah and Julia H. Flanders created the following sample TEI header of a journal article to use in a tutorial (Mah and Flanders 2003):

```
<teiHeader id="TR00412.hdr">

 <fileDesc>

  <titleStmt>

    <title type="main">The Cook's Guide: Or, Rare Receipts for

    Cookery, 1664</title>

  <title type="sub">&subtitle;</title>

    <author><persName key="HWolley.neb">Wolley,
Hannah</persName></author>

    <sponsor>Brown University</sponsor>

    <funder>U.S. National Endowment for the Humanities</funder>

  </titleStmt>

  <editionStmt>

    <edition>%%%%% unreleased work in progress %%%%%</edition>

  </editionStmt>

  <publicationStmt>

    <publisher>Brown University Women Writers Project</publisher>

    <address>

     <addrLine>Box 1841</addrLine>
```

```
      <addrLine>Brown University</addrLine>

      <addrLine>Providence, RI 02912-1841</addrLine>

      <addrLine>USA</addrLine>

      <addrLine>url:mailto:wwp@brown.edu</addrline>

      <addrline>url:http://www.wwp.brown.edu</addrline>

      <addrline>401-863-3619</addrLine>

      </address>

      <idno type="WWP">TR00412</idno>

      <availability>&legalese;</availability>

      <date value="%%%%%"></date>

   </publicationStmt>

   <sourceDesc n="OT00412">

    <biblStruct>

    <monogr>

      <author><persName key="HWolley.neb">Wolley,
Hannah</persName></author>

      <title>The Cook's Guide: Or, Rare Receipts for Cookery
</title>

      <imprint>

       <pubPlace>London</pubPlace>

       <publisher>Peter Dring</publisher>

       <date value="1664"></date>

      </imprint>

      <extent><measure type="pagination">127 pp.</measure></extent>

      <extent><measure type="format">octavo</measure></extent>

    </monogr>

    <idno type="L">1037.a.22</idno>

    <idno type="Wing">W3276</idno>

   </biblStruct>

  </sourceDesc>

</fileDesc>

<encodingDesc>

 <projectDesc>&projDesc;</projectDesc>

 <samplingDecl>&sampling;</samplingDecl>

 <editorialDecl>&editorial;</editorialDecl>
```

```
<tagsDecl>

  <rendition id="r.it">slant(italic)</rendition>

  <rendition id="r.up">slant(upright)</rendition>

  <rendition id="r.centit">slant(italic)align(center)</rendition>

  <rendition id="r.break">break(yes)</rendition>

  <rendition id="r.nobreak">break(no)</rendition>

  <rendition id="r.alrightbreak">break(yes)align(right)
</rendition>

  <tagusage gi="placename" render="r.it"></tagusage>

  <tagusage gi="label" render="r.it"></tagusage>

  <tagusage gi="head" render="r.centit"></tagusage>

  <tagusage gi="p" render="r.up"></tagusage>

  <tagusage gi="fw" render="r.alrightbreak"></tagusage>

 </tagsDecl>

</encodingDesc>

 <profileDesc>

  <langUsage>

   <language id="eng">British English circa

    <date value="1664">1664</date></language>

   </langUsage>

 </profileDesc>

<revisionDesc>

 <change>

  <date value="1997-07-31">31 Jul 97</date>

  <respStmt>

   <name key="FHalpern.ahl">Faye Halpern</name><resp>Encoder
</resp>

  </respStmt>

  <item>Began capture using emacs with psgml on Unix with

  version 1.1.4a of wwp-store DTD.</item>

 </change>

</revisionDesc>

</teiHeader>
```

The design of the TEI Header was based on ISBD and is intended to supply information suitable for creating a catalog record. Like MARC, TEI distinguishes between

required, recommended, and optional encoding practices, and contains a mechanism
for user-defined extensions of the scheme. However, the TEI Header contains a number of field categories that cannot be captured in MARC, for instance, the *change
history section* can record the changes made to an electronic text, including the date,
the responsible party, and the nature of the change. The *source desc* within the *file desc*
permits a detailed and richly content-designated description, particularly for nonprint
sources. "The *encoding desc* provides for a lengthy and detailed description of the encoding of the electronic file including the data about the project, the purpose for which
it was created, the editorial decisions that were made, and the transcription practices that
were used" (Sperberg-McQueen and Burnard 2003b).

3.5 EAD

The EAD DTD is a standard for encoding archival finding aids using SGML/XML.
The standard is maintained in the Network Development and MARC Standards Office of
the LC, in partnership with the Society of American Archivists. Development of the EAD
DTD began in 1993, with a project initiated by the Library of the University of California,
Berkeley (Library of Congress 2003a). Using the syntax of the SGML, the EAD DTD
defines the structural elements and designates the content of descriptive guides within
archival and manuscript holdings (SGML—ISO 8879). The latest edition of the standard
is EAD DTD Version 2002. Initially, EAD DTD was created on the basis of SGML and,
because of the wide use of XML, the XML version of EAD DTD is now available.

"EAD enables standardized exchange of descriptive data contained in specific types
of archival finding aids known either as archival inventories or manuscript registers. It
provides tools for a detailed, multilevel description, structured display, navigation, and
searching" (MIT Libraries 2004a). While the MARC format is used for encoding bibliographic records, the EAD DTD is used for encoding archival finding aids.

EAD is ideally suited to archival descriptive practices. EAD-encoded finding aids
serve the same purpose for archival materials as MARC 21 records do for traditional library materials. EAD provides a standardized structure for descriptive data and a mechanism for communicating that data via computers. Just as a MARC record contains the
metadata of a library book, the EAD-encoded online finding aid is a record of the metadata of an archival collection. In addition, "EAD-encoded finding aids contain metadata
about themselves in a header section" (Kiesling 2001, 85).

In principle, encoded finding aids consist of three parts. The first part contains information about the finding aid itself (<eadheader>), the second describes the prefatory
matter useful for the display or publication of the finding aid (<frontmatter>), and the
third describes the archival records or manuscript papers (<archdesc>).

"The EAD header, encoded as <eadheader>, is a wrapper element for bibliographic
and descriptive information about the finding aid document rather than the archival
materials being described. The <eadheader> is modeled on the Text Encoding Initiative (TEI) header element to encourage uniformity in the provision of metadata across
document types" (Society of American Archivists 2002). The EAD header contains the
finding aid's title and author, its date of creation, its language, and its Web publication
information, as well as data about the encoding, such as who performed it and when.

The <eadheader> is essential to finding aids in a machine-readable environment because it records information that was often omitted in local paper finding aids. Typically,
its content is not displayed to users as part of the finding aid proper, although it can be

used for retrieval and its contents can be used to provide a brief citation to the finding aid, as in a search result set. The <eadheader> is also used by repository staff to control the EAD instance. The four available subelements of the <eadheader> must occur in the following order: <eadid> (required), <filedesc> (required), <profiledesc> (optional), and <revisiondesc> (optional). These elements and their subelements provide a unique identification code for the finding aid, bibliographic information such as the author and title of the finding aid, information about the encoding of the finding aid, and statements about significant revisions (Society of American Archivists 2002).

The required <eadheader> elements are listed below:

```
<eadheader>

 <eadid>[...]</eadid>

 <filedesc>

  <titlestmt>

   <titleproper>[...]</titleproper>

  </titlestmt>

 </filedesc>

</eadheader>
```

The following example of an <eadheader> was extracted from the Minnesota Territorial Archives records of Territorial Governor Willis A. Gorman. It describes a minimally encoded series of government records.

```
<?xml version="1.0" encoding="utf-8"?>

<!DOCTYPE EAD PUBLIC "+//ISBN 1-931666-00-8//DTD ead.dtd (En-
coded Archival Description (EAD)

Version 2002)//EN">

<ead>

 <eadheader countryencoding="iso3166-1" repositoryencoding="iso
15511" langencoding="iso639-2b"

 relatedencoding="marc">

  <eadid countrycode="us" repositorycode="mnhi">terr06</eadid>

 <filedesc>

  <titlestmt>

   <titleproper>MINNESOTA TERRITORIAL ARCHIVES. Territorial
Governor:

   </titleproper>

   <subtitle> An Inventory of Territorial Governor Willis A.
Gorman</subtitle>

   <author>Finding aid prepared by Lydia Lucas.</author>

  </titlestmt>

 </filedesc>
```

```
<profiledesc>

  <creation>Finding aid encoded by Lyda Morehouse,

    <date>July 17, 2002.</date></creation>

</profiledesc>

</eadheader>
```

Though EAD fully supports archival descriptive practices, it "lacks the robust mechanisms for Web resource discovery that DC provides" (Burnard and Light 1996).

3.6 RDF

Unlike the previous sections, which describe encoding standards, this section will introduce a logical structure for metadata, the RDF.

The RDF emerged from W3C's Platform for Internet Content Selection (PICS). It is the result of a number of metadata communities combining their needs to produce a robust and flexible architecture for supporting metadata on the Web. "Developed under the auspices of the W3C, RDF is an infrastructure that enables the encoding, exchange, and reuse of structured metadata. This infrastructure enables metadata interoperability through the design of mechanisms that support common conventions of semantics, syntax, and structure" (Miller 1998). The effective use of metadata across various applications requires common conventions for semantics, syntax, and structure. Such conventions provide the framework for exchanging and reusing metadata between different communities. RDF was invented in response to the desire to share metadata between communities. Web architects can use RDF to easily provide useful Web metadata without divine intervention. In addition, RDF is important to the Semantic Web, which will prove more transformative than the current World Wide Web. The W3C defines the Semantic Web as "the representation of data on the World Wide Web" (Matt 2004). The RDF integrates a variety of applications using XML for syntax and URIs for naming, and is the backbone of the Semantic Web.

The following is the definition of RDF in the "Dublin Core Metadata Glossary."

Resource Description Framework (RDF)

The basic language for writing metadata; a foundation which provides a robust flexible architecture for processing metadata on the Internet. RDF will retain the capability to exchange metadata between application communities, while allowing each community to define and use the metadata that best serves their needs (User Guide Committee 2001).

In its latest recommendation on RDF, "RDF Primer," the W3C describes RDF as "a language for representing information about resources in the World Wide Web. It is particularly intended for representing metadata about Web resources, such as the title, author, and modification date of a Web page, copyright and licensing information about a Web document, or the availability schedule for some shared resource" (Manola and Miller 2004). Compared with its predecessor, which was also created by Eric Miller, this recommendation had an increased emphasis on the World Wide Web as the forum where RDF exists and functions.

RDF is based on the premise that the resource being described has properties and those properties have values. The resource can be described by statements specifying the properties and values of the resource. A statement is comprised of three parts, the subject, predicate, and object. The part designated as "subject" identifies the resource described by the statement. The "predicate" identifies the properties or characteristics of the subject, and the "object" identifies the value of the resource. Figure 3.4 illustrates the simplest RDF statement.

In Figure 3.4, the object takes the form of a link to an authority record or document portion identifying Mr. Smith, the predicate is a link to the creator element in the Dublin Core Metadata Specification, and the subject is a link to the document. Computer programs can follow these links to obtain additional information about John Smith or the object's creators.

URIs form the mechanism by which RDF identifies a statement's subject, predicate, and object. To be more precise, RDF uses URI references (Manola and Miller 2004).

RDF provides a data model that supports the graphic description of a resource. A data model is a collection of triples, each composed of nodes and arcs. In the triple illustrated in Figure 3.5, one node represents the subject and the other represents the object. The arc identifies the predicate that denotes the relationship between the subject and object. The direction of the arc is significant and always points from the subject toward the object.

Therefore the data model of Figure 3.4 is illustrated in Figure 3.6.

A single data model might contain more than one triple. This occurs when a node functions simultaneously as both the subject of one statement and the object of another. Figure 3.7 is an example of a data model containing four triples. The first triple is constituted by the resource subject, "An introduction to the Resource Description

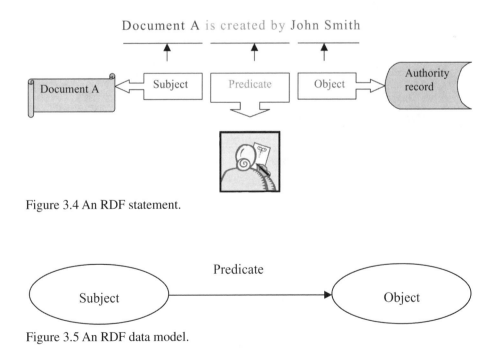

Figure 3.4 An RDF statement.

Figure 3.5 An RDF data model.

Framework," the predicate, "Creator," above the arc, and the "creator" in one node. However, in the other three triples, the "Creator" node is the subject of the other three statements whose objects are "Eric Miller," "emiller@oclc.org," and "Research scientist" respectively. The level can be further increased as required.

Figure 3.7 demonstrates that RDF is a simple, yet powerful, model for describing resources. RDF provides the XML syntax necessary to represent this model in such a way that it can be stored in machine-readable files and communicated between applications. This exact syntax is called RDF/XML, which is defined in the RDF/XML Syntax Specification (Beckett 2004). RDF imposes a formal structure on XML, thereby allowing the consistent representation of semantics.

The following is the RDF/XML description of the statement in Figure 3.4:

```
<?xml version="1.0"?>

<rdf:RDF xmlns:rdf=http://www.w3.org/1999/02/22-rdf-syntax-ns#

    xmlns:dc="http://purl.org/dc/elements/1.1/"

<rdf:Description rdf:about="http://uri-of-Document-A">

  <dc:creator>John Smith</dc:creator>

  </rdf:Description>

</rdf:RDF>
```

If each statement is represented separately, an RDF model consisting of multiple statements can be represented in RDF/XML. The example below includes two statements.

```
<?xml version="1.0"?>

<rdf:RDF xmlns:rdf="http://www.w3.org/1999/02/22-rdf-syntax-ns#"

xmlns:dc=http://purl.org/dc/elements/1.1/

xmlns:exterms="http://www.example.org/terms/">

<rdf:Description rdf:about="http://www.example.org/index.html">

<exterms:creation-date>August 16, 1999</exterms:creation-date>

</rdf:Description>

<rdf:Description rdf:about="http://www.example.org/index.html">

<dc:language>en</dc:language>

</rdf:Description>

</rdf:RDF>
```

Each statement can be represented with RDF/XML using a separate rdf:Description element. These statements can also be expressed in an abbreviated style.

In the above example, the second through fourth lines are used to declare the XML namespaces. RDF uses the XML namespace mechanism to uniquely identify property types. "XML namespaces provide a method for unambiguously identifying the semantics and conventions governing the particular use of property types by uniquely identifying the governing authority of the vocabulary" (Miller 1998). For example, Figure 3.8 specifies the property types in Figure 3.7 with two kinds of namespaces, the Dublin

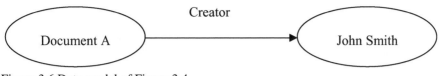

Figure 3.6 Data model of Figure 3.4.

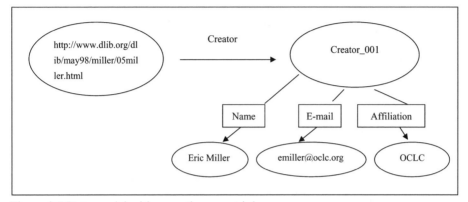

Figure 3.7 Data model with more than one triple.

Core and CARD schemas. In Figure 3.8, the more explicit declaration identifies the resource, "http://www.dlib.org/dlib/may98/miller/05miller.html," with the semantics of property type "Creator," unambiguously defined in DC or the Dublin Core vocabulary. The value of the property type is "Creator_001." In this example, an additional resource description standard, CARD specification, was used instead of Dublin Core to define the semantics of the elements "name," "email," and "affiliation." CARD is designed to automate the exchange of the personal information typically found on a business card. In this case, the business card schema was defined as CARD.

The data model illustrated in Figure 3.8 can be represented syntactically as follows:

```
<?xml version="1.0"?>
<rdf:RDF xmlns:rdf="http://www.w3.org/1999/02/22-rdf-syntax-ns#"
        xmlns:dc="http://purl.org/dc/elements/1.1/"
        xmlns:card="http://person.org/BusinessCard/">

 <rdf:Description rdf:about="http://www.dlib.org/dlib/may98/
miller/05miller.html">
    <dc:creator>Creator_001</dc:creator>
 </rdf:Description>

 <rdf:Description rdf:about="Creator_001">
    <card:name>Eric Miller</card:name>
```

```
    <card:email>emiller@oclc.org</card:email>

    <card:affiliation>OCLC</card:affiliation>

  </rdf:Description>

</rdf:RDF>
```

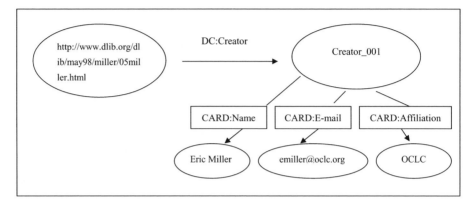

Figure 3.8 Data model with more than one XML namespace.

RDF schemas are used to denote vocabularies, the sets of semantic property types defined by a particular community. RDF schemas define the valid properties in an RDF description, as well as any characteristics or restrictions of the property type values themselves. The XML namespace mechanism identifies RDF schemas.

As Eric Miller concluded, the World Wide Web affords unprecedented access to distributed information. Metadata improves access to this information, and RDF is a W3C proposed standard for defining the architecture necessary to support Web metadata. RDF is an XML application that imposes the structural constraints required to express semantics unambiguously, so that metadata can be consistently encoded, exchanged, and machine processed. Additionally, RDF is a tool for publishing a vocabulary that is both human readable and machine processable, and is designed to encourage the exchange, use, and extension of metadata semantics among disparate information communities.

REFERENCES

Associated Universities Inc. 1999. XML *in 10 points. Version 1.9, Build 275. Introduction*. Available at: http://aips2.nrao.edu/docs/reference/Coding/node39.html#SECTION0281210000 0000000000. Accessed 3 February 2004.

Beckett, Dave. 2004. *RDF/XML Syntax Specification (Revised): W3C Recommendation 10 February 2004*. Available at: http://www.w3.org/TR/2004/REC-rdf-syntax-grammar-20040210/. Accessed 2 March 2004.

Biddulph, Matt. 2004. *Crawling the Semantic Web*. Available at: http://www.idealliance.org/papers/ dx_xmle04/papers/03-06-03/03-06-03.html.Accessed 15 April 2007.

Bos, Bert. 2001. *XML in 10 Points*. Available at: http://www.w3.org/XML/1999/XML-in-10-points. html.en. Accessed 9 February 2004.

Bray, Tim, Jean Paoli, C. M. Sperberg-McQueen, Eve Maler, and François Yergeau. 2004. *Extensible Markup Language (XML) 1.0: W3C Recommendation 04 February 2004*, 3rd ed. Available at: http://www.w3.org/TR/REC-xml/. Accessed 14 October 2005.

Burnard, Lou. 2004. *Digital Texts with XML and the TEI*. Available at: http://www.tei-c.org/Talks/ OUCS/2004–02/One/teixml-one.pdf. Accessed 23 February 2004.

Burnard, Lou. n.d. What is SGML and How Does It Help? Available at: http://www.oasis-open. org/cover/burnardw25-index.html. Accessed 20 October 2004.

Burnard, Lou, and Richard Light. 1996. *Three SGML Metadata Formats: TEI, EAD, and CIMI: A Study for BIBLINK Work Package 1.1*. Available at: http://www.ifla.org/documents/ libraries/cataloging/metadata/biblink2.pdf. Accessed 3 February 2004.

California Digital Library. 2001. *California Digital Library Digital Object Standard: Metadata, Content, and Encoding*. Available at: http://www.cdlib.org/news/pdf/CDLObjectStd-2001. pdf. Accessed 30 January 2004.

Canadian Heritage Information Network. 2002. Standards for encoding metadata. Available at: http://www.chin.gc.ca/English/Standards/metadata_encoding.html. Accessed 3 February 2004.

Cover, Robin, ed. 2002. *Standard Generalized Markup Language (SGML): SGML and XML as (Meta-) Markup Languages*. Available at: http://xml.coverpages.org/sgml.html. Accessed 15 April 2007.

Dempsey, Lorcan, and Rachel Heery. 1997. *DESIRE: Project Deliverable*. Available at: http:// www.ukoln.ac.uk/metadata/desire/overview/overview.rtf. Accessed 30 March 2003.

Fietzer, William. 2002. "Interpretive Encoding of Electronic Texts Using TEI Lite." In *Cataloging the Web: Metadata, AACR, and MARC 21*, eds. Wayne Jones, Jodith R. Ahronheim, and Joesephine Crawford, 103. Lanha, Md., and London: The Scarecrow Press, Inc.

Gartner, Richard. 2003. *METS: Metadata Encoding and Transmission Standard*. Available at: http://post-ifla.sub.uni-goettingen.de/agenda/gartner.ppt. Accessed 4 May 2004.

Goldfarb, Charles. n.d. *SGML User's Group History*. Available at: http://xml.coverpages.org/ sgmlhist0.html. Accessed 9 February 2004.

Guenther, Rebecca, and Sally McCallum. 2003. "New Metadata Standards for Digital Resources: MODS and METS." *Bulletin of the American Society for Information Science and Technology* December/January: 12.

Kiesling, Kristi. 2001. "Metadata, Metadata, Everywhere: But Where Is the Hook?" *OCLC Systems & Services* 17 (2): 84–88.

Library of Congress. 2003a. *Development of the Encoded Archival Description DTD*. Available at: http://www.loc.gov/ead/eaddev.html. Accessed 24 February 2004.

Library of Congress. 2003b. *METS: An Overview & Tutorial*. Available at: http://www.loc.gov/ standards/mets/METSOverview.v2.html. Accessed 5 February 2004.

Mah, Carole E., and Julia H. Flanders. 2003. *The TEI Header: A Tutorial with Examples*. Available at: http://www.wwp.brown.edu/encoding/training/teiheader/teiHeader.html. Accessed 23 February 2004.

Manola, Frank, and Eric Miller, eds. 2004. *RDF Primer: W3C Recommendation*. Available at: http://www.w3.org/TR/2004/REC-rdf-primer-20040210/. Accessed 26 February 2004.

Miller, Eric. 1998. "An Introduction to the Resource Description Framework," *D-Lib Magazine* (May). Available at: http://www.dlib.org/dlib/may98/miller/05miller.html. Accessed 4 November 2003.

MIT Libraries. 2004a. *EAD: Encoded Archival Description*. Available at: http://libraries.mit.edu/ guides/subjects/metadata/standards/ead.html. Accessed 24 February 2004.

MIT Libraries. 2004b. *Metadata Reference Guide: TEI (Text Encoding Initiative) Metadata*. Available at: http://libraries.mit.edu/guides/subjects/metadata/standards/tei.html#3. Accessed 23 February 2004.

Mueller, Martin. *A Very Gentle Introduction to the TEI Markup Language*. n.d. Available at: http:// www.tei-c.org/Sample_Manuals/mueller-main.htm. Accessed 24 February 2004.

Napier, Marieke. 2001. *Metadata Resources: Metadata Encoding and Transmission Standard (METS)*. Available at: http://www.ukoln.ac.uk/metadata/resources/mets/. Accessed 5 February 2004.

OASIS. 2004. *Extensible Markup Language (XML)*. Available at: http://xml.coverpages.org/xml. html. Accessed 10 February 2004.

OASIS. n.d. *Standard Generalized Markup Language (SGML)*. Available at: http://xml.coverpages. org/sgml.html/. Accessed 8 February 2004.

Powell, Andy, and Pete Johnston. 2003. Guidelines for Implementing Dublin Core in XML. Available at: http://dublincore.org/documents/dc-xml-guidelines/. Accessed 15 April 2007.

Seadle, Michael. 2002. "METS and the Metadata Marketplace," *Library Hi Tech* 20 (3): 255–257.

Society of American Archivists. 2002. *Encoded Archival Description Tag Library. EAD Elements: <eadheader> EAD header*. Available at: http://www.loc.gov/ead/tglib/elements/eadheader. html. Accessed 24 February 2004.

Sperberg-McQueen, C. M., and Lou Burnard. 1994. "1, A Gentle Introduction to SGML." In *A Gentle Introduction to SGML*. Available at: http://www.isgmlug.org/sgmlhelp/g-sg.htm. Accessed 15 April 2007.

Sperberg-McQueen, C. M., and Lou Burnard, eds. 2003a. *The XML Version of the TEI Guidelines. 1, About These Guidelines*. Available at: http://www.tei-c.org/P4X/AB.html#ABTEI. Accessed 23 February 2004.

Sperberg-McQueen, C. M., and Lou Burnard, eds. 2003b. *The XML Version of the TEI Guidelines. 5, The TEI header*. Available at: http://www.tei-c.org/P4X/HD.html. Accessed 23 February 2004.

Sperberg-McQueen, C. M., and Lou Burnard. n.d. *TEI P3. Chapter 2, A Gentle Introduction to SGML*. Available at: http://www-sul.stanford.edu/tools/tutorials/html2.0/gentle.html. Accessed 9 February 2004.

Text Encoding Initiative. 2001. *Welcome to the TEI Website*. Available at: http://www.tei-c.org/. Accessed 23 February 2004.

Text Encoding Initiative. 2002. *A Gentle Introduction to XML. May 2002*. Available at: http:// www.tei-c.org/Guidelines2/gentleintro.html#Note2. Accessed 10 February 2004.

User Guide Committee. 2001. *Dublin Core Metadata Glossary: Final Draft*. Available at: http:// library.csun.edu/mwoodley/dublincoreglossary.html. Accessed 30 June 2004.

Walsh, Norman, and Leonard Muellner. 2002. *DocBook: The Definitive Guide. 1, Getting Started with SGML/XML*. Available at: http://www.docbook.org/tdg/en/html/ch01.html. Accessed 9 February 2004.

World Wide Web Consortium. 1999. *Terms and Definitions*. Available at: http://www.w3.org/ TR/1999/WD-xhtml-building-19990910/terms.html. Accessed 3 February 2004.

World Wide Web Consortium. 2003. *HyperText Markup Language Activity Statement*. Available at: http://www.w3.org/MarkUp/Activity. Accessed 20 February 2004.

World Wide Web Consortium. 2004. *HyperText Markup Language (HTML) Home Page*. Available at: http://www.w3.org/MarkUp/. Accessed 20 February 2004.

4

Metadata Implementation

Metadata implementation is a broad concept, but is used here for lack of a better title to encompass all the topics discussed in this chapter. However, only limited aspects of metadata implementation are mentioned in this book. The first two sections of this chapter will discuss namespace and application profile respectively. The third section of this chapter will expand on the discussion of encoding metadata standards and metadata syntax in chapter 3, and will address the semantics of metadata, or metadata schema registry. Discussions on the generation and harvesting of metadata and other practical issues will be woven throughout this chapter.

4.1 NAMESPACE

In the computing disciplines, the term "namespace" conventionally refers to a *set* of names, that is, a collection containing no duplicates. Namespace is more precisely described as a collection of terms identified by a Uniform Reference Identifier (URI) reference. In short, a namespace is a formal collection of terms managed according to a policy or algorithm. *Namespaces for the Dublin Core Metadata Initiative (DCMI)*, gives the following definition of a namespace: "A DCMI namespace is a collection of DCMI terms and each DCMI namespace is identified by a URI" (Powell and Wagner 2001). For example, the URI "http://purl.org/dc/elements/1.1/" identifies the namespace "Dublin Core Metadata Element Set, Version 1.1," which comprises all the DCMI elements specified in the Dublin Core Metadata Element Set, Version 1.1. Namespaces allow the unambiguous identification of an element's definition with a URI, even though the label "title" alone might occur in many metadata sets. In a more general sense, one can take any closed set of names as a namespace. Thus, a controlled vocabulary such as the Library of Congress Subject Headings, a set of metadata elements such as DC, or the set of all URLs in a given domain can be thought of as namespaces that are managed by the authority in charge of that particular set of terms.

"Namespace" is defined in the W3C XML schema activity (Bray et al. 2006), and allows for the unique identification of elements. Within the W3C XML and RDF schema specifications, "Namespaces are the domain names associated with elements which, along with the individual element name, produce a URL that uniquely identifies the element" (Research and Development Group of UKOLN 1999).

The XML namespace is a common example. "An XML namespace is a collection of names, identified by a URI reference [RFC2396], that are used in XML documents as element types and attribute names. The use of XML namespaces to uniquely identify metadata terms allows those terms to be unambiguously used across applications, promoting the possibility of shared semantics" (Powell and Wagner 2001). XML namespaces, by associating the elements and names in XML documents with the namespaces identified by URL references, are a simple way to qualify elements and attribute names in XML documents. The following example is a section of an RDF structure with XML syntax. This RDF structure was generated for a document description in CURD (Carmen[1] Uploader with RDF and DIGSIG Generator), which contains DC, vCard, and Open Archives Metadata Set (OAMS).

```
<rdf:RDF xmlns:rdf = "http://www.w3c.org/1999/02/22-rdf-synax-
ns#"

    xmlns:dc = "http://purl.org/de/elements/1.0/#"

    xmlns:vcard = "http://imc.org/Vcard/3.0#"

    xmlns:oams= "http://www.openarchives.org/sfc/sfc_oams.htm#">

<rdf:Description>

 <rdf:Description xml:lang="en" rdf:about="http://xxx.lanl.gov/
 abs/cond-mat/9909184">

   <dc:Title>

     <rdf:alt>

       <rdf:li xml:lang="en"> Classification of phase transi-
       tions in small systems

 . . .

   <oams:title> Classification of phase transitions in small sys-
   tems </oams:title>

   <oams:accession date="1992-01-30">
```

```
<oams:displayId> http://xxx.lanl.gov/abs/cond-mat/9909184
</oams:displayID>

<oams:fullId> arXiv:cond-mat/9909184 </oams:fullId>

<oams:author>

  <oams:name> Peter Borrmann </oams:name>

. . .

</rdf:RDF>
```

Three kinds of namespaces identified with various URLs are included in the above example of RDF framework. The elements (such as Description) and terms used in the application above have been included in these three metadata schemas, that is, DC, vCard and OAMS.

Namespaces are a fundamental part of the Web's infrastructure. Simply put, a namespace is a formal collection of terms managed according to a policy or algorithm. All metadata element sets are namespaces bound by the rules and conventions of their maintenance agency. Namespace designations allow the metadata schema designer to define the context of a particular term, thereby assuring that the term has a unique definition within the bounds of the designated namespace. Thus, the designation of various namespaces within a block of metadata allows the identification of elements within that metadata as belonging to a particular element set. "Using the namespace metadata system designers can select elements from suitable existing metadata element sets, taking advantage of the investment of existing communities of expertise, and thereby avoid reinventing well-established metadata sets for each new deployment domain" (Duval et al. 2002).

Namespaces allow us to:

- identify the management authority for an element set,

- support the definition of unique identifiers for elements,

- and uniquely define particular data element sets or vocabularies (Research and Development Group of UKOLN 1999).

4.2 APPLICATION PROFILE

The concept of application profiles grew out of the UK Office for Library and Information Networking's (UKOLN) work on the DESIRE project. "An application profile is an assemblage of metadata elements selected from one or more metadata schemas and combined in a compound schema" (Duval et al. 2002). In the final draft of the "Dublin Core Metadata Glossary," an application profile is defined as "a set of metadata elements, policies, and guidelines defined for a particular application. The elements may be from one or more element sets, thus allowing a given application to meet its functional requirements by using metadata from several element sets including locally defined sets" (User Guide Committee 2001). For the purposes of the DCMI Usage Board review, an application profile is defined as "a declaration of which metadata terms an organization, information resource, application, or user community uses in its metadata" (Baker 2002). Thomas Baker, in a so-called strawman proposal to the Dublin Core Registry working group, defines application profiles as "entities that declare which elements from which namespaces underlie the local schema used in a particular application or project" (UK Office for Library and Information Networking 2004). In his view, application profiles "reuse" semantics from namespaces and repackage them for a particular purpose. This interpretation is in accordance with that of Rachel Heery and Manjula Patel, who define application profiles as "schemas consisting of elements drawn from one or more namespaces, combined together and optimised for a particular application" (Heery and Patel 2000).

Application profiles provide the means to express principles of modularity and extensibility. "The purpose of an application profile is to adapt or combine existing schemas into a package that is tailored to the functional requirements of a particular application, while retaining interoperability with the original base schemas" (Duval et al. 2002). Application profiles' main purpose is to increase the so-called semantic interoperability of the resulting metadata instances within a community of practice, thus maintaining the basic interoperability between communities without relying on a single standard.

The application profile consists of combining, through implementers, and optimizing data elements extracted from one or more namespaces or schemas for a particular local application. One useful feature of application profiles is that they allow the implementer to customize its use of standard schemas. Two situations necessitate application profiles. The first is when no ready-made schema exists that is capable of completely fulfilling a local need. The second is when some elements of several kinds of existing metadata schemas are appropriate for one task. Combining, harmonizing, and optimizing the relevant elements from different schemas with some self-made terms is an economical way to meet a local need. Obviously, using one or more ready-made metadata schemas saves the resources that would be required to develop a completely new one and also, in a sense, establishes a common platform for communication with other applications. In practice, it is very common for a particular metadata application to require domain-specific metadata elements or controlled vocabularies in addition to more generic elements. The application profile facilitates the combination and reuse of different metadata element sets. For example, the application profile of European Libraries and Electronics Resources in Mathematical Sciences (EULER)[2] consists of the several namespaces listed below:

- Dublin Core Metadata Element Set, Version 1.1 (dc1.1;
- Dublin Core Qualifiers (dcterms;
- EULER Element Set, Version 0.1 (euler0.1)
- EULER Qualifiers, Version 0.1 (eulerq0.1)

As shown above, the implementation of the EULER project combines metadata elements and terms from four different schemas. Generally, the project uses the metadata

---

2. EULER is a project cofunded by the European Commission in the Telematics for Libraries sector. The project started in April 1998, and after 30 months, completed in September 2000. The successor project, EULER-TAKEUP, began in December 2001.

terms specified in the standard DC terms, Dublin Core Metadata Element Set, Version 1.1 and Dublin Core Qualifiers (dcterms). However, since the application deals with electronic resources in a specialized discipline, in this case mathematics, it requires some domain-specific additions to the standard DC terms. It is undoubtedly necessary to define some local elements to express particular professional concepts only used in a particular field. In this case, EULER Element Set, Version 0.1 (euler0.1) and EULER Qualifiers, Version 0.1 are the namespaces created specifically to define the necessary local elements. The generic elements such as "Title" and "Creator" are within the scope of the namespace Dublin Core Metadata Element Set, Version 1.1, while "EULER identifier" and "Event name" are part of the namespace "euler0.1."

When one considers the current implementation of metadata schemas, it is clear that the complete standard schema is rarely used. Implementers identify useful elements in existing schemas, which are typically subsets of an existing standard. Then they might add a variety of local extensions to the standard for their own specific requirements, refine existing definitions in order to tailor elements to a specific purpose, and combine elements from more than one standard. "The implementor will formulate 'local' rules for content whether these are mandatory use of particular encoding rules (structure of names, dates) or use of particular controlled vocabularies such as classification schemes, permitted values" (Heery and Patel 2000).

Dublin Core Metadata Elements Set might be the metadata schema most commonly absorbed into specific application profiles, which is appropriate considering that the primary concern of DCMI when developing Dublin Core was that it be a simple yet effective element set for describing a wide range of networked resources. DCMI is continually trying to develop various kinds of terms for special implementations or different kinds of application profiles. The DC Library Application Profile is one example. "In the DC Library Application Profile in addition to the namespace the Dublin Core Metadata Element Set, Version 1.1 and Dublin Core Qualifiers, there are also other two namespace developed focusing on the library world. They are DC-Library Metadata Element Set and the DC-Library Metadata Element Set Qualifiers" (Guenther 2002). The DCMI-Libraries Working Group has explored various uses of the Dublin Core Metadata Element Set in the library.

Metadata schema designers have a fairly standard process for designing application profiles, the steps for which are the following (Dekkers 2001):

- Define metadata requirements
- Select most appropriate existing standard metadata element set
- Where possible, use standard elements for locally required elements, possibly narrowing semantics and adding local rules and vocabularies
- Define remaining elements in private namespace

This process results in the creation of application profiles for local implementation that reuse elements from existing sets and add custom elements when no existing equivalents can be found. The first and second steps are crucial in the process described above. In practice, the order listed above is not always followed, for example, when adhering to a dominant metadata standard in the particular application domain is a strategic objective.

There are two possible schema languages for expressing application profiles: RDF Schema and XML Schema. XML DTDs cannot seriously be considered an alternative since they do not explicitly support namespaces. Each schema language offers its own advantages. For example:

- RDF Schemas provide support for rich semantic descriptions.
- XML Schemas provide support for explicit structural, cardinality, and datatyping constraints.

"The SCHEMAS project is using RDF Schemas both for the namespace definitions and the registry of application profile definitions—because they 'would like to harvest distributed application profiles automatically'" (Heery and Patel 2000). However, using only RDF Schemas can severely compromise diversity and interoperability:

- Compared with XML Schema, RDF Schema provides limited support for specifying local usage constraints or refining existing namespace elements.
- Many domains use XML Schema to define their metadata description standards. An approach based purely on RDF Schema will automatically prevent these communities from publishing their standards in a registry.
- Effective automatic harvesting should understand both RDF Schema– and XML Schema– specified namespaces and application profiles.

Based on the limits of RDF Schema, Jane Hunter suggests using an XML Schema to approach applications. Studies have demonstrated that XML Schema has features that satisfy a significant number of application profile requirements. Nevertheless, there are problems associated with XML Schema, such as complexity, instability, and lack of tools. Therefore, "The importance of including support for both RDF Schema and XML Schema definitions in frameworks for metadata interoperability was highlighted" (Hunter 2000). Carl Lagoze and Jane Hunter therefore advocate "combining RDF and XML schemas to enhance interoperability between metadata application profiles" (Hunter and Lagoze n.d.).

4.3 METADATA SCHEMA REGISTRY

Before describing the metadata schema registry, this section will discuss the difference between the terms "scheme" and "schema."

The final draft of the Dublin Core Glossary defines 'scheme' as follows:

Scheme

A scheme, or schema, is a systematic, orderly combination of elements. A set of rules for encoding information that supports a specific community of users (User Guide Committee 2001).

This particular definition considers scheme and schema to be synonyms; however, this analysis is rare.

The 10th edition of the *Concise Oxford Dictionary*'s explanation of the words "schema" and "scheme" is the following:

schema (technical) a representation of a plan or theory in the form of an outline or model.

scheme a systematic plan or arrangement for attaining some particular object or putting a particular idea effect a particular ordered system or arrangement: *a classical rhyme scheme.* (Pearsall 2000)

In the widely used *Kingsoft Electronic Dictionary,* the definitions of schema and scheme are the following:

- *Schema:* The set of statements, expressed in data definition language, that completely describe the structure of a database.
- *Scheme:* The overall logical organization of a database.

The definition of metadata schema used for the purposes of the present discussion is most consistent with the Kingsoft definition. The metadata schema can be defined as a logical organization consisting of a group of certain metadata elements.

The final draft of the "Dublin Core Metadata Glossary" defines the metadata schema registry, or metadata registry for short, as follows:

A system to provide management of metadata elements. Metadata registries are formal systems that provide authoritative information about the semantics and structure of data elements. Each element will include the definition of the element, the qualifiers associated with it, mappings to multilingual versions and elements in other schema (User Guide Committee 2001).

The metadata schema registry is a database of metadata schemas and application profiles. It is widely recognized as an important mechanism not only for sharing authoritative information about metadata schema, but also for enhancing the reusability and interoperability of metadata schemas. The metadata registry provides the tools for managing and disclosing metadata schema declarations, application profile declarations, and value space declarations. As metadata schemas and application profiles are continuously evolving, metadata registries maintain the relationships among a schema's various versions in order to promote semantic and machine interoperability over time.

"Metadata schema registries enable the publication, navigation and sharing of information about metadata" (Johnston 2004). They provide indexes of terms and access to those terms across a variety of domains for different purposes. Some of the purposes of a metadata schema registry are (Research and Development Group of UKOLN 1999):

- authoritative definition of schema,
- change control,
- evolution of metadata language,
- declared relationships between different metadata schemas,
- best practices, and
- promoting existing schema to avoid duplicated effort.

Metadata registries exist at a variety of places and levels as part of the infrastructure for supporting digital information management. A metadata registry might be a richly functional database (the DESIRE registry is a prototype of such a registry), or it might be thin, meaning it only provides links to schema declarations. It can exist at the namespace level (e.g., DC Version 1.1) or registration authority level (e.g., DCMI). "A registry might have an ambition to register all schemas associated with a namespace concept (e.g., DC) and all application profiles containing elements associated with that namespace. Or there might be separate registries for namespaces and for 'communities of use,' the latter containing application profiles used by a particular implementor community" (Heery and Patel 2000).

Metadata registries are presently an important topic of digital library research. As the number of metadata and application-profile schemas designed to meet the needs of particular discourses and practice communities increases, the importance of registries' management and disclosure roles will similarly increase. The expectation is that registries will provide the tools for identifying and referencing established schemas and application profiles, potentially allowing machine mapping among different schemas. In addition, it is expected that such registries will contain, or link to, important controlled vocabularies from which the values of metadata fields can be selected.

In summary, the benefits of schema registries are (Heery 2003):

- increased interoperability between schemas as a result of reuse across many applications,
- less duplication of effort amongst implementers,
- promotion of existing solutions, and
- harmonization between competing. standards.

The metadata schema registries listed below have gained wide-ranging attention.

- *DESIRE Metadata Registry*

  The DESIRE project developed a model metadata registry. Needless to say, this is a pioneer among metadata schema registries. In order to demonstrate the feasibility of creating a useful and scalable metadata registry, the DESIRE project has developed a prototype metadata registry. It has been implemented using a relational database (mySQL) but a standard Web browser provides both administrative and user interfaces. ISO/IEC 11179 was used as a guide when constructing the registry, and strongly influenced the choice of data model. The project ended in March 2000, and related work in the form of implementing an RDF metadata schema registry was undertaken as part of the SCHEMAS project.

- *SCHEMAS Registry*

  The SCHEMAS Registry contains several metadata element sets as well as a large number of activity reports that describe and comment on various metadata-related activities and initiatives. The purpose of the SCHEMAS Registry is to approach the diverse and often confusing landscape of new and emerging metadata standards from the perspective of project or service implementers who must use these standards to design their own interoperable schemas. Additionally, as a part of the more general registry, a Multilingual RDF Registry focuses specifically on the use of RDF. A metadata schema registry is an important focus of the SCHEMAS project. This registry contains links to elements and definitions of both formal standards and schemas designed for specific projects. The registry also links to metadata activity reports derived from the SCHEMAS Metadata Watch service. The registry covers metadata relating to a broad range of functional requirements, from resource discovery to rights management and digital preservation. The registry itself will serve as a good-practice example of registry use and benefits; details of its configuration will be made available as a technology baseline for other registry implementers. The SCHEMAS Registry is a human readable registry, and is based on the DESIRE prototype. Work on the SCHEMAS Registry continued as part of the later CORES project.

- *MEG Registry*

  MEG, facilitated by the Interoperability Focus, is a forum for discussing the provision of educational resources at all levels across the United Kingdom. The MEG Registry project was funded by Joint Information Systems Committee (JISC)/Becta, and the project proposal was submitted in February 2002. The project was completed one year later. The MEG Registry is for educational metadata schemas. It has delivered a prototype registry and schema creation tools. UKOLN staff seeded the registry with Dublin Core and IEEE/LOM schemas. The MEG Registry project provided an opportunity to implement a prototype schema registry based on the recently stabilized RDF specifications and tools. The goal of the MEG Registry was to develop a more sustainable and scaleable solution than those already in existence. Essentially, the project reengineered the DESIRE Registry as an RDF application. It was shaped by, but also refined, the SCHEMAS project data model. The registry reads and then indexes machine-readable descriptions of metadata vocabularies. It provides browse/search interfaces for human readers (HTML) and software tools (query API <HTTP GET>).

- *CORES Registry*

    Funded by the European Community, the CORES project provides a forum that encourages the sharing of metadata semantics. The CORES project hosted a metadata schemas registry designed to enable users to discover and navigate metadata element sets. It is a registry of core vocabularies and profiles that enables projects and services to use a common model to declare their use of standards in schemas. CORES maintains a registry of core vocabularies and profiles, thereby encouraging the uptake and use of the registration model developed by the SCHEMAS project. Projects and services can register their schemas using the schema creation tool and Web interface provided by CORES. According to the report on DC-2003 prepared by Rachael Heery and other professionals, "CORES continued work on the MEG Registry code base, enhancing the software by adding two main pieces of functionality: authentication and annotation, and also enabling the display of administrative metadata associated with schemas. User registration data, annotations and the schema registry are all stored in an RDF database. The registry is implemented as a set of Perl scripts, using the Redland RDF toolkit to query and manipulate the RDF databases" (Herry et al. 2003).

- *MetaForm*

    Metaform was launched in the Goettingen State and University Library in Germany. It is a database for metadata formats that places a special emphasis on the expression of Dublin Core and its manifestations in various implementations. The formats are registered with their elements and definitions. This database allows for crosswalks between the DCMES and its various dialects, as well as for crosscuts of a particular Dublin Core element (e.g., DC.Creator) through all of the formats. The user may also view mappings between DC applications and other formats. This service is part of the Metadata Initiative of German Libraries (META-LIB) Project. This was conceived as a database that would identify the core elements used for the description of networked resources. It should be noted that, in principle, MetaForm is a highly dynamic instrument subject to frequent adaptation to the metadata formats that are themselves in flux.

- *DCMI Metadata Schemas Registry*

    DCMI's Metadata Registry is designed to promote the discovery and reuse of existing metadata definitions. By March 2004, it was providing users and applications with an authoritative source of information about the Dublin Core element set and related vocabularies in 23 languages. This registry simplifies the discovery of terms and related definitions and illustrates the relationship between terms. The reuse of existing metadata terms is essential for standardization and promotes greater interoperability between metadata element sets. The discovery of existing terms is an essential prerequisite step in this process. This application promotes the wider adaptation, standardization, and interoperability of metadata by facilitating its discovery and reuse across diverse disciplines and communities of practice. The DCMI Metadata Schemas Registry was developed by the Dublin Core Metadata Registry Working Group. It was developed, and is distributed, as an open-source project, built entirely upon open-source/open-standards software. The original mandate of the DCMI Registry Working Group was to establish a metadata registry to support the activities of the DCMI. The goal was to enable the registration, discovery, and navigation of semantics defined by the DCMI in order to provide an authoritative source of information regarding the DCMI vocabulary. Emphasis was placed on promoting the use of the Dublin Core and managing the change and evolution of the DCMI vocabulary. The overriding goal has been the development of a generic registry tool useful for registry applications in general, not just for the DCMI. The most recent activity directly related to DCMI Metadata Schemas Registry was the installation of a DCMI Metadata Schemas Registry by the Library of the Chinese Academy of Science (LCAS) in July 2004. The LCAS is leading a national digital library standards development project that involves the participation of all the major libraries in China. Part of this project involves the development of a metadata registry. The recently installed DCMI Metadata Schemas Registry will serve that purpose.

- *ULIS Open Metadata Registry*

  In addition to providing information about metadata schemas, metadata schema registries also play important roles in the interoperation of metadata among communities that speak different languages. The international implementation of the terms DCMI Metadata Schema Registry has contributed a lot to this effort. The Open Metadata Registry of the Japanese University of Library and Information Science (ULIS), a multilingual metadata schemas registry based on RDF schema, is another step in this direction. The goal of this project is to develop an open metadata schema registry. The ULIS Open Metadata Registry provides reference descriptions of the basic 15 elements of Dublin Core Metadata Elements Set (DCMES), Dublin Core qualifiers, and a controlled vocabulary for the Type element recommended by the DCMI. As of June 2001, the 15 elements are described in 22 languages, and the qualifiers are expressed in English and Japanese. As an experiment, the registry also includes descriptive elements of Nippon Cataloging Rules. The RDF schema language is used for the metadata schemas. The registry is composed using XML technologies, such as XML Stylesheet Language for Transformations (XSLT) and Document Object Model (DOM). Reference descriptions are encoded in multiple languages with Unicode (UTF8) in the current version, while the previous version used local character encoding schemes.

Generally, metadata schema registries can take different forms and function as some or all of the following (Heery 2003):

- An authoritative source for a particular standard such as the DCMI Registry
- A repository of schemas (both element sets and application profiles) relevant to a particular sector or domain such as the MEG registry itself which focuses on the requirements of UK educational services
- A mapping and crosswalk registry such as explored within the DESIRE project

If we take MetaForm as example, we will find that registration is the first step for setting up a metadata registry service. As mentioned above, MetaForm is a tool that offers a comparative analysis of different Dublin Core applications. It enables the analysis and comparison of different metadata formats. Figure 4.1 is a MetaForm entry form for registering a new metadata format. With this template, the user can register a metadata or related format that will then be included in the MetaForm database.

4.4 METADATA WORKING FLOW

During its life cycle, metadata proceeds through five stages: generation, harvesting, storage, management, and usage. The first two procedures are crucial to the whole life cycle of metadata because they form the basis of the next three stages. Therefore, this section will focus only on metadata generating and harvesting.

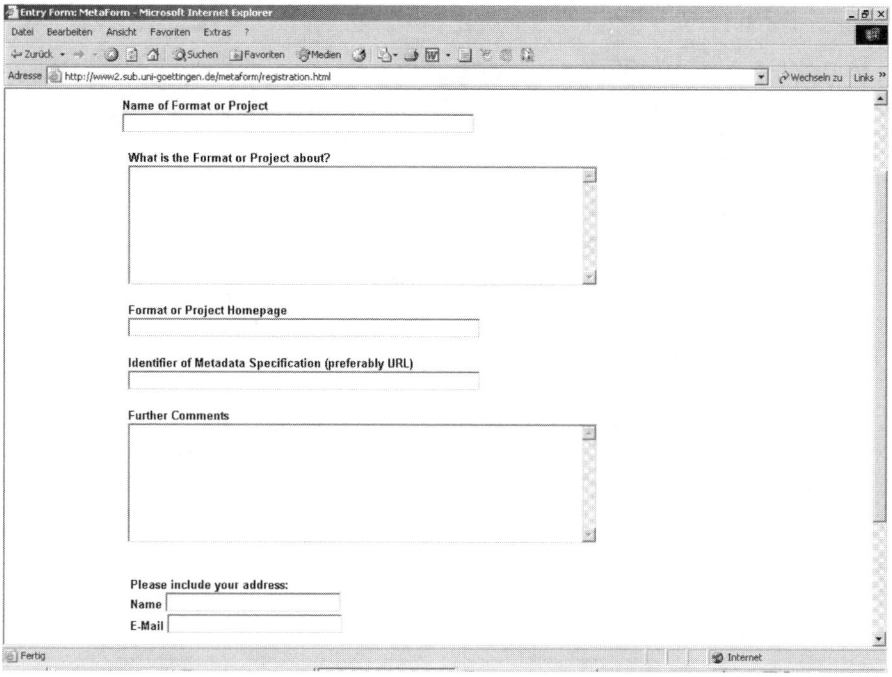

Figure 4.1 A Metaform entry form.

4.4.1 Metadata Creation

When considering metadata creation, three basic questions must be answered:

- Is it necessary to create metadata?
- If so, who should create the metadata?
- How is metadata created?

This chapter has already addressed the importance, necessity, and functions of metadata and, in the process, has provided an affirmative answer to the first question. Therefore, we are free to concentrate on the second and third questions.

"In any case, all agree that one of the greatest challenges to achieving the vision of the Semantic Web lies not in the development of ontologies, inference engines, or intelligent agents, but rather in encouraging authors to provide meaningful metadata along with their web resources" (Caplan 2003, 52). Normally, an information resource's metadata can be created by the resource creator, the Web crawler, or the professional metadata creator. Table 4.1, based on Dempsey and Heery's description, illustrates the methods by which the three kinds of metadata are generated. They classified the metadata formats into three brands, and differentiated between the creation methods based on the level of manual involvement. The two professionals thought this "in turn would affect level and type of resource required for record creation and the cost" (Dempsey and Heery 1998).

Table 4.1 Typology of metadata formats with regard to creation method

	Origin	**Format**	**Creation method**
Brand one	Full text indexes	Proprietary formats	Created automatically by a gathering process involving web crawlers
Brand two	Simple structured generic formats	Proprietary formats Dublin Core IAFA/WHOIS++ templates RFC 1807	Manually created or manually enhanced on the basis of automatically extracted descriptions
Brand three	More complex structure, domain specific	FGDC MARC GILS ...	Created manually, probably requiring knowledge of the format and some familiarity with cataloging rules, in order to achieve high quality consistent results
	Part of a larger semantic framework	TEI headers ICPSR EAD CIMI ...	

4.4.1.1 Creating Metadata with Web Crawlers

Web resource metadata can be generated via automatic or human processes. Within the Web, search engine spiders and HTML and XML editors and generators produce various types of metadata automatically.

There are so many information resources within the Web that it is impossible to create metadata manually for each of them. Search engines are one way to make the Web accessible automatically. "Web search engines harvest and index a significant portion of the Internet and provide low cost index access to it, generally in an advertiser-supported model" (Duval et al. 2002). Such an index can be considered a kind of metadata and it provides a surprisingly cost-effective solution to resource discovery for many information needs.

Within the search engine, Web crawlers, also known as spiders or indexing robots, are responsible for searching the Web and collecting metadata. This software automatically extracts data from Web pages, often using the content of the HTML title tag and the first body section of the text. "Crawlers are smart pieces of software that 'traverse' the web, visiting sites continuously, saving copies of the resources and their locations as they go in order to build up a huge catalog of fully indexed pages. They typically provide powerful searching facilities and extremely large result sets, which are 'relevance-ranked' in an effort to make them useable" (Gill 1998, 12). Crawlers provide high recall, but offer less precision than directories, which are human-created lists of network resources that use metadata in order to classify and catalog Web resources. Directories are more precise than crawlers, but have a smaller recall and are dependent on human insight.

The following example is one search result for DCMI using Google, currently one of the most famous search engines.

Example of Metadata included in one record located by the Google search engine

```
Dublin Core Metadata Initiative (DCMI)
... 2003-09-15, Makx Dekkers, DCMI Managing Director, has pub-
lished the next status report
of the Dublin Core Metadata Initiative, with highlights of the
last year...
Description: Open forum to develop the Dublin Core metadata
standard.
Category: Reference>Libraries>...>CataloguingCataloging>Metada
ta>DublinCore
dublincore.org/ - 13k - 13 Oct 2003 - Cached - Similar pages
```

From the above example, we can observe that the metadata generated by a Web crawler is unstructured and very rough. That's the main reason that such data are not always considered to be metadata.

Though creating metadata with Web crawlers has the great advantages of low cost and high efficiency, it has some limitations. Firstly, the Web crawler is only valid for creating metadata for Web resources. Secondly, the quality of some of the metadata generated by Web crawlers is doubtful. The metadata created by Web crawlers is often incomplete. Inconsistent use of HTML by authors may even lead to incomplete and unhelpful content. Lastly, not all metadata can be generated automatically, especially metadata that requires high intelligence, for example, subject, coverage, and so forth. However, this method of generating metadata is necessary only when faced with dramatically large numbers of information resources. "A hybrid approach of having a tool automatically generate metadata and then allowing users to check and modify this metadata would seem to offer the best of both automatic and manual worlds" (Wood 1997).

4.4.1.2 Creating Metadata with Resource Creators

Previously, two opposing opinions existed with regards to author-generated metadata. On one hand, there is a long-standing suspicion that when a resource author is also tapped for metadata creation, the author-generated metadata could be of poor quality and might actually hamper rather than aid the resource (Thomas and Griffin 1998). Most resource authors have little previous knowledge of metadata creation. They encounter difficulties when indexing their own information resources. For example, it's easy for a novice creator to understand the meaning of the element "title" in the DC metadata schema. However, without any instructions, the meaning of the element "coverage" in the same schema is not so implicitly understood. It's quite possible that some metadata elements created by the authors themselves mislead users rather than help them find what they really need.

Conversely, some believe that the Web resource author is a good candidate for metadata creation. Jane Greenberg, in collaboration with three colleagues, once conducted an experiment to determine the resource author's ability to create acceptable metadata in an organizational setting. Their research shows that the participating authors were capable of creating acceptable metadata for the National Institute of Environmental Health Sciences (NIEHS) Dublin Core metadata schema. The metadata generally required only minor, if any, revision. "The quality of the metadata produced clearly suggests authors in an organizational setting can create good quality metadata and that they have the ability to create professional level metadata" (Greenberg et al. 2001). Authors have the best understanding of the resource they produced, so their knowledge should be valuable for Web resource metadata creation. An author should be the best choice for creating some select elements. An author's unique understanding of his or her own resource and the enormous amount of available information resources are the two most important reasons for encouraging author-generated metadata.

However, the above statement fails to consider the two following points.

The first is whether the author wants to create the metadata for his or her own resources. The Internet is such a free realm, that no one can be forced to do anything in the virtual world. An author's incentive for creating metadata is the desire to ensure that his or her own resources get higher and more accurate hits and are available for as many users as possible. Besides, the premise is that there is a helpful tool that could be easily used by the author, who may be a layperson, of the metadata creation to index his or her own resources The availability and usability of such a tool have a great effect on author-generated metadata. A tool for creating metadata is a necessity, not only for ease in cataloging, but also for data integrity and other quality assurance matters. So far, a lot of tools have been developed for the purpose of creating metadata. A helpful lists of the tools and templates for creating metadata can be found at <http://dublincore.org/tools/>. The Dublin Core Metadata Template provided by the Nordic Metadata Project is a very good example from the list, and is shown in Figure 4.2. A brief description of each element is offered in addition to its name. This service assures the quality creation of Dublin Core metadata by the Nordic "Net-publisher" community. Additionally the template's drop-down menus (shown in Figure 4.3) provide not only good assistance in generating metadata, but also a valid method for authority control.

At present, although tools exist for the creation of metadata in some of the more complex schemes, Dublin Core–style metadata must still be entered by hand. "Work is currently underway within projects such as the European-funded DESIRE to investigate means by which much of this metadata creation may be automated. Such automation will undoubtedly make the creation and upkeep of useful metadata more straightforward, and therefore hopefully more commonplace" (Miller 1996).

The second question is whether author-generated metadata is acceptable or usable. It is likely that providing more guidance for authors would ensure that more of the metadata elements that they created would be acceptable. HotMeta is primarily designed for the descriptive metadata of various kinds of information resources, and it provides a very detailed and easily understood user guide to assist the metadata creator. Furthermore, "Validation of metadata records can happen in three places, depending on how HotMeta is configured" (Distributed System Technology Center 2003):

- Metadata records that are created or updated by MetaEdit are validated before they are saved to the repository or to a file. The user can ignore this and (attempt to) save a record with validation errors.

- Depending on its configuration settings, the HotMeta Broker will validate new records and updates to records, rejecting any with errors. This applies to metadata from MetaEdit, the Gatherer, and the import utility.

- Depending on its configuration settings, the HotMeta Gatherer will validate records before sending them to the Broker or writing them to an output file.

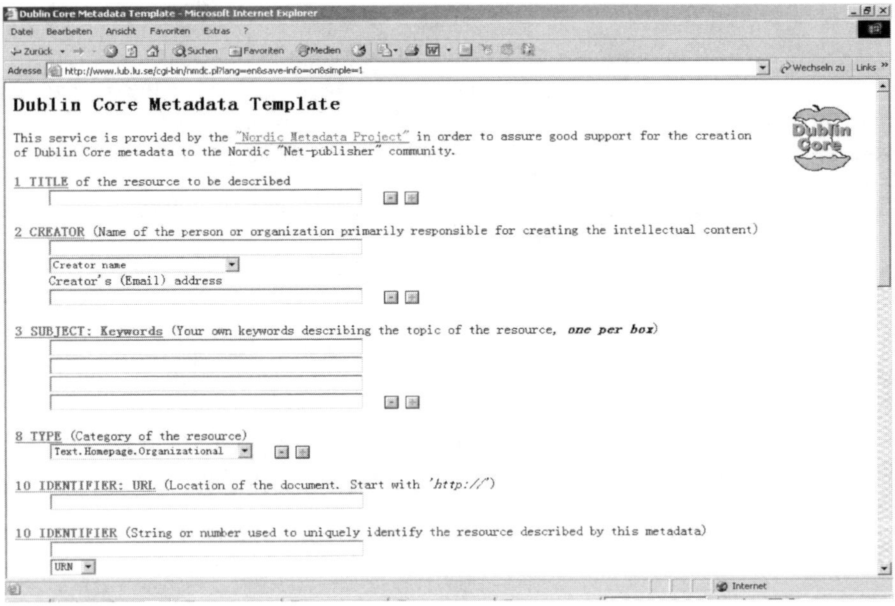

Figure 4.2 The short Dublin Core Metadata Template.

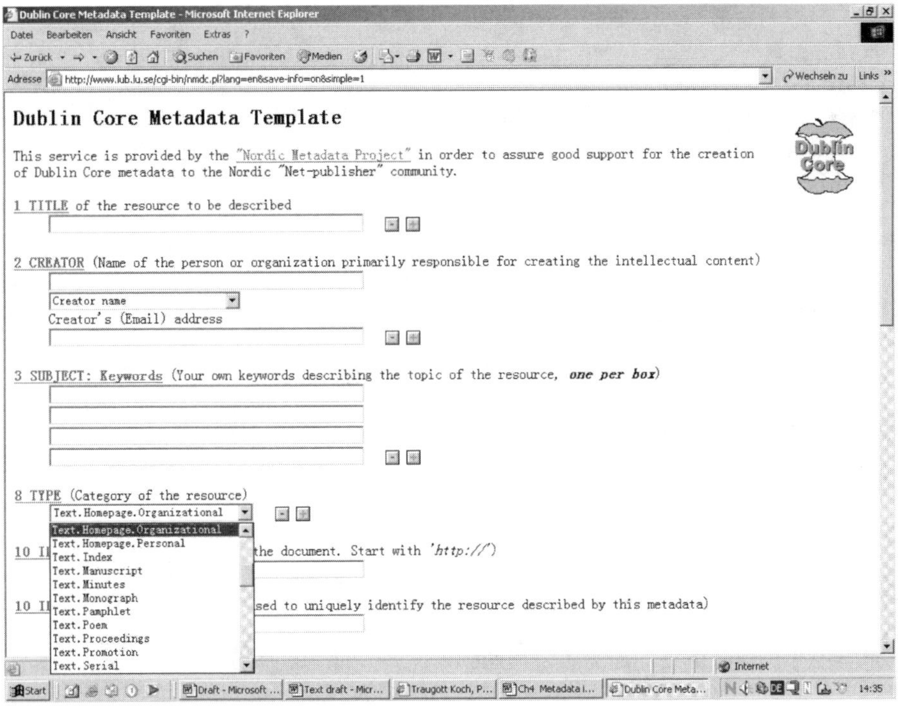

Figure 4.3 The drop-down menu of the Dublin Core Metadata Template.

This validation mechanism doubtlessly improves the quality of the metadata stored in the HotMeta database.

Currently, a number of digital library projects support author-generated metadata. This practice makes sense when the rapid growth of the Internet is weighed against the economics of hiring metadata professionals. Two examples of digital library projects that support author-generated metadata are the National Digital Library of Theses and Dissertations (NDLTD) and the Synthesis Coalition's National Engineering Education Delivery System (NEEDS)a digital library for engineering education. These projects both have Web forms that help authors to create consistent and accurate metadata for theses and dissertations contributed to, respectively, the NDLTD and courseware contributed to NEEDS.

In a few years, there will be thousands of authors and publishers providing metadata in Dublin Core and local formats based on it. It is important to support metadata creation with appropriate user guides and tools. The resulting metadata must be properly indexed so that the resources can be searched. "The experience from the Nordic metadata has shown that the applications and documentation required for Dublin Core production and use can be developed very effectively in international co-operation, and then adapted according to the local needs for national and regional projects" (Hakala et al. 1998).

4.4.1.3 Creating Metadata with Professional Metadata Creators

Prior to the Web, most metadata for resource discovery was created manually by labor-intensive library cataloging. Some cataloging rules remain the most successful standards for describing books and periodicals, though catalogs are costly to create and impractical for many materials available on the Internet. Web crawlers are capable of producing fairly accurate metadata for certain elements, such as "date produced" or "MIME type," but their results are inconsistent for more intellectually demanding metadata, such as "subject descriptions" or "author." As a result, many environments are better suited to human intellectual processing for the production of schema-specific metadata.

In a paper in *D-Lib Magazine*, Godfrey Rust (1998) proposed an integrated model for descriptive and rights metadata. Rust is primarily concerned with metadata-related activity in the rights-owning communities. He argues that creators and rights owners will become the principal sources of core metadata in the Web environment, and that "metadata will be generated *simultaneously* and *at source* to meet the requirements of discovery, access, protection and reward" (Rust 1998).

Professional metadata creators and resource authors represent two main classes of metadata creators. "Metadata professionals, such as catalogers and indexers, are people who have had formal training and are proficient in the use of descriptive and content-value standards. Although researchers have noted problems with inter-indexer consistency, professionals generally produce high quality metadata" (Greenberg et al. 2001). As discussed in the previous section, resource authors create the intellectual content of a work. Researchers regularly produce abstracts, keywords, and other types of metadata for their scientific and scholarly publications. Visual artists, another class of authors, generally sign and date their works. In the Web environment, authors can provide metadata via a template or editor, while turning to Webmasters or other skilled people to make their work Web accessible.

Many kinds of metadata created by experts are extremely complicated. They have been developed to operate within a narrowly defined field of work, and are poorly suited to describing a wide range of resources. However, sometimes it is imperative for a professional to create metadata. If it were feasible for an author to generate metadata, there would be two levels for one kind of metadata, just like Cataloging in Publication (CIP) records and the records in OPAC in the library world. The two levels data might differ in quality and serve different purposes.

Between the two extremes of automatically and manually generated metadata lies a broad range of metadata that can be created automatically to some degree, and which can be expected to grow in importance with advances in areas such as natural language processing, data mining, and profile and pattern recognition algorithms.

"Content creation applications (word processors, electronic paper such as PDF, and Website creation tools) often have facilities for author-supplied attributes or automated capture of attributes that can simplify the creation of metadata. As these facilities grow more sophisticated, it will be easier and more natural to combine application-supplied metadata (e.g., creation dates, tagged structural elements, file formats and related information), creator-supplied metadata (keywords, authors, affiliations, for example) and inference-based metadata (classification metadata based on automated classification algorithms, for example)" (Duval et al. 2002). Combining attributes of these approaches will increase the quality and reduce the cost of metadata creation.

In short, a tripartite division exits in the area of metadata creation. Web indexes based on the robotic extraction of (currently unstructured) metadata are automatic and cheap to create. Documentation of a particular collection by specialists is expensive. So-called information gateway services add value through intellectual effort, and are correspondingly expensive. These factors will drive the creation of both author-produced metadata and more sophisticated automatic extraction techniques. However, the creation of full, structured metadata will remain expensive.

Ultimately, the richness of metadata descriptions will be determined by the policies and practices designated by the agency creating the metadata, which are guided by the functional requirements of services or applications. Some of the tradeoffs for systems and searchers are listed below (Duval et al. 2002):

Detailed metadata descriptions:

- May improve searching precision
- Require higher investment in creation of metadata
- Make it more difficult to promote consistency in creation of metadata

Simple descriptions:

- Are easier and less costly to generate
- May result in more false results, or more effort on the part of searchers to identify most relevant results
- Improve probability of cross-disciplinary interoperability

It's obvious the balance between the richness and completeness of the metadata and the velocity of metadata creation has to be considered when deciding by which method the metadata will be created.

The need for quality assurance in metadata creation was raised during the 2003 Dublin Core Conference in Seattle, Washington, United States. The presenter commented that "some problems arose due to errors, omissions and ambiguities in the metadata" (Barton, Currier, and Hey 2003). Solutions to this problem should be seriously sought.

4.4.2 Metadata Harvesting

Before discussing the harvesting of metadata, it's necessary to establish where metadata exists. Metadata can exist separately from the resources it describes and, in some cases, it may be included as part of the resource. Generally, metadata exists in the following three locations:

- embedded in the Web resource headers,
- standing alone in separate files, and
- connected with the resource.

Therefore, on the World Wide Web, there are currently three ways to access metadata.

The first is through embedded metadata, the metadata describing the document within which it is contained. For example, a TEI header might accompany conformant TEI documents. However, independent TEI headers, which describe remote documents, may also exist. Metadata can also be included in the HEAD part of an HTML document, or within documents generated by word processors. The embedded HTML tag is the simplest example of embedded metadata, and it is common in some of the domain-specific SGML frameworks. The following is an example of such embedded metadata.

Figure 4.4 is the home page of Electronic Mathematical Archiving Network Initiative (EMANI). The head area of the HTML document for Figure 4.4 appears below. As displayed in the document, HTML <META> tags are placed within the page's <HEAD> </HEAD> area. Dublin Core metadata is often stored in the <HEAD> </HEAD> area of a Web page, and may be viewed simply by selecting View...| Source from the Web browser's menu bar.

Example of Metadata Embedded in the HTML Document

```
<!DOCTYPE HTML PUBLIC "-//SoftQuad Software//DTD HoTMetaL PRO
6.0::19990601::extensions to HTML 4.0//EN" "hmpro6.dtd">

<HTML>

 <HEAD>

    <TITLE>EMANI Home Page</TITLE>

    <META HTTP-EQUIV="Content-Type" CONTENT="text/html;
    charset=iso-8859-1">
```

```
<META NAME="author" CONTENT="Bernd Walser">

<META NAME="description" CONTENT="EMANI home page">

<META NAME="keywords" CONTENT="EMANI, emani, Mathematics,
digital">

<META NAME="language" CONTENT="EN">

</HEAD>
```

Resource creators are encouraged to insert the metadata about their resources in the resources' HTML documents. Metadata incorporated within resources is easiest to harvest.

The second way to access metadata is during Hypertext Transfer Protocol (HTTP) transfer, when the server transfers some metadata to the client about the object being transferred. During an HTTP GET, some metadata is transferred from the server to the client, while during a PUT or a POST, metadata is transferred from the client to the server. The information about who exactly is making a statement must be part of the architecture of the World Wide Web. Whose statement, whose property is that metadata?

The third way to find metadata is to look it up in another document. This practice was not very common until the Platform for Internet Content Selection (PICS) initiative defined label formats specifically to represent information about World Wide Web resources. "The PICS architecture specifically allows for PICS labels that are resources about other resources to be buried within the resource itself, to be retrieved as separate resources, or to be passed over during the http transaction" (Berners-Lee 1997).

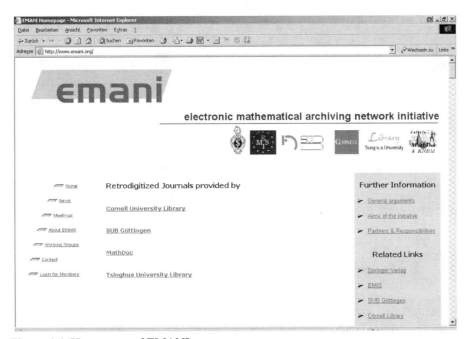

Figure 4.4 Home page of EMANI.

One comparison has been made on the basis of the Nordic Metadata Project's practice for gathering metadata between the circumstance before the invention of Open Archives Initiative (OAI) and that after its invention. During the earlier stages, there is no OAI, but later, with OAI, it becomes easier to harvest metadata by automatically granting permission to access metadata when the resource is provided on the Web and eliminating the need to seek permission to access metadata. OAI is a common framework for Web communities, allowing them to harvest metadata in a standard manner.

Robots are the most common tools for harvesting metadata on the World Wide Web. There are some other tools for harvesting metadata in the virtual world. However, "Robots and some harvesting tools only index static and fixed documents. Great many other useful Web-based information resources in the 'deep web', including the contents of databases and library catalogues are very often accessible through a local interface" (Graham 2001, 291). In order to expose the contents of the rich database repositories on the Web, the OAI has developed a Protocol for Metadata Harvesting, OAI-PMH, which uses Dublin Core and XML. This program, which is somewhat technical in focus, features four leading implementers of the Protocol, who offer practical perspectives on this OAI application. The OAI-PMH supplies a formalized framework for the coordinated exchange of metadata in the distributed and decentralized electronic information environments. The key features of the OAI-PMH are (Fast 2003):

- low barrier to entry,
- application-independent, and
- open standards (XML, HTTP).

The OAI-PMH provides an application-independent interoperability framework for metadata harvesting. It is a tool for illuminating the above-mentioned resources through a low-overhead standards-based interoperability framework (see Figures 4.5 and 4.6).

There are two classes of participants in the OAI-PMH framework (The OAI Executive 2002):

- *Data providers* administer systems that support the OAI-PMH as a means of exposing metadata. It uses the protocol to reveal metadata about content in their collections; and

- *Service providers* use metadata harvested via the OAI-PMH as a basis for building value-added services.

Dublin Core has been established as the common metadata set for the protocol, and, as such, allows simple cross-discipline searching. As noted earlier, the framework supports the use of discipline- or domain-specific metadata sets as well.

4.5 OTHER ISSUES

Other issues concerning metadata implementation will be discussed briefly in the following sections.

4.5.1 Vocabulary

Vocabularies are the set of properties, or metadata elements, defined by resource description communities. It is hoped that standardizing metadata vocabularies will encourage the reuse and extension of semantics among disparate information communities.

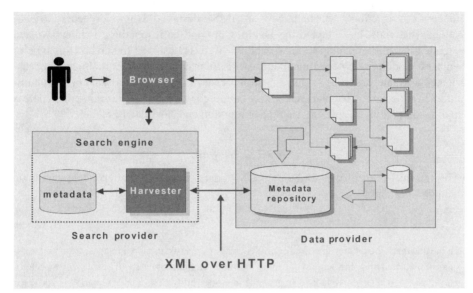

Figure 4.5 The OAI protocol model for metadata harvesting.
Source: Fast 2003

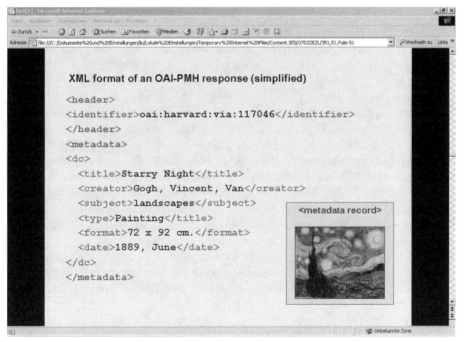

Figure 4.6 XML format of an OAI-PMH response (simplified).

For example, the DCMI, an international resource description community that focuses on simple resource description for discovery, has adopted RDF, which, additionally, is a tool for publishing both human-readable and machine-processable vocabularies.

Educom's Instructional Metadata System (IMS), designed to provide access to educational materials, has adopted the Dublin Core and corresponding architecture, and extended it with domain-specific semantics. "RDF is designed to support this type of semantic modularity by creating an infrastructure that supports the combination of distributed attribute registries. Thus, a central registry is not required. This permits communities to declare vocabularies that may be reused, extended and/or refined to address application or domain specific descriptive requirements" (Miller 1998).

4.5.2 Crosswalk

In the final draft of the "Dublin Core Metadata Glossary," the term "crosswalk" is defined as follows:

Crosswalk

A table that maps the relationships and equivalencies between two or more metadata formats. Crosswalks or metadata mapping support the ability of search engines to search effectively across heterogeneous databases, i.e. crosswalks help promote interoperability (User Guide Committee 2001).

Crosswork is a high level mapping table for conversion. Undoubtedly, it more or less means a sacrifice, because when one metadata schema is mapped into another one, it's almost impossible to find all elements in the original schema completely matching with those of the other. Under such a case, some elements disappear after mapping.

Crosswalks require some degree of sacrifice because it's almost impossible for two metadata standards to be completely equivalent. When data is transferred from one metadata standard to another, it's normal for some original fields or elements to be lost.

A number of projects use crosswalks to transform one form of metadata to another. For example, Michigan State University developed the Innovative Interfaces XML Harvester, a tool to help convert the collection-level information in EAD records into MARC communication format. This permitted the loading of records that refer to the more detailed EAD record into Michigan State University's online catalog. Other projects have developed crosswalks that convert DC records into MARC, and that adapt header information from TEI into MARC. None of these transformations is easy. EAD, for instance, handles the date information for personal names differently from the MARC 100 field, and it has a very unique treatment of subjects. DC simplifies the basic set of MARC tags greatly, which tempts coders to enter a broader range of information than would be acceptable in many well-regulated MARC databases.

METS is a kind of standard designed for transforming metadata across various applications. It avoids transformation problems by accepting descriptive metadata in any format and with any local rules or specific standards. "This liberal approach makes sense in an environment where standards are evolving too rapidly for crosswalk development, and where the point is to ingest some form of description without misleading implications from overly simplistic copying of one field to another in a format with different standards" (Seadle 2002, 257).

The use and promotion of metadata across a networked information environment poses significant challenges, although potential solutions are being developed. Currently, a number of crosswalks are available and are accepted in most of the metadata schema registries discussed in section 4.3.

4.5.3 Authority Control

Authority control over metadata content is usually optional. The Dublin Core, for example, allows the specification of authoritative sources for elements such as Creator and Subject, but does not require content to emanate from an authoritative source. When metadata lacks authority control, either that control should be applied before the metadata records are added to the library catalog, or the records should be stored in a separate database in which consistency of content is not expected.

Metadata's unsuitability for direct use in library catalogs is primarily a result of the fact that library catalogs use semantic or content standards and data registries, whereas metadata does not. The integrity of a library catalog is dependent upon the consistent application of a well-defined set of standards and the utilization of carefully maintained data registries, such as name authority files and controlled vocabulary lists. Though authority control is not required or expected in metadata, metadata element sets do permit the use of authorized forms of names and subjects, and provide conventions to indicate authoritative sources when controlled headings are used. "When a significant portion of the records in a database fails to meet the criteria for consistency and standardization, the database loses its integrity and can fulfill neither the objectives defined by Cutter and others, nor those expected by the users of the database" (American Library Association 1998).

4.5.4 Multilingualism

Increasing attention has been focused on the current domination of the metadata world by one language. In response to the strong appeal for the equal treatment of different kinds of languages, multilingualism has become an important topic in metadata implementation. "Some standards typically deal with multilingualism through the complementary processes of *internationalization* and *localization:* the former process relates to the creation of 'neutral' standards, whereas the latter refers to the adaptation of such a neutral standard to a local context" (Duval et al. 2002).

Multilingualism is one aspect of the broader issue of multiculturalism, which is concerned with, amongst other things,

- the way in which dates are represented in different calendars,
- the direction in which text is displayed and read,
- the cultural connotations of certain icons and pictograms, and
- standards of practice (name order, collation standards, leading article standards).

Clearly, many of these concerns exceed the immediate context of metadata. However, as mentioned above, it is important that metadata describes relevant characteristics, and that it does so in ways that respect cultural and language differences.

REFERENCES

American Library Association. Committee on Cataloging: Description and Access. 1998. *Task Force on Metadata and the Cataloging Rules. Final Report, Section 4*. Available at: http://www.ala.org/Content/NavigationMenu/ALCTS/Division_groups/MARBI/Next_Section_4.htm. Accessed 14 May 2003.

Baker, Thomas. 2002. *DCMI Usage Board Review of Application Profiles.* Available at: http://dublincore.org/usage/documents/profiles/. Accessed 9 March 2004.

Barton, Jane, Sarah Currier, and Jessie M. N. Hey. 2003. "Building Quality Assurance into Metadata Creation: An Analysis Based on the Learning Objects and e-Prints Communities of Practice." In *DC-2003: Proceedings of the International DCMI Conference and Workshop,* September 28–October 2, 2003, Seattle, Washington, 39–48. Syracuse, N.Y.: Information Institute of Syracuse.

Berners-Lee, Tim. 1997. *Metadata Architecture.* Available at: http://www.w3.org/DesignIssues/Metadata.html. Accessed 25 February 2003.

Bray, Tim, Dave Hollander, Andrew Layman, and Richard Tobin, eds. 2006. *Namespaces in XML 1.0 (Second Edition): W3C Recommendation 16 August.* Available at: http://www.w3.org/TR/REC-xml-names/. Accessed 15 April 2007.

Caplan, Priscilla. 2003. *Metadata Fundamentals for All Librarians.* Chicago, Ill.: The American Library Association.

Dekkers, Makx. 2001. *Application Profiles, or How to Mix and Match Metadata Schema.* Available at: http://www.cultivate-int.org/issue3/schemas/#ref-03. Accessed 9 March 2004.

Dempsey, Lorcan, and Rachel Heery. 1998. "Metadata: A Current View of Practice and Issues." *Journal of Documentation* (March): 145–72.

Distributed System Technology Centre. 2003. *HotMeta: User Guide. Version 3.2.2.* Available at: http://www.dstc.edu.au/Downloads/metasuite/HMUserGuide-3.2.2.pdf. Accessed 1 October 2003.

Duval, Erik, Wayne Hodgins, Stuart Sutton, and Stuart L. Weibel. 2002. "Metadata Principles and Practicalities," *D-Lib Magazine* 8 (4). Available at: http://webdoc.sub.gwdg.de/edoc/aw/d-lib/dlib/april02/weibel/04weibel.html. Accessed 25 February 2003.

Fast, Karl. 2003. *Metadata Harvesting: Reflections on Metadata in a Networked World.* Available at: www.asis.org/IA03/fast.ppt. Accessed 22 October 2003.

Gill, Tony. 1998. "Metadata and the World Wide Web." In *Introduction to Metadata: Pathway to Digital Information,* ed. Los Angeles, CA. USA: Getty Information Institute.

Graham, Rebecca A. 2001. "Metadata Harvesting," *Library Hi Tech* 19 (3): 290–295.

Greenberg, Jane, Maria Cristina Pattuelli, Bijan Parsia, and W. Davenport Robertson. 2001. Author-generated Dublin Core Metadata for Web Resources: A Baseline Study in an Organization," *Journal of Digital Information* 2 (2). Available at: http://jodi.ecs.soton.ac.uk/Articles/v02/i02/Greenberg/. Accessed 13 June 2003.

Guenther, Rebecca. 2002. *Library Application Profile.* Available at: http://dublincore.org/documents/2002/04/16/library-application-profile/index.shtml. Accessed 9 March 2004.

Hakala, Juha, Preben Hansen, Ole Husby, Traugott Koch, and Susanne Thorborg. 1998. *The Nordic Metadata Project: Final Report.* Available at: http://www.lib.helsinki.fi/meta/nmfinal.doc. Accessed 28 October 2003.

Heery, Rachel. 2003. *Registry for Educational Metadata Schemas: Final Project Report and Recommendations.* Available at: http://www.ukoln.ac.uk/metadata/education/regproj/report.pdf. Accessed 2 April 2004.

Heery, Rachel, Pete Johnston, Csaba Fülöp, and András Micsik. 2003. *Metadata Schema Registries in the Partially Semantic Web: The CORES Experience.* Available at: http://dc2003.ischool.washington.edu/Archive-03/03heery.pdf. Accessed 1 April 2004.

Heery, Rachel, and Manjula Patel. 2000. "Application Profiles: Mixing and Matching Metadata Schemas," *Ariadne* 25. Available at: http://www.ariadne.ac.uk/issue25/app-profiles/intro.html. Accessed 29 October 2003.

Hunter, Jane. 2000. *An XML Schema Approach to Application Profiles.* Available at: http://archive.dstc.edu.au/maenad/appln_profiles.html. Accessed 29 October 2003.

Hunter, Jane, and Carl Lagoze. n.d. *Combing RDF and XML Schemas to Enhance Interoperability between Metadata Application Profiles.* Available at: http://www.org/cdrom/papers/572/index.html. Accessed 29 October 2003.

Johnston, Pete. 2004. *JISC IE Metadata Schema Registry*. Available at: http://www.ukoln.ac.uk/ projects/iemsr/. Accessed 4 March 2004.

Miller, Eric. 1998. "An Introduction to the Resource Description Framework," *D-Lib Magazine* (May). Available at: http://www.dlib.org/dlib/may98/miller/05miller.html. Accessed 4 November 2003.

Miller, Paul. 1996. *Metadata for the Masses*. Available at: http://www.ariadne.ac.uk/issue5/ metadata-masses/. Accessed 7 December 2003

Open Archives Initiative Executive. 2002. *The Open Archives Initiative Protocol for Metadata Harvesting: Protocol Version 2.0 of 2002–06–01*. Available at: http://www.openarchives. org/OAI/openarchivesprotocol.htm. Accessed 10 June 2003.

Pearsall, Judy, ed. 2000. *Concise Oxford Dictionary Tenth Edition for 2000* (CD-ROM). Oxford.

Powell, Andy, and Harry Wagner, ed. 2001. *Namespaces Policy for the Dublin Core Metadata Initiative (DCMI)*. Available at: http://dublincore.org/documents/dcmi-namespace/. Accessed 4 March 2004.

Research and Development Group of UKOLN. 1999. *DESIRE Metadata Registry*. Available at: http://desire.ukoln.ac.uk/registry/. Accessed 10 March 2004.

Rust, Godfrey. 1998. "Metadata: The Right Approach: An integrated Model for Descriptive and Rights Metadata in e-Commerce." *D-Lib Magazine* (July/August). Available at: http:// www.dlib.org/dlib/july98/rust/07rust.html. Accessed 4 November 2003.

Seadle, Michael. 2002. "METS and the Metadata Marketplace," *Library Hi Tech* 20 (3): 255–257.

Thomas, Charles F., and Linda S. Griffin. 1998. *Who Will Create the Metadata for the Internet?* Available at: http://www.firstmonday.dk/issues/issue3_12/thomas/index.html. Accessed 17 May 2003.

UK Office for Library and Information Networking. 2004. *Metadata Watch Report #3. Section 2, The Concept of Application Profiles*. Available at: http://www.schemas-forum.org/metadata-watch/third/section2.html. Accessed 26 August 2004.

User Guide Committee. 2001. *Dublin Core Metadata Glossary: Final Draft*. Available at: http:// library.csun.edu/mwoodley/dublincoreglossary.html. Accessed 30 June 2004.

Wood, Andrew. 1997. *Metadata: The Ghosts of Data Past, Present, and Future*. Available at: http:// archive.dstc.edu.au/RDU/reports/Sympos97/metafuture.html. Accessed 25 June 2003.

PART 2
Metadata Projects and Their Applications in the Digital Library

5

Metadata Projects

This chapter will focus on projects dealing especially with metadata. Numerous metadata projects have commenced all over the world since metadata began generating significant attention. Due to the sheer number of metadata projects, it is nearly impossible to draw a panorama of the topic. Therefore, several representative examples will be discussed in this chapter.

Research on metadata has been within the scope of many previous large-scale projects. One significant example is DESIRE, which is an EU project involving cooperation between England, the Netherlands, Sweden, and Norway. One of the most important and impressive outcomes of the project is a review of metadata, which has been used as a significant reference by many other projects and studies. It is unnecessary for metadata projects to be conducted by a single community. Metadata exists everywhere. Cooperation across several domains brings a variety of needs, interests, and experiences together, creating a more comprehensive output.

The following sections will briefly introduce four metadata projects that occurred in different parts of the world and have had a worldwide influence. First, we will examine the BIBLINK project, a European project linking libraries and publishers. Next, we will study the MetaLib project, the first metadata project implemented in Germany. The Australian MetaWeb project, with its varied approaches to metadata is third. Finally, there is the Nordic Metadata Project, the largest metadata project launched in northern Europe.

Though each metadata project has its own focus, these projects share some common concerns, such as surveying existing metadata formats, creating and harvesting metadata, and so forth. It is no longer usual for a project to focus exclusively on metadata. Normally, projects focusing solely on metadata are merged into bigger infrastructures or discussed in specific contexts.

5.1 BIBLINK

BIBLINK is an early metadata project, which ran from April 1, 1996, to February 15, 2000. It was sponsored by the European Commission and funded under the Telematics Application Programme of the European Union Fourth Framework Programmes.

The concept of the BIBLINK project crystallized from the work of an EU concerted action, known as Computerised Bibliographic Actions (CoBRA), which addressed the issues raised by the tremendous growth of electronic publications. When electronic publishing emerged, electronic publications, like many kinds of grey literature, were omitted from the bibliographic procedures of national libraries. However with the explosion of electronic publications and their increasingly important status in both the academic world and society at large, these resources can no longer be neglected. Therefore, a proposal for establishing a prototype system that would provide an automated flow of metadata between publishers and national bibliographic agencies was presented. The system established by the BIBLINK project was intended to be a mutually beneficial link between electronic resource publishers and national bibliographic agencies. The integration of the electronic publications' bibliographic records into the national bibliography, a kind of official channel, undoubtedly increased both the public awareness and the accessibility of electronic publications. Furthermore, authority control within the workspace guarantees the quality and reliability of the electronic publications' bibliographic information. However, it was already well known that electronic publications had become an important kind of information resource. Cooperation between publishers and national bibliographic agencies would certainly enrich the national bibliography's collection and would, in turn, improve its bibliographic service.

The BIBLINK project, led by the British Library and the BIBLINK Consortium, was composed of the following three groups:

- Five European national libraries

  - The British Library, London, United Kingdom
  - Biblioteca Nacional (The Spanish National Library), Madrid, Spain
  - Bibliothèque Nationale de France (The French National Library), Paris, France
  - Koninklijke Bibliotheek (or The National Library of the Netherlands), Den Haag, the Netherlands
  - Nasjonalbiblioteket (The National Library of Norway), Rana, Norway
- Two academic institutions

  - UKOLN, University of Bath, United Kingdom
  - Universitat Oberta de Catalunya (Open University of Catalonia), Barcelona, Spain
- Two publishing trade organizations

  - Book Industry Communication
  - CD-ROM Standards and Practices Action Group

The project's goal was to establish a relationship between national bibliographic agencies and publishers of electronic material in order to establish authoritative bibliographic information beneficial to both sectors. The overall objectives of the project are summarized as follows (Patel and Clayphan n.d.):

- To create a direct bibliographic link between publishers and national bibliographic agencies, which will facilitate bibliographic control over electronic publications
- To develop an agreed upon bibliographic description for electronic resources to assist with bibliographic control
- To meet the needs of the national libraries for securing authoritative advanced information about new electronic publications
- To enable publishers of electronic materials to register new electronic publications (whether online, through the Internet, or offline on a medium such as CD-ROM)
- To enable publications to carry enriched bibliographic data as an integral part of the electronic publication in order to aid the process of resource discovery
- To help library utilities meet an increasing demand for information about electronic publications
- To be able to identify such publications uniquely
- to supply libraries with bibliographic records relating to such material for integration into their own catalogs

The BIBLINK project lasted for a little more than 47 months, and was divided into two phases. Both phases had durations of 18 months, though the second phase required an extension. The first phase focused on research and consensus building, and a demonstration system was developed during the second phase.

The BIBLINK Core metadata set was the most important outcome of the first stage of the project. A metadata study was undertaken during the first phase. Based on a comparative analysis, the BIBLINK Core metadata set (see Table 5.1) was created with both online and offline publications in mind. The element set comprises 12 of the 15 Dublin Core elements, plus 10 elements defined by the partners as the minimum data set required by libraries. In order to cover the range of resources included in the scope of the identifier, the project adopted several established schemes—Serial Item and Contribution Identifier (SICI), International Standard Book Number (ISBN), and International Standard Serial Number (ISSN), as well as those currently under development for digital items, URN, DOI, and URL.

The UNIversal MARC (UNIMARC) format was chosen as the central format, and conversion is possible between several national MARC formats and BIBLINK Core. "For the conversion the USEMARCON software is used. For transmission of data e-mail or a Web form can be used. For authentication of publications and corresponding metadata a hash value is calculated" (Noordermeer 2000).

The BIBLINK demonstrator was developed, tested, and implemented during the extended second stage. The BIBLINK demonstrator primarily consists of the BIBLINK workspace (see Figure 5.1), a shared, virtual workspace for the exchange of metadata between publishers, National Bibliographic Agencies (NBAs), and other third parties, such as the ISSN International Centre. The workspace allows publishers to upload electronic publication metadata using e-mail or the Web. NBAs and third parties are able to download this metadata, enhance it in various ways, and then upload the enhanced metadata back to the workspace. The intention is for NBAs to

Table 5.1 BIBLINK Core metadata set

Element name	Element definition
DC.Title	The name by which the resource is known.
BIBLINK.TitleAlternate	A title other than the main title, including subtitle.
DC.Creator	The person primarily responsible for the intellectual content.
BIBLINK.CreatorOrganization	The organization primarily responsible for the intellectual content.
DC.Contributor	A person responsible for making contributions to the content.
BIBLINK.ContributorOrganization	An organization responsible for making contributions.
DC.Identifier	A unique number or alphanumeric string, e.g., DOI, ISBN, URN.
DC.Publisher	The agent responsible for making the resource available.
DC.Date	The date of availability of the resource.
DC.Format	The physical or digital manifestation of the resource.
DC.Subject	The topic of the resource. Key words or phrases.
DC.Description	Description of content or an abstract.
DC.Language	The language of the content.
DC.Rights	A rights management statement or link to it.
DC.Source	Information about another resource from which the present resource is derived.
BIBLINK.Price	A simple retail price—for physical resources such as CD-ROMs.
BIBLINK.Extent	The size of the resource—in bytes, number of files, or CD-ROMs.
BIBLINK.Checksum	A hash value computed for authentication purposes.
BIBLINK.Frequency	The frequency of issue for serials.
BIBLINK.Edition	A statement indicating the version or edition of the resource.
BIBLINK.PlacePublication	Geographic location of the publisher.
BIBLINK.SystemRequirements	Hardware or software requirements for the system needed to view the resource.

use the enhanced metadata as the basis for appropriate national bibliography records. Publishers are also able to download the enhanced metadata for use in their own systems. "The metadata is stored and exchanged in several syntaxes, including HTML, SGML, UNIMARC and the national MARC formats of the participating partners"

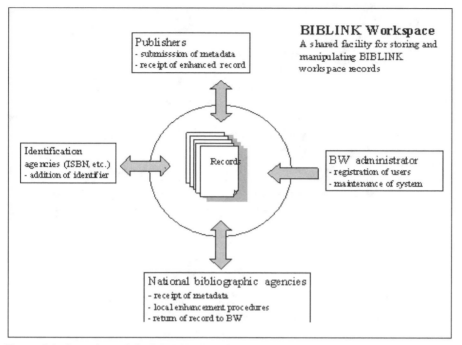

Figure 5.1 Overview of the BIBLINK workspace.
Source: Patel and Clayphan n.d.

(Powell 2000). The Parisian company Jouve developed the software in collaboration with the project partners.

Cooperation might be more fruitful and less labor intensive if the recently developed Electronic Cataloging in Print (E-CIP) could be integrated into the scope of projects like the BIBLINK project.

5.2 THE METALIB PROJECT

In 1997, having recognized both the challenges introduced by the new information infrastructure and the importance of metadata, German libraries began to implement a project, the MetaLib Project (Metadaten—Initiative deutscher Bibliotheken, or, in English, Metadata Initiative of German Libraries; see Figure 5.2), focused especially on metadata. The project contributes to the provision of not only a panorama of the global research on and applications of metadata, but also to the foundation of a digital library in which metadata play key roles at multiple levels.

5.2.1 MetaLib Project

The MetaLib project analyses the increasing importance of metadata for libraries and learned societies. The project partners developed guidelines, based on the DCMES, for using metadata in the indexing of electronic documents. In addition, the partners provided information on the discussion of metadata and various metadata formats. The executing organization of the MetaLib Project is the German Research

Figure 5.2 Home page of the MetaLib project.

Foundation (Die Deutsche Forschungsgemeinschaft, DFG). The MetaLib Project is part of the Modernisation and Rationalisation in the Scientific Libraries program within the framework of the Distributed Digital Research Library.

The first phase of the MetaLib Project was from 1997 to 1999. During that period, the following institutions were involved in the project:

- The German Library Institute (Das Deutsche Bibliotehkinstitut, DBI)
- The Goettingen State and University Library (Die Niedersächsische Staats- und Universitätsbibliothek Goettingen, SUB)
- The German Library (Die Deutsche Bibliothek, DDB)
- The Bavarian State Library (Die Bayerische Staatsbibliothek, BSB)

DBI was the coordinator for the first phase of the project.

After the extension of the project in 1999/2000, SUB and DDB continued running the subprojects. The cooperation of BSB and DBI ended in 1999. The project was finally completed in January 2002. However, neither DDB nor SUB completely halted their work after the termination of financial support. DDB continues to engage in the standardization of metadata, while the result of the subproject at SUB, MetaServer, continues to operate.

The goal of the MetaLib Project is to determine effective guidelines for metadata elements set, especially DCMES, that promote the development of digital and digitalized resources in academic libraries. Its long-term objective is ultimately the convergence of metadata elements sets into a single core standard that will serve all documents and facilitate transnational data exchange.

5.2.2 Subproject of MetaLib at the Goettingen State and University Library

The task of the subproject of MetaLib at the Goettingen State and University Library is to develop the basic rules for a code that will index digital objects based on both current metadata discussions in their entirety and recommendations for dealing with metadata in the library. When analyzing metadata formats, the project concentrates on applications in German learned society. The project focuses on the Dublin Core metadata scheme.

The Goettingen metadata project concentrates on the following points (SUB Goettingen 2002):

- Analyzing the current metadata discussion, in particular, the Dublin Core initiative and the Resource Description Framework;
- Analyzing the metadata applications in German learned societies and consideration of applications in other national and international learned societies;
- Developing application models for digital objects;
- Comparing these models with bibliothecarial codes;
- Supporting a uniform use of the Dublin Core metadata scheme by potential users (libraries, compound systems, and learned societies).

An internal document prepared by the subproject of the MetaLib at the Goettingen State and University Library, "MetaLib 'Best Practice Guide': Recommendations for the Use of Metadata for the Individual Users, Library and Library Networks" (Meta-Lib "Best Practice Guide": "Empfehlungen für die Nutzung von Metadaten für Einzelanwender, Bibliotheken und Bibliotheksverbünde"), described the subproject's activities with regards to the three aspects listed below.

- Survey of existing metadata workflows in Germany

  The experience of the OCLC project Cooperative Online Resource Catalog (CORC) shows that Dublin Core may be considered a good importing format for integrating electronic resources into the databases of library networks. In Germany, both the Library Service Center Baden-Wuerttemberg (Das Bibliotheksservice-Zentrum Baden-Wuerttemberg, BSZ) and the North Rhine-Westphalia Digital Library Foundation (Die Digitale Bibliothek Nordrhein-Westfalen Grundlagen) have adopted such a workflow. The metadata-creating workflow of the Southwest Germany Library Consortium (Der Südwestdeutsche Bibliotheksverbund, SWB) and the Digital Library of the University Library Center in North Rhine-Westphalia (Die Digitale Bibliothek des Hochschulbibliothekszentrums Nordrhein-Westfalen, HBZ) were reviewed by the subproject. The adaptability of the BSZ workflow to the other German library networks was also analyzed.

- Survey of the situation of online publications in German universities

  After describing the general situation of online publications in German universities and, more specifically, that of dissertations and documents in the mathematics and physics areas, the subproject explained how the Goettingen State and University Library deals with such publications online.

- Recommendations

  Recommendations were made at two levels—that of individual users, such as departments and university libraries, and that of the library network. In addition to the general recommendations about data format and document drafts, the subproject concentrated its recommendations on metadata, including the gathering and storing of metadata, the elements and qualifiers of Dublin Core and more local elements, qualifications of the Dublin Core Elements Set, syntax of Dublin Core, and so forth. With respect to recommendations for the library network, the subproject still left some questions open for discussion.

In addition to the surveys and recommendations described above, the Metadata Server is a major output of the subproject of MetaLib at the Goettingen State and University Library. There are two databases developed by the Library within the Metadata Server, MetaGuide and MetaForm, which offer information about metadata and metadata applications.

MetaGuide (see Figure 5.3) provides comprehensive information on national and international metadata issues and developments from a library's perspective. Special emphasis has been laid upon the development of the Dublin Core Metadata Elements Set. MetaGuide provides two kinds of catalogs and one search engine. On October 15, 2004, there were 579 records in the MetaGuide database. MetaGuide can also be considered an introduction to four special subject guides developed by another project of the Goettingen State and University Library, the Special Subject Guides/Fachinformation (SSG-FI) project.

MetaForm is a tool that offers a comparative analysis of different Dublin Core applications. It enables the analysis and comparison of different metadata formats. More specifically, MetaForm is a database for metadata formats, with a special emphasis on the Dublin Core and its manifestations as they are expressed in various implementations. The formats are registered with their elements and definitions. This database allows for crosswalks between the Dublin Core Metadata Elements Set and its various dialects, as well as for crosscuts of a particular Dublin Core element (e.g., DC.Creator) through all of the formats. As a third option, the user may also view mappings between DC applications and other formats. In addition, the MetaForm Web site offers the opportunity to register a metadata or related format. The registration may be completed just by filling out an entry form.

5.3 THE METAWEB PROJECT

The increase in metadata-based projects in Australia has been significant since the Dublin Core Metadata Initiative began in 1995, "resulting in Australia becoming a center of excellence in standard metadata deployment" (Campbell 1999a). In 1997 and 1998, a small group of Australian institutions joined forces on the MetaWeb Project to facilitate the advancement of metadata initiatives.

The goal of the Metadata Tools and Services project, known as MetaWeb, was to "develop indexing services, user tools, and metadata element sets in order to promote the use of, and exploitation of metadata on the Internet" (Campbell 1999b). It began in October 1997 and was successfully completed on June 30, 1998.

The MetaWeb project was partially funded by the National Priority (Reserve) Fund allocation for Improved Library Infrastructure, which is administered by the Australian Vice Chancellors (AV-CC) Standing Committee on Information Resources. The four participants on the project were the Australian Defence Force Academy, the Charles Sturt University, the Distributed Systems Technology Centre, and the National Library of Australia.

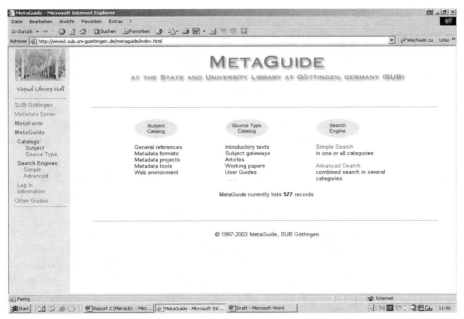

Figure 5.3 Home page of the MetaGuide.

All of MetaWeb's activities can be classified into two general functions: creating metadata tools and providing related services. The activities of the project can be described as follows (Campbell 1997):

- Establishing an Australian metadata Web site

- Establishing an Australian metadata electronic discussion list

- Developing a pilot Australian metadata repository using a suitable subject-related testbed

- Developing and/or modifying a suite of management and technical tools to facilitate the creation and maintenance of metadata

- Developing a generic Australian metadata repository model and associated software

- Developing metadata standards for Australian resource discovery, including extensions to the Dublin Core standard

- Applying the generic Australian metadata repository model and associated software and standards to more testbed applications

- Promulgating the use of digital signatures for the authentication of networked electronic information

- Deciding future directions and ongoing support arrangements for maintenance of products and facilities

The project provided the following metadata tools:

- A gatherer—the MetaWeb project created some specialized, but standards-compliant, tools to exploit the investment in metadata creation. A tool called a gatherer visits some predetermined Web sites and transports the metadata to a central repository or database where it is indexed for subsequent searching. The gathered metadata may be updated at any time, and the gatherer retrieves metadata at regular intervals. "The tool which does the indexing is called a broker, and the indexes it creates are managed in a similar way to those supported behind the scenes in public access catalogues. A search interface is then supplied to query the metadata, which may be executed across the whole of the metadata set for a particular item, or by specifying a single element to be searched" (Campbell 1999a). For the documents for which metadata in a standard such as the Dublin Core (for generic metadata) or the Australian Government Locator Service (for government resources metadata) have already been created, the gatherer scoops up the documents with one or more <META> tags, throws away the full text, and stores the documents' metadata in a repository.

- A broker—a behind-the-scenes processor that indexes the metadata and makes it available for subsequent querying.

- A repository—a database software which stores the metadata and its indexes.

- A creation tool—the MetaWeb project has conducted a separate analysis of creation tools and generators that work at the document level. Under the auspices of the MetaWeb Project, the Distributed Systems Technology Centre (DSTC) launched an Australian tool known as Reggie. It provides standard templates for the creation of metadata in several schemas, page by page. The goal of the Reggie Metadata Editor is to enable the easy creation of various forms of metadata using the one flexible program. At present, the Reggie applet can create metadata using the HTML 3.2 standard, the HTML 4.0 standard, the RDF format, and the RDF Abbreviated format.

- A site-level metadata generator—some sites have metadata locked away as system file parameters or in early implementations of noncompliant Dublin Core elements. A site-level generator can be made available to the Web administrator of a user who wants to unlock the potential of this metadata by creating default Dublin Core values. The site-level metadata generator permits the retrospective conversion of all the pages at a prespecified URL. It embeds metadata in each page for 6 of the 15 unqualified Dublin Core elements that can be provided without human intervention.

- A metadata search engine—HotMeta is a metadata search engine. "It gathers metadata from resources on the Internet or Intranet and provides a user interface to search the resources" (Distributed Systems Technology Centre n.d.). HotMeta crawls specified sites, extracts and indexes metadata from the embedded HTML meta tags, and saves it in a metadata repository. It provides interfaces that enable users to browse, find, and search the metadata stored in the repository.

- A subject gateway—a subject gateway, entitled Meta Matters, was originally developed as part of the MetaWeb project and is now maintained by the Dublin Core ANZ Group. It is a subject gateway to metadata resources in Australia and New Zealand and overseas subject-related links.

The MetaWeb project provided a lot of useful services, such as:

- Australian metadata discussion list

  It was used to discuss and disseminate information and services to the Australian public concerning metadata issues and technologies. Though it has been closed since August 2002, a Web archive of all postings on the list is still available on the Internet.

- Analysis of metadata creation tools

  The report actually consists of the MetaWeb Project's good faith evaluations for the purpose of assisting the Australian metadata community to choose the tools most suitable for in-house use.

- List of Australian metadata creators

  The project provided a list of the Australian sites currently supporting Dublin Core metadata and some brief information about these sites.

- Interpretation rules used by different Australian creators

  The interpretation rules, which come from three institutions in Australia and are used by different Australian creators, were provided.

Since the completion of the MetaWeb Project, the MetaWeb tools and principles have been adopted and adapted by several subject gateway projects for the purposes of experimenting with discipline-oriented sites, which were proposed to facilitate research by various communities in Australia. Though the MetaWeb project lasted less than a year and was not a relatively large project, it has drawn much attention from colleagues all over the world. For instance, UKOLN even conducted some exercises on the project and had a discussion about whether there should be a project similar to MetaWeb in the United Kingdom.

5.4 THE NORDIC METADATA PROJECT

The Nordic Metadata Project is a metadata project that is well known, not only in Scandinavia, but also all over the world. It has contributed so much to the development of the DCMES that it was considered "the first international Dublin Core project" (Hakala n.d.).

The project was divided into the two phases described below:

- Nordic Metadata Project I—intended to create a Nordic Metadata production, indexing, and retrieval environment. It began on November 1, 1996, and ended on May 31, 1998.
- Nordic Metadata Project II—enhanced the tools developed in the Nordic Metadata Project I. This part of the project ran from January 1999 until 2002.

Both phases of the project were supported by the Nordic Council for Scientific Information (NORDINFO). The seven institutions involved in the first stage of the project are shown in Table 5.2.

The Nordic Metadata Project I created the basic elements of a metadata production and utilization system based on the DCMES. The goal of the Nordic Metadata Project I was to enhance end-user services by making digital documents more easily searchable and deliverable over the Web (Koch 1998). The participants cooperated with the international metadata community, especially regarding the Dublin Core specification. A few subtasks were derived from the basic goal of the project (Hakala n.d.):

- Evaluation of existing metadata formats
- Enhancement of the existing Dublin Core specification

Table 5.2 Participants of the Nordic Metadata project

Project participants	
Bibsys, Norway	Ole Husby
The Danish Library Center, Denmark	Susanne Thorborg
Helsinki University Library, Finland	Juha Hakala
Lund University Library, NetLab, Sweden	Traugott Koch
Munksgaard, Denmark	Anders Geertsen
The National and University Library of Iceland, Iceland	Sigbergur Fridriksson
The Swedish Institute of Computer Science, Sweden	Preben Hansen

- Conversion from Dublin Core to Nordic MARC formats, and vice versa
- Creation of a DC Metadata Syntax, User Environment, and User Interaction
- Improvement of the discovery and retrieval of Nordic Internet documents through a metadata aware search service
- Management of documentation and projects

The first subtask mentioned above somewhat overlaps with part of the DESIRE project's work, which focused on enhancing existing European information networks for research users across Europe through research and development. The combined result of the third, fourth, and fifth tasks formed a set of tools known as the Dublin Core toolbox. This toolbox enables users to create, harvest, and index Dublin Core metadata and to convert this data into MARC format. The tools available in the public domain are:

- The metadata template (see Figure 5.4)

  The user can create Dublin Core metadata for an HTML document by completing this template, and then this quality metadata will be carried with the document. A short, simple template, with an easy add-on feature for individual fields is also offered as an alternative if only a less-detailed description of the resource is needed.

- The metadata harvesting and indexing application

  In practice this application is an enhanced version of the Nordic Web Index[1] that can extract metadata from HTML documents in Dublin Core and other formats and make this information searchable via metadata databases. In other words, through this application, metadata can be extracted from HTML documents and indexed into separate national metadata databases. The project provided an alternative method to OAI metadata harvesting;

---

1. The Nordic Web Index (NWI) is a project within the Nordic Net Center (NNC) for Libraries aimed at establishing a distributing service that continuously and automatically finds and indexes all information available on the World Wide Web in Nordic countries.

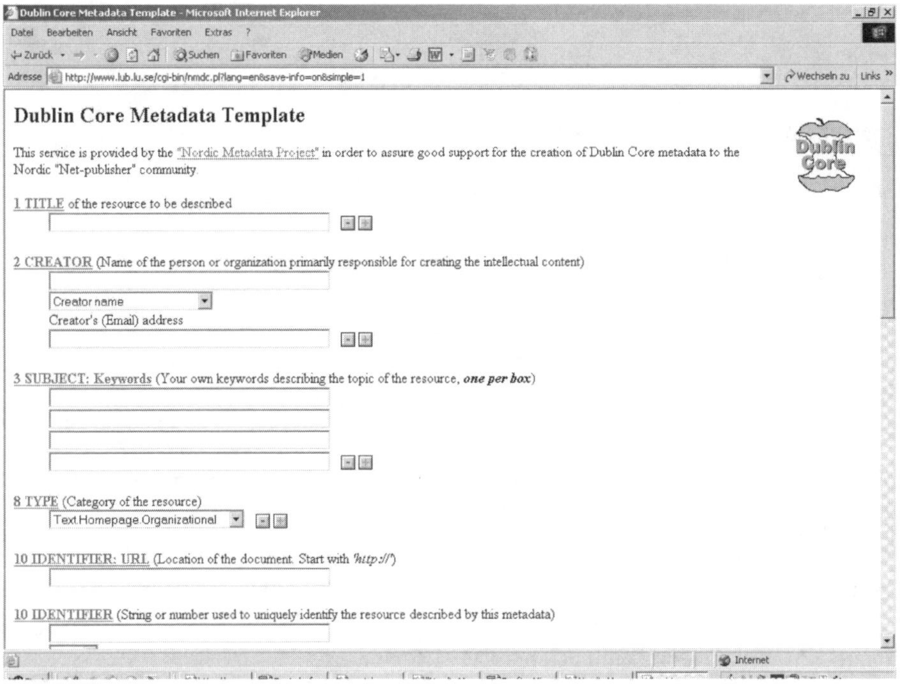

Figure 5.4 Short and simple version of the Dublin Core Metadata Template.

- The Dublin Core to MARC converter (see Figure 5.5)

    This converter can extract Dublin Core data from a document and convert it into a MARC record. The converter is capable of converting records from Dublin Core to USMARC and all Nordic MARC formats. The designers' goal was to build both a stand-alone converter and a C library that can be plugged into existing applications. The NORMARC to DC converter was also built to test the feasibility of MARC to DC conversion. Because of the magnitude of this task, no other conversions were built during this project.

- The Uniform Resource Names (URN) generator (see Figure 5.6)

    This generator can build URNs based on National Bibliography Numbers (NBNs). A goal of the Nordic metadata project was to enable users to obtain decent identification of their documents as part of the metadata creation process. Therefore, when the URN syntax was finished in the autumn of 1997, negotiations began with the Internet Engineering Task Force's (IETF) URN working group on how national bibliography numbers could be used as URNs. The resulting syntax looks like this URN:NBN:xx-yy.

    The project partners for the Nordic Metadata Project II were almost the same as those in the first stage, except that Munksgaard, Denmark left and the contact at the National and University Library of Iceland, Iceland changed to Andrea Johannsdottir.

    In short, the Nordic Metadata Project II had two main tasks. The first was to further develop the tools built by the Nordic Metadata Project I, and the second was to improve the Dublin Core. As a result of Nordic Metadata I, several project team members hold important positions in the global Dublin Core community, and

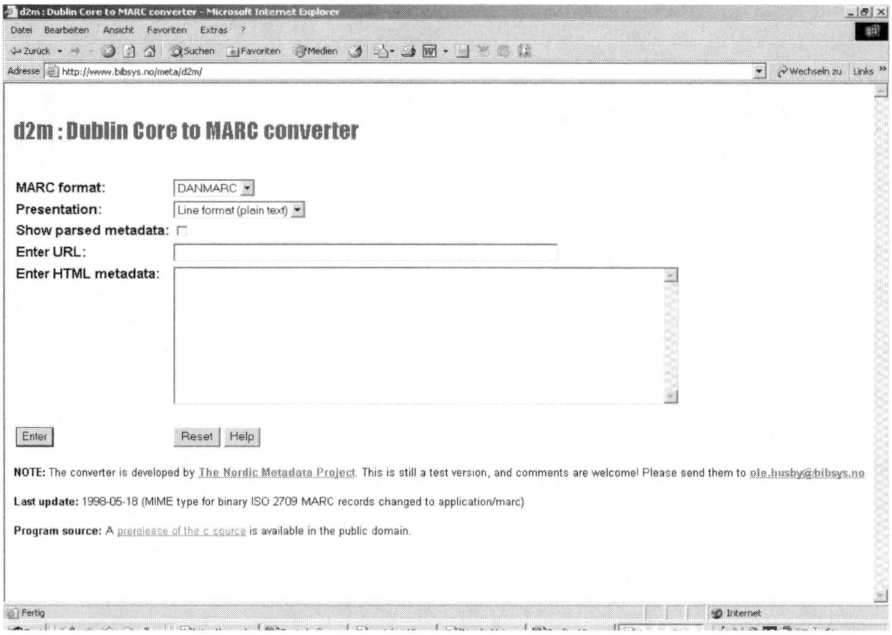

Figure 5.5 Web page of Dublin Core to MARC converter.

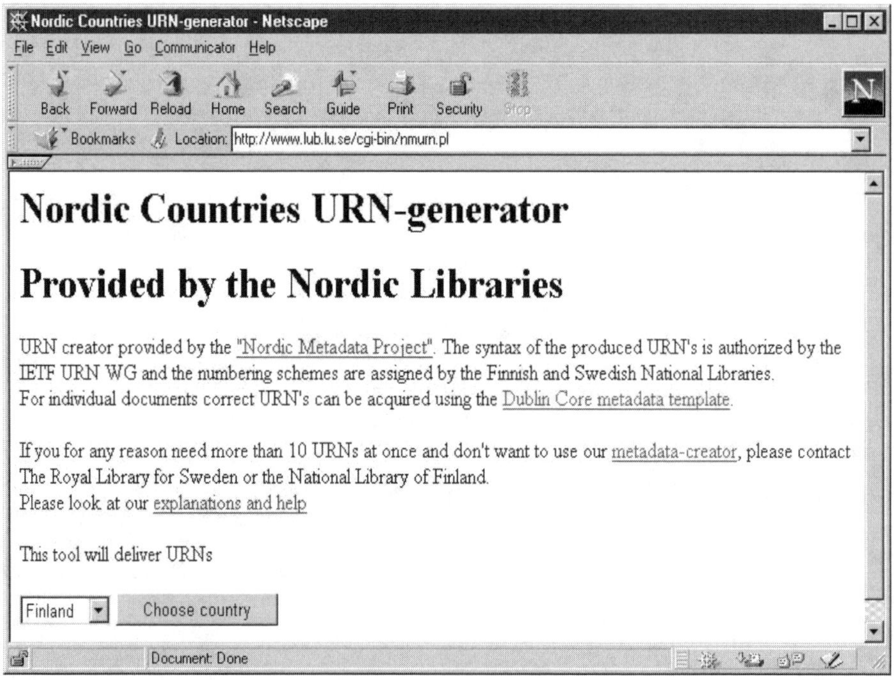

Figure 5.6 The URN generator user interface.

are therefore able to access the format features that are valuable from the Nordic perspective.

Although the Nordic Metadata Project I implemented metadata tools that are currently used by a large number of users in Scandinavia and elsewhere, it has not organized long-time maintenance of the tools that have been developed. The project participants believed that the continuing Dublin Core development meant a project was the ideal way to further develop the tools. On the basis of these two thoughts, the Nordic Metadata Project II outlined the concrete tasks listed below:

Enhancement of the Existing Dublin Core Specification

When the Nordic Metadata Project II began, there were 15 defined Dublin Core elements. The project participated in the task of defining a core set of Dublin Core qualifiers with which one could further specify the semantic content of a given element. Another area of Nordic Metadata II activity was the specification of Dublin Core syntaxes for new document formats such as XML.

Improvement of the Dublin Core to MARC Converter

The Nordic Metadata I built the first publicly available Dublin Core to MARC converter. Although this application was fully functional, it had to be rebuilt in order to make it table driven, rendering the maintenance of the converter software a lot easier. As a part of this task, a standard conversion table was defined, which could be used in all projects that prepare Dublin Core to MARC conversions. As a separate task, a MARC to Dublin Core converter was built. An experimental NORMARC to DC converter has proved the feasibility of such an application.

Dublin Core User Support and Tools Evaluation

A DC user guide was built within the project to assist the user in creating high-quality metadata. A wide range of tool evaluations were conducted during this period, in order to improve services.

- *DC user guide*—The Nordic Metadata produced full and short versions of the Dublin Core user guide. These documents have been actively used because they are linked to the metadata templates and thus form an integral part of the service. In addition to the template guide, there are also user guides linked to the URN generator and the DC to MARC converter.

- *Evaluation of tools*—In Nordic Metadata Project I, the users were asked to evaluate the metadata template. Although the number of respondents was small when compared with the number of people who used the tool to provide metadata, the feedback received gave the project participants valuable insight on how to improve the service. The evaluation continued in the Nordic Metadata II, but in this project, not only the template, but also other services, such as, in the following order, national metadata databases, the DC to MARC converter, and URN, were evaluated.

Maintenance and Development of Metadata Tools

- Metadata template

  The metadata template was improved during this second stage. The functions that were deemed necessary to add to the template included:

  - support for Dublin Core elements' core qualifiers,
  - support for new Dublin Core syntaxes for XML and RDF and for modified HTML 4.0 syntax,
  - support for AltaVista-supported metadata syntax, and
  - development of new functionality, such as extraction of existing metadata from the document to be described.

- Metadata harvesting and indexing tools

  The service was improved the following ways:

  - Improvement of NWI's harvesting and indexing software
  - Adaptation and improvement of the retrieval system
  - Adaptation of the user interface and search support
  - Establishment and maintenance of national metadata databases

As stated in the final report of the Nordic Metadata Project, the project "has been an excellent example of Nordic co-operation" (Hakala n.d.). It has enabled the Nordic countries to show a unified front to the international Dublin Core community. The applications developed by the project are still being actively used in national or regional metadata initiatives in Scandinavian countries. Therefore, the Nordic Metadata Project, in spite of its significant experimental aspects, has also been a fruitful initiative from a practical point of view.

REFERENCES

Campbell, Debbie. 1997. *The MetaWeb Project*. Available at: http://www.dstc.edu.au/Research/Projects/metaweb/timeline.html. Accessed 27 April 2004.

Campbell, Debbie. 1999a. *Dublin Core Metadata and Australian MetaWeb Project*. Available at: http://www.nla.gov.au/nla/staffpaper/dcampbell1.html. Accessed 28 April 2004.

Campbell, Debbie. 1999b. *The MetaWeb Project*. Available at: http://www.dstc.edu.au/Research/Projects/metaweb/. Accessed 27 April 2004.

Distributed Systems Technology Centre. n.d. *HotMeta: HotMeta Overview and Capabilities*. Available at: http://www.dstc.edu.au/cgi-bin/redirect/rd.cgi?http://archive.dstc.edu.au/RDU/HotMeta/. Accessed 28 April 2004.

Hakala, Juha. n.d. *The Nordic Metadata II Project: Cataloguing, Indexing and Retrieval of Network Documents*. Available at: http://www.lib.helsinki.fi/meta/nm2plan.html. Accessed 30 April 2004.

Koch, Traugott. 1998. *Nordic Metadata Project: A Presentation*. Available at: http://www.ub2.lu.se/tk/metadata/NMDPpres.html. Accessed 29 April 2004.

Noordermeer, Trudi. 2000. "A Bibliographic Link Publishers of Electronic Resources and National Bibliographic Agencies: Project BIBLINK," *Exploit Interactive* 4. Available at: http://www.exploit-lib.org/issue4/biblink/. Accessed 16 April 2004.

Patel, Manjula, and Robina Clayphan. n.d. *Project BIBLINK: Linking Publishers and National Bibliographic Agencies*. Available at: http://www.ukoln.ac.uk/metadata/publications/biblink/proj-biblink.html. Accessed 16 April 2004.

Powell, Andy. 2000. *The BIBLINK Demonstrator*. Available at: http://hosted.ukoln.ac.uk/biblink/wp11/. Accessed 16 April 2004.

SUB Goettingen. 2002. *Metadata Server: Metadata at SUB Goettingen*. Available at: http://www2.sub.uni-goettingen.de/sub_en.html#meta. Accessed 5 May 2003.

6

Metadata Applications in the Digital Library

With the emergence of tremendous amounts of digital information, different methods of organizing meaningful information resources have been developed, such as subject gateway, digital library, and so forth. In a sense the digital library is a kind of digital collection, where digital information is collected and organized in an efficient way. However, a digital library is much more than a digital collection since it also deals with digitization, preservation, service, and other related issues. Metadata is essential to the digital library. It is so important that it was once declared that the digital library "is all about metadata" (Russell 2000).

This chapter will first briefly introduce the digital library and its metadata applications. Then some representative examples of the metadata applications used in the digital library projects taking place in different parts of the world will be described in the sections to follow.

6.1 METADATA APPLICATIONS IN THE DIGITAL LIBRARY

Taking S. R. Ranganathan's *Five Laws of Library Science*, published in 1963, as reference, the digital library can be described as an organic system that provides information services based on digitized or born-digital collections via computer network. Basically, it is a system within which various parts have closed relationships with each other. Its ultimate aim is to provide information services, and it functions on computer networks. Digitized or born-digital collections are the materials and foundations of the whole system.

The development of the digital library is a process that has taken more than 10 years. In the last decade the digital library has grown from an infant to a mature adult. Currently, the digital library is one of society's stable information infrastructures.

6.1.1 Definitions of the Digital Library

Simply put, the fundamental content of the digital library is born-digital materials or digitized materials and digital services. The context of the digital library is the computer network. People from different domains have different visions of the digital library. Currently, there are a number of definitions of the digital library, and many of them were formulated during the implementation of digital library projects. Some of the definitions are comprehensive, while some of them focus on one or more aspects of the digital library. Here are some representative examples of the various definitions.

The Digital Library Federation (DLF) has crafted a full definition that is considered broad enough to comprehend other uses of the term.

Digital libraries are organizations that provide the resources, including the specialized staff, to select, structure, offer intellectual access to, interpret, distribute, preserve the integrity of, and ensure the persistence over time of collections of digital works so that they are readily and economically available for use by a defined community or set of communities (Digital Library Federation 1999).

More recently, William Arms advanced the following informal definition of the digital library in his monograph, "Digital Libraries":

An informal definition of a digital library is a managed collection of information, with associated services, where the information is stored in digital formats and accessible over a network (Arms 2003).

Additionally, in order to distinguish the term "digital library" from "electronic library" and "virtual library," Roy Tennant defined the digital library as follows:

A *digital library* is a library consisting of digital materials and services. Digital materials are items that are stored, processed and transferred via digital (binary) devices and networks. Digital services are services (such as reference assistance) that are delivered digitally over computer networks (Tennant 1999).

Common elements of the existing definitions of the digital library are (Association of Research Libraries 1995):

- The digital library is not a single entity.
- The digital library requires technology to link the resources of many.
- The linkages between the many digital libraries and information services are transparent to the end users.
- Universal access to digital libraries and information services is a goal.
- Digital library collections are not limited to document surrogates—they extend to digital artifacts that cannot be represented or distributed in printed formats.

To summarize, from the above definitions, one can observe that the key factors of a digital library are the management of digital collections, the provision of services based on digital collections, and the use of computer networks as a platform. However, in practice, experts from different communities have their own emphases when dealing with the digital library. Computer scientists and engineers might place more emphasis on access to and retrieval of the digital content of digital libraries, while library and information professionals might pay more attention to the digital collection and the services based on it. Both aspects are of equal importance, and the above three definitions were selected accordingly.

6.1.2 Metadata in the Digital Library

"The concept of metadata, when applied in the context of current libraries, digital or traditional, typically refers to information that provides a (usually brief) characterization of the individual information object's in the collections of a library" (Smith 1996). Metadata is ubiquitous in a digital library setting. For instance, digital preservation is one of the most crucial aspects for establishing and maintaining a digital library. It depends, to some extent, on the creation, capture, and maintenance of suitable metadata. Preserving the right metadata is key to preserving digital objects. Metadata fulfils various roles within the digital repository. "[M]etadata accompanies and makes reference to each digital object and provides associated descriptive, structural, administrative, rights management, and other kinds of information. This metadata will also be maintained and will be migrated from format to format and standard to standard, independently of the base object it describes" (Lynch 1999).

In general, three types of metadata are included in the digital library, which are (California Digital Library 2001):

- *Descriptive metadata*—information about intellectual content (analogous to standard catalog record). Such metadata is used in the discovery and identification of a digital object. Examples include EAD, MARC, and Dublin Core records. Additionally, descriptive metadata for digital objects applies to information on the full collection of files associated with the digital object and their relationships to one another. The descriptive metadata actually stored within a digital library object is minimal; most of the descriptive metadata regarding the object is stored externally from the object and is only referenced, or, is an indirect package.

- *Structural metadata*—information for handling, maintaining, and archiving a digital object. It is used to display and navigate a particular object for a user, and includes information on the internal organization of that object, similar to a book's introduction, chapters, pages, and index.

- *Administrative metadata*—description of the internal structure of a digital object. Administrative metadata represents the management information for this object, including the date it was created, the format of its content file (JPEG, GIF, etc.), the scanning resolutions used, the rights information, and so forth.

The general functions of these three types of metadata include description, access management, administration, discovery, persistent identifier, presentation, digital preservation, and preservation reformatting.

Metadata exists at different levels in the digital library. A hierarchy of information is used to accommodate the diversity of digital objects and to efficiently propagate data. Metadata elements may be supplied at multiple and various levels. Nesting of objects is expected and is further clarified during the pilot phase of metadata capture and deposit.

Information may be inherited from parent levels or may be specific to single objects at a lower level. For example, a collection may have general access rights, but some of its items may be restricted. The access_rights attribute value on the collection (set or aggregate level) may be public, but a single title (primary object level) in the collection may be restricted.

In the case of the Library of Congress Digital Repository, the levels of metadata are (Library of Congress 2004):

- *Set*—Set-level metadata applies to what is currently known as a digital collection, for example, *Alexander Graham Bell Family Papers.* Digital collections are formed from aggregates that group digital items by original content type, such as nonmotion visual, text, motion visual, or audio, and by custodial responsibility as well as by collection. A collection may be determined from an archival series or from a topical bibliography. Some digital collections are contained within a single aggregate. Others are formed by numerous aggregates. Set-level metadata applies to all aggregates within the set regardless of content or responsibility.

- *Aggregate*—An aggregate organizes digital objects by digital type and by digital custodial responsibility. A single aggregate may be a digital collection. Aggregate-level metadata applies to all primary objects within an aggregate.

- *Primary object*—The specific item identified by the online collection access aid as a coherent whole is known as the primary object. Primary objects are usually the digital equivalents of physical library items, such as a book, a sound recording, a movie, a single title of sheet music, a folder of letters, a photograph, or a map. This metadata level applies to all the intermediate and terminal objects of a particular primary object.

- *Intermediate object*—The intermediate object is a view or component of the primary object. A book that can be presented as page images or as searchable text has two intermediate objects. One points to all the page images of the book, the other to an encoded text file. Complex primary objects such as sound recordings offer many intermediate object possibilities. Multiple sides or tracks of a recording, each with sound and label components, may be captured in several formats. A single 78 rpm record with two sides will have several audio files in both streaming and higher resolution formats, as well as the image and text of the label for each side and the jacket or album cover. Metadata for an intermediate object allows the gathering of digital files and metadata for the creation of presentations.

- *Terminal object*—The terminal object is the digital content file or files that form the object. There is at least one terminal for each object. Terminal object-level metadata is primarily structural, supplying the digital attributes of each file such as size, extension, bit depth, and so forth.

There are many choices for different kinds of collections, with respect to the choice of metadata schemas in the digital library. As a report about metadata in the digital library concludes, "The Dublin Core seems poised to provide a metadata system for resource discovery that is consistent across a wide range of applications and domains, usable by both experts and non-experts, interoperable with existing library catalogs and legacy databases, and coherent across many languages (over twenty to date)" (EU-NSF Working Group on Metadata n.d.). It is for these reasons that so many digital libraries choose Dublin Core as their metadata standard.

Currently, digitization technology is well established and well understood in the digital library field. Standards for digitization processes have become entrenched and are widely recognized. However, there is still no common standard with respect to metadata. In other words, there is no MARC standard for the digital library.

The absence of a standard for the digital library means (Gartner 2003):

- poor cross-searching,
- limited interchange facilities,
- metadata tied to proprietary packages, and
- consequent obsolescence and conversion costs.

Two things are urgently needed for the digital library: a standard for metadata content that is analogous to AACR2 and a standardized framework for holding and exchanging metadata that is analogous to MARC.

METS, which is introduced in the third chapter of this book, was therefore designed to meet the need for a digital library metadata standard. "METS is the first widely-accepted standard designed specifically for digital library metadata. It attempts to address the lack of standardization in digital library metadata practices, which is currently inhibiting the growth of coherent digital collections. Written in XML schema, METS offers a coherent overall structure for encoding all relevant types of metadata (descriptive, administrative, and structural) used to describe digital library objects. It also allows for the encoding of specific behaviours necessary for the rendering of these objects" (Gartner 2002).

The most important reasons for the choice of METS by the digital library are the following (Gartner 2003):

- It provides a framework for holding all types of metadata for the digital object.
- It is written in XML.
- It recommends a number of schemes for the content of metadata, but does not prescribe them.

METS will undoubtedly be the MARC of the digital library world, the central format for digital library metadata.

6.2 METADATA IN PANDORA

So far, many digital library projects have been conducted in Australia. Early statistics provided by Renato Iannella showed that there had been 18 digital library initiatives in Australia by the end of 1996 (Iannella 1996). Increasing numbers of digital library projects have been subsequently implemented on the continent. A staff member of the National Library of Australia described Australia's vision for a digital library as "a national library infrastructure that uses digital technology to enhance the preservation of and access to both traditional collections and emerging digital collections" (Phillips 1998).

Generally, two methods are used to describe the digital library resources in Australia. Traditional cataloging tools are still being used, while other metadata schemes such as Dublin Core and Australian Government Locator Service (AGLS)[1] have been adopted.

---

1. The AGLS metadata standard is a set of 19 descriptive elements that government departments and agencies can use to improve the visibility and accessibility of their services and information over the Internet. It has been mandated for use by Commonwealth government agencies. The National Archives of Australia is the maintenance agency for the AGLS metadata standard.

For example, the resources collected in the Preserving and Accessing Networked Documentary Resources of Australia (PANDORA) project have been cataloged in a traditional way (which will be discussed in detail later), while projects such as the Australian Digital Theses Project use the Dublin Core standard.

The top level of the Australian librarianship, the National Library of Australia, has played a key role with respect to metadata activities in the digital library. In 2002, the National Library of Australia published *Guidelines for the Creation of Content for Resource Discovery Metadata*, which it had prepared with the State Library of Tasmania. The document is intended to assist with the creation of descriptive metadata of consistent quality for online resources that will improve resource discovery services for these resources. It is based on one of the most widely used metadata schemes—the Dublin Core. The guidelines are designed with the goal of providing advice on determining the *content* for the most useful Dublin Core/AGLS metadata elements for resource discovery. The guidelines addresses the title, creator, subject, description, publisher, date, identifier, and coverage elements (National Library of Australia 2002). Since its publication, the guidelines has often been used in metadata descriptions of the digital objects in the Australian digital libraries.

In addition, the National Library of Australia "is committed to developing services to share metadata describing electronic information resources and seeks the support of Australian libraries and other organizations to achieve this" (National Library of Australia n.d.). Specifically, the National Library of Australia adopts strategies that facilitate the sharing of electronic information resources in Australia, such as (National Library of Australia n.d.):

- Extend the concept of resource sharing among Australian libraries to include electronic resources, by undertaking a range of activities which facilitate the use of nationally operated bibliographic and metadata services for the description, discovery, and delivery of electronic information resources.

- Make available subsets, in MARC and non-MARC formats, of national bibliographic/metadata services for repurposing to form part of other services tailored to provide a deeper and/or broader level of access to resources in a given format or on a given subject.

The National Library of Australia is also a leader among Australian libraries and other relevant organizations in developing policies and techniques for preserving electronic resources. It participates in international forums aimed at developing electronic preservation metadata standards. It tests and promotes the use of the internationally developed Preservation Metadata Set for electronic resources recommended by the OCLC/RLG Preservation Metadata Working Group. The work of the OCLC/RLG Working Group on Preservation Metadata culminated in the 2001 to 2002 production of draft reports on the two broad kinds of preservation metadata prescribed by the Open Archival Information Systems Reference Model. The draft reports address content information, the data object and the information needed to present it, and preservation description information, the additional required information for managing the preservation of a digital object.

PANDORA is another effort of the National Library of Australia. The project was developed by the National Library of Australia, in collaboration with its partners, to ensure long-term access to select Australian online publications. The National Library, other deposit libraries, and other cultural collecting agencies are responsible for collecting and preserving these publications, which are an important part of Australia's publishing heritage. The work began in 1996, when it had become clear that an increasing amount of Australian information was being made available via the Web instead of in print publications. The National Library developed policy, procedures, and a digital archiving system for building and managing an archive of Web publications. It invited the state and territory libraries and other cultural collecting agencies to join the undertaking. The State Library of Victoria was the first partner to join the invitation in 1998, and, one by one, all of the mainland state libraries have joined, as well as ScreenSound Australia and the Australian War Memorial (National Library of Australia 2003). Metadata for the objects collected within the PANDORA project is created in a traditional way. The PANDORA project clearly proves that traditional cataloging has followed the development of online resources and is still valid for describing such resources accurately and properly.

The "Electronic Cataloguing Manual" is an essential document that provides instructions for describing the electronic information resources within the PANDORA project. The manual includes the following four sections:

• Cataloging—General

• Cataloging— Nonserials

• Cataloging—Serials

• Cataloging—Collections

The manual also addresses the issues surrounding changes in the existence and availability of Internet resources.

The manual generally prescribes adopting the following cataloging tools during original cataloging

• "AACR2," [Anglo-American Cataloging Rules] 2nd edition, 1998 revision, amendments 2001 to chapter 9, "'Electronic Resources' and relevant CSBs."

• *CONSER cataloging manual*, "Module 31: Remote Access Electronic Serials."

• OCLC's "Cataloging Internet Resources: A Manual and Practical Guide," 2nd edition.

• "Cataloguing Electronic Resources: OCLC-MARC Coding Guidelines," revised July 1999.

• LC's "Guidelines for the Use of field 856," revised August 1999.

• "Guidelines for Coding Electronic Resources in Leader/06."

• "Use of Fixed Fields 006/007/008 and Leader Codes in CONSER Records."

• "USMARC Format for Bibliographic Data: Field List," 1994 edition, including updates 1 to 3.

• Kinetica[2] "Guidelines for the Cataloguing of Electronic Resources."[3] Policy on the use of separate and single records for resources that exist in both electronic and nonelectronic format can be found in the following guidelines:

    • Kinetica client cataloguing

---

2. Kinetica is a modern Internet-based service for Australian libraries and their users. It provides access to the national database of material held in Australian libraries, known as the National Bibliographic Database.

3. The guidelines have been tailored to provide specific help with cataloging remote access electronic resources. They apply to a range of electronic resources, including e-books, e-journals, titles supplied by aggregator services, databases, Web sites, images, and sound files. They are not intended for use in the cataloging of locally accessed electronic resources, such as CD-ROMs, or electronic resources that do not require a computer for access, such as videodiscs.

- Serials work sheet
- Nonserials work sheet

In addition, the first section of the manual contains rules dealing with the chief sources of information, such as general title information, imprint, URLs, and the creation of records with Kinetica. Furthermore, prescriptions for cataloging nonserials, serials, and collections are found in subsequent sections of the manual.

An Access database, operating independently of the archiving system and Pantrack, was subsequently created to manage administrative metadata. The system's lack of integration was further compounded by the adoption of desktop harvesting robots (initially the offline browsing software WebZIPthen HTTrack).

The PANDORA archive contains two preservation copies of each archived instance, together with associated metadata, including a metadata master and shadow copy for each archived instance.

In broad terms, PANDORA supports workflows, which include managing administrative metadata about titles that have been either selected for national preservation, considered but rejected for national preservation, or monitored pending a selection decision.

6.3 METADATA IN THE OXFORD DIGITAL LIBRARY

The Oxford Digital Library (ODL) is a core service of Oxford University Libraries Services (OULS) and offers central access to the digital collections of Oxford University Libraries. The current ODL core team is a unit within the OULS System and Electronic Resources Service (SERS).

Between 1998 and 1999, the former deputy of the Bodleian Library of Oxford University advanced the idea of creating a digital library. A comprehensive survey investigating the necessity and possibility for setting up a digital library was undertaken both within and outside of Oxford. By 2002, 33 libraries had joined the OULS Libraries and Departments group. Currently, the number has reached 38. Furthermore, increasing numbers of college libraries are also involved in the group. The group has undertaken extensive digitization work aimed at preserving, archiving, and promoting access. The Bodleian Library does not allow its books to be removed from the library. This policy has been in place for years, and the Bodleian Library does not entrust its resources to any outside company or institution. However, this policy is an internal reason for the Bodleian Library to be eager for a digital library. The Bodleian Library hopes to establish digital collections and to develop a digital library on the basis of those collections. Since 2001 or 2002, the working parties have begun to be concerned with both digitized collection development and services. In 2002, three million pounds were invested to construct a hybrid library. Also in 2002, the American Andrew W. Mellon Foundation invested a sum of money to set up the ODL (Popham 2004). "The ODL aims to offer a Digital Library architecture which will allow centralized access to digital resources, both those it creates itself and those acquired from outside. The use of established standards for descriptive metadata (i.e., EAD, TEI) is a precondition for this integration process. Existing digital library collections may be transferred step by step into a common architecture with an integrated retrieval mechanism" (Oxford Digital Library 2002b). Currently, 20 projects are running in the ODL. It is "currently establishing a range of core services to support the creation of digital resources from Oxford University Libraries Services holdings" (Oxford Digital Library 2002a).

The ODL's adoption of the METS mechanism, which began three year ago, makes it a little different from many current digital libraries. It adopted this metadata standard soon after it was available. The ODL is quite closely related to the development of METS.

In the ODL, METS files have been generated by an automated Web-based cataloguing system. The ODL produces DC-based descriptive metadata (see Figure 6.1), a core of qualified DC data but are more qualified than the standard. Table 6.1 displays the three categories of DC fields used in ODL records. ODL-record description follows strict cataloguing guidelines that are designed to map to AACR2.

As previously described, METS provides a framework capable of holding all types of metadata for digital objects. In the opinion of a metadata specialist working in ODL, "The benefit of METS is that it doesn't tell you how to do something. Many things within METS are not prescribed. It does not prescribe content of metadata, but recommends a number of schemes for this. There is nothing about what should contain or how to create the record. They are up to the adopter. METS is pretty flexible" (Huber 2004a). The METS schema is a flexible mechanism for encoding descriptive, administrative, and structural metadata for a digital library object, and for expressing the complex links between these various forms of metadata. It is, therefore, a useful standard for the exchange of digital library objects between repositories. In addition, METS is able to associate a digital object with behaviors or services. METS was created to be universal, and at least one ODL metadata specialist believes that it will be adopted widely. In practice, ODL is an example of the successful employment of the METS scheme (Huber 2004b).

The long-term goal of ODL is to establish a hybrid library that provides integrated access to *ALL* library resources, including paper, microforms, manuscripts, maps, born-digital and digitized collections, and other materials. Printed books occupy a very important status at Oxford. The records of these printed books must be integrated into the hybrid library. The Oxford libraries use MARC 21 for printed books. ODL, accordingly, exploits MODS, which is compatible with MARC, to transform the ODL-created digital object records to the Oxford library catalogs. MODS is a

Table 6.1 DC fields in the ODL records

Mandatory for all records	Title
(Every record must contain at least a minimal entry in each of these fields.)	Subject
	Type
	Description
Mandatory where applicable	Creator
(Where an item has an identifiable creator, is datable, is digitized from	Date
a surrogate, has a corresponding record on OLIS, or has restrictions on access	Identifier
over and above those which apply to the entire collection, the relevant field in	Right
this category must be filled in. The **Format** field may also be used to indicate	Format
the physical extent of the original item.)	Source
Recommended where applicable	Contributor
(It is strongly recommended to fill in these fields if they are applicable	Publisher
to this item.)	Language
	Coverage
	Relation

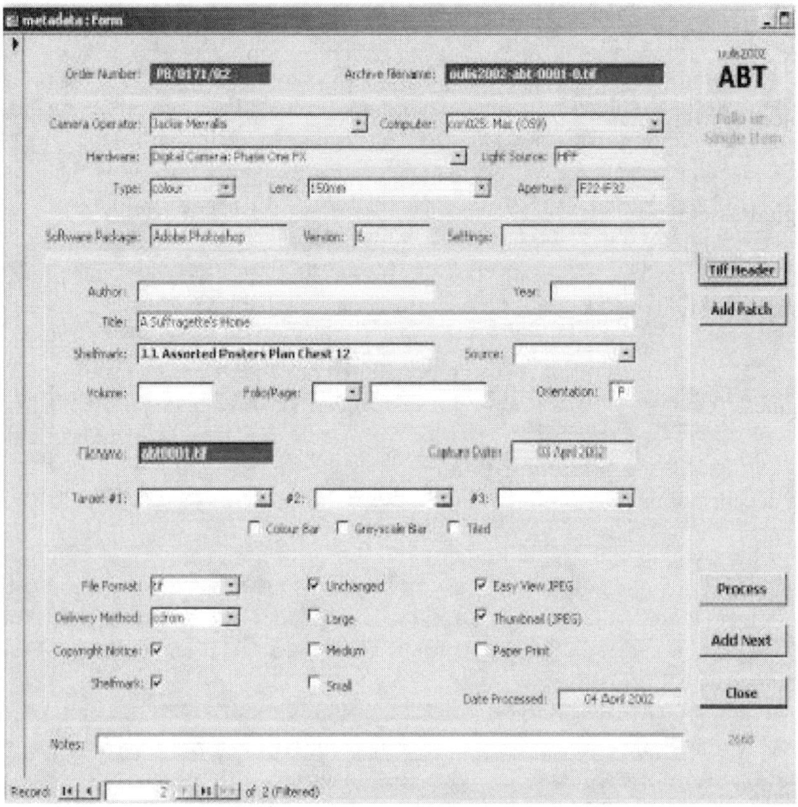

Figure 6.1 Metadata form of a digital object in the ODL.

useful tool for integrating the library records and metadata of the digital library. It is stable and has a very logical organization. In addition, it provides practical feedback. ODL practices have proven that MODS is a useful procedure. "The use of MODS will allow for a relatively uncomplicated integration of ODL's item-level descriptions into the library system provided it is able to handle XML data, as MODS is basically a way of using MARC 21 in XML and provides for an easy cross-walk from ODL's initial DC-based records" (Huber 2004b). Furthermore, "MODS offers the option to use authorities such as LC-NAF[4] by providing for an 'authority' attribute for its name-element. ODL uses this mechanism to integrate LCNAF for all its collections" (Huber 2004b).

Additionally, a number of digital library projects support author-generated metadata. This practice is logical when the rapid growth of the Internet is weighed against the economics of hiring metadata professionals. The ODL also supports author-created metadata.

---

4. LC-NAF is the Library of Congress Name Authority File.

6.4 DSPACE METADATA

DSpace is a newly developed digital repository created to capture, distribute, and preserve the intellectual output of the Massachusetts Institute of Technology (MIT). "As a joint project of MIT Libraries and the Hewlett-Packard Company (HP), DSpace provides stable long-term storage needed to house the digital products of MIT faculty and researchers" (MIT Libraries and Hewlett-Packard Company 2002a). It is a specialized type of digital-asset or content-management system; it manages and distributes digital items comprised of digital files (or bit streams), and allows for the creation, indexing, and searching of associated metadata. Despite its recent arrival in the digital library world, DSpace is highly reputed all over the world because of its advantages, such as an increased number of more powerful functions, continual development that is better supported, and digital preservation. It was reported that one of the current most popular search engines, "Google[,] has begun to do on campus search over DSpace including using the metadata as well as free-text since April 2004. The search includes cross searches over 17 DSpace repositories" (Young 2004).

DSpace accepts all manner of digital formats. Some examples of items that DSpace can accommodate are:

- Documents (e.g., articles, preprints, working papers, technical reports, conference papers)
- Books
- Theses
- Data sets
- Computer programs
- Visualizations, simulations, and other models
- Multimedia publications
- Learning objects

"By 'support' for a given metadata schema the DSpace means that metadata can be entered into DSpace, stored in the database, indexed appropriately, and made searchable through the public UI.[5] At the present time, this applies mainly to descriptive metadata, although as standards emerge it could also include technical, rights, preservation, structural and behavioral metadata" (MIT Libraries and Hewlett-Packard Company 2002b).

Currently, DSpace supports only the Dublin Core Metadata Elements Set, with a few additional qualifications conforming to library application profiles. The DSpace Libraries Working Group Application Profile (LAP) was used as a starting point for the DSpace application of Dublin Core, borrowing most of DC's qualifiers and adapting others to fit. Some qualifiers were added to suit DSpace's needs. DSpace metadata is listed in Table 6.2.

Plans for developing a method of supporting a subset of the Internet Protocol (IP) Multimedia Subsystem/Sharable Content Object Reference Model (IMS/SCORM) element set (for describing education material) will be formulated in the coming year.

---

5. UI is user interface.

Table 6.2 DSpace metadata list

Element	Qualifier	Scope note
Contributor		A person, organization, or service responsible for the content of the resource. Catchall for unspecified contributors.
	advisor author editor illustrator other	Use primarily for thesis advisor.
Coverage	spatial	Spatial characteristics of content.
	temporal	Temporal characteristics of content.
Creator		Do not use; only for harvested metadata.
Date		Use qualified form if possible.
	accessioned	Date DSpace takes possession of item.
	available	Date or date range item became available to the public.
	copyright	Date of copyright.
	created	Date of creation or manufacture of intellectual content if different from date issued.
	issued	Date of publication or distribution.
	submitted	Recommend for theses/dissertations.
Identifier		Catchall for unambiguous identifiers not defined by qualified form; use identifier. other for a known identifier common to a local collection instead of unqualified form.
	citation	Bibliographic citation for works that have been published as a part of a larger work, e.g., journal articles, book chapters.
	govdoc	Government document number.
	isbn	International Standard Book Number.
	issn	International Standard Serial Number.
	sici	Serial Item and Contribution Identifier.
	ismn	International Standard Music Number.
	other	A known identifier type common to a local collection.
	uri	Uniform Resource Identifier.
Description		Catchall for any description not defined by qu Catchall for any description not defined by qualifiers alifiers
	abstract	Abstract or summary.

(continued)

Description	provenance	The history of custody of the item since its creation, including any changes successive custodians made to it.
	sponsorship	Information about sponsoring agencies, individuals, or contractual arrangements for the item.
	statementofresponsibility	To preserve statement of responsibility from MARC records.
	tableofcontents	A table of contents for this item.
	uri	Uniform Resource Identifier pointing to description of this item.
Format		Catchall for any format information not defined by qualifiers.
	extent	Size or duration.
	medium	Physical medium.
	mimetype	Registered MIME type identifiers.
Language		Catchall for non-ISO forms of the language of the item, accommodating harvested values.
	iso	Current ISO standard for language of intellectual content, including country codes (e.g., "en_US").
Publisher		Entity responsible for publication, distribution, or imprint.
Relation		Catchall for references to other related items.
	isformatof	References additional physical form.
	ispartof	References physically or logically containing item.
	ispartofseries	Series name and number within that series, if available.
	haspart	References physically or logically contained item.
	isversionof	References earlier version.
	hasversion	References later version.
	isbasedon	References source.
	isreferencedby	Pointed to by referenced resource.
	requires	Reference resource is required to support function, delivery, or coherence of item.
	replaces	References preceding item.
	isreplacedby	References succeeding item.
	uri	References Uniform Resource Identifier for related item.

(continued)

Table 6.2 (continued)

Element	Qualifier	Scope note
Rights		Terms governing use and reproduction.
	uri	References terms governing use and reproduction.
Source		Do not use; only for harvested metadata.
	uri	Do not use; only for harvested metadata.
Subject		Uncontrolled index term.
	classification	Catchall for value from local classification system; global classification systems will receive specific qualifier.
	ddc	Dewey Decimal Classification Number.
	lcc	Library of Congress Classification Number.
	lcsh	Library of Congress Subject Heading.
	mesh	Medical Subject Headings.
	other	Local controlled vocabulary.
Title		Title statement/title proper.
	alternative	Varying (or substitute) form of title proper appearing in item, e.g., abbreviation or translation.
Type		Nature or genre of content.

HP and MIT also have a research project called Semantic Interoperability of Metadata and Information in unLike Environments (SIMILE) that is investigating methods that will support arbitrary metadata schemas using RDF, as applied by the Haystack research project in the Lab for Computer Science, and some of the Semantic Web technologies being developed by the W3C.

6.5 METADATA IN THE PEKING UNIVERSITY RARE BOOK DIGITAL LIBRARY

Chinese researchers and practitioners began to focus on the subject of metadata for both traditional and digital resources in the mid-1990s. For the next several years, they felt perplexed, and sometimes anxious, about how to create and manage metadata in a manner that would most effectively enable networked resource sharing. In mainland China, in addition to the use of metadata (such as catalog records) in traditional libraries, digital libraries is one of the metadata application areas that receives intense focus. Chinese research on the digital library began in 1995, and the first digital library project in China was launched at the beginning of 1996 by the National Library of China. Work on establishing the Chinese Digital Library Standards, the most important standard series in the Chinese digital library field, started in October 2002 and ended in September 2004. The project was initiated by the Institute of Scientific and

Technical Information of China, the Library of Chinese Academy of Sciences, and the National Library of China. At present, nearly 20 institutions have participated in the establishment and development of the Standards (Institute of Scientific and Technical Information of China 2003). As in other parts of the world, research and practice related to the digital library have drawn ever-increasing attention in China.

In China, the Institute of Digital Library (IDL) at Peking University was one of the pioneer institutions in metadata and digital library research and practice. It was established in September 1999 and colaunched and organized by the Administrative Center of the China Academic Library and Information System (CALIS), Peking University Library, and the Center of Information Science of Peking University. The Peking University Rare Book Digital Library (RBDL) is one of the practical achievements of IDL.

RBDL was built based on the large special collection of Peking University Library, totalling 180,000 titles and 1,600,000 items, including Chinese rare books, rubbings,[6] ancient atlases, Dunhuang scrolls, and old journals published before 1949. The Peking University Library has a rubbing collection of some 60,000 items. The Digital Rubbing Collection (DRC) was the pilot project of RBDL. Within the DRC project, the rubbing metadata standard was designed under the instructions of the Metadata Standard Framework of Peking University Digital Library, and was later defined as the RBDL Rubbing Metadata Standard Version 1.0 (Xiao and Chen. n.d.).

In accordance with the Metadata Standard Framework of the Peking University Digital Library, the RBDL rubbing metadata is composed of descriptive, administrative, and geographic information systems (GIS) metadata (Figure 6.2).

According to the definition of ISO/IEC 11179, every element is defined by the 10 following facets:

- Name
- Identifier
- Version
- Registration authority
- Language
- Definition
- Obligation
- Data type
- Maximum occurrence
- Comment

---

6. A rubbing is an imprint taken from calligraphy on stone or wood (http://www.britannica.com/needmoreengraved). The practice emerged in the Tang Dynasty (618–907) in China as a method of studying the style of earlier calligraphers, and later developed into an important art form in itself. Rubbings are made by carefully pressing paper onto a carved or incised surface so that the paper conforms to the features to be copied. The paper is then blacked and the projected areas of the surface become dark, while indented areas remain white. Simply put, rubbing is "a representation of a raised or indented surface made by placing paper over the surface and rubbing the paper gently with a marking agent such as charcoal or chalk" ().

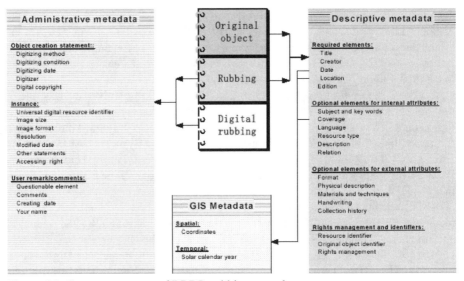

Figure 6.2 Content structure of RBDL rubbing metadata.
Source: Research Group of the Chinese Metadata Standards 2001.

In the RBDL Rubbing Metadata Version 1.0, each element is defined by the four facets below:

- Version: RBDL Rubbing Metadata Version 1.0
- Registration authority: Peking University Library
- Language: ch
- Data type: Character string

The 19 descriptive metadata elements (see Table 6.3) were divided into three categories for the RBDL rubbing collection, which are core element, local core element, and unique element. The 12 core elements were designed on the basis of the Dublin Core metadata standard. The following is the Peking University Library's rubbing collection's list of descriptive metadata elements:

- Object creation statement: digitizing method, condition, date, digitizer, digital copyright, and so forth.
- Instance: universal digital resource identifier, like Document Object Identifier (DOI), URI, URN or URL, image size, image format, resolution, modified date, other statements, accessing rights.
- User remark/comments: for the feedback or comments of end users.
- Structure of file: description of the relationship between the multiple digital files that constitute the complete digital object.

The GIS metadata matches the temporal and spatial information elements in descriptive metadata, and is operated by data processing technicians. GIS metadata is composed of two elements: *spatial* (coordinates) and *temporal.*

Table 6.3 Descriptive metadata elements of the RBDL Digital Rubbing Collection

Core element	Title Creator Subject and Key words Description Date Resource type (type of original object) Format (Rubbing) Resource identifier Language Relation Coverage Rights management
Local core element	Edition Physical description
Unique element	Collection history Handwriting Location (place of origin) Materials and techniques (materials of original object) Original object identifier

Some metadata-related technology had to be considered when the rubbing metadata standard was designed:

- GIS applications: GIS metadata is designed for it.

- Chronological mapping list: used to convert between the Chinese lunar calendar and the solar calendar in date and coverage elements.

- Mapping list: used to map Chinese ancient and current place names that appear in the location and coverage elements of the place name authority.

- Networked knowledge organization systems/schemes/services (NKOS): an open thesaurus/ subject/classification/taxonomy system applied in subject element.

REFERENCES

Arms, William. 2003. *Digital Libraries. Chapter 1: Background*. Available at: http://www. cs.cornell.edu/wya/DigLib/new/Chapter1.html. Accessed 19 March 2004.

Association of Research Libraries. 1995. *Definition and Purposes of a Digital Library*. Available at: http://www.arl.org/sunsite/definition.html#1. Accessed 5 May 2004.

California Digital Library. 2001. *California Digital Library Digital Object Standard: Metadata, Content, and Encoding*. Available at: http://www.cdlib.org/news/pdf/CDLObjectStd-2001. pdf. Accessed 30 January 2004.

Digital Library Federation. 1999. *Annual Report 1998–1999. Introduction*. Available at: http:// www.diglib.org/pubs/AR9899p1.html. Accessed 5 May 2004.

EU-NSF Working Group on Metadata. n.d. *Metadata for Digital Libraries: A Research Agenda*. Available at: http://www.ercim.org/publication/ws-proceedings/EU-NSF/metadata.html. Accessed 23 June 2003.

Gartner, Richard. 2002. *METS: Metadata Encoding and Transmission Standard. October 2002*. Available at: http://www.jisc.ac.uk/index.cfm?name=techwatch_report_0205. Accessed 9 March 2004.

Gartner, Richard. 2003. METS*: Metadata Encoding and Transmission Standard*. Available at: http://post-ifla.sub.uni-goettingen.de/agenda/gartner.ppt. Accessed 4 May 2004.

Huber, Alexander. 2004a. Interview by author. METS. Oxford, the United Kingdom, 1 September.

Huber, Alexander. 2004b. "Re: Two more questions, plz." E-mail to Jia Liu. 4 October.

Iannella, Renato. 1996. "Australian Digital Library Initiative," *D-Lib Magazine* (December). Available at: http://www.dlib.org/dlib/december96/12iannella.html. Accessed 13 May 2004.

Institute of Scientific and Technical Information of China. 2003. *Chinese Digital Library Standards*. Available at: http://cdls.nstl.gov.cn/cdls2/w3c/. Accessed 24 May 2004.

Library of Congress. 2004. *Library of Congress Digital Repository Development: Core Metadata Elements*. Available at: http://www.loc.gov/standards/metadata.html. Accessed 5 May 2004.

Lynch, Clifford. 1999. "Canonicalization: A Fundamental Tool to Facilitate Preservation and Management of Digital Information," *D-Lib Magazine* 5 (9). Available at: http://www.dlib.org/dlib/september99/09lynch.html. Accessed 28 June 2004.

MIT Libraries and Hewlett-Packard Company. 2002a. *DSpace: Durable Digital Depository*. Available at: http://libraries.mit.edu/dspace-mit/index.html. Accessed 21 May 2004.

MIT Libraries and Hewlett-Packard Company. 2002b. *DSpace FAQ*. Available at: http://libraries.mit.edu/dspace-mit/what/faq.html. Accessed 21 May 2004.

National Library of Australia. 2002. *Guidelines for the Creation of Content for Resource Discovery Metadata*. Available at: http://www.nla.gov.au/guidelines/metaguide.html. Accessed 13 May 2004.

National Library of Australia. 2003. *PANDORA, Australia's Web Archive: An Overview*. Available at: http://pandora.nla.gov.au/background.html. Accessed 12 May 2004.

National Library of Australia. n.d. *Electronic Information Resources Strategies and Action Plan 2002–2003*. Available at: http://www.nla.gov.au/policy/electronic/eirsap/. Accessed 13 May 2004.

Oxford Digital Library. 2002a. *Digital Collections*. Available at: http://www.odl.ox.ac.uk/collections.htm. Accessed 17 May 2004.

Oxford Digital Library. 2002b. *Services*. Available at: http://www.odl.ox.ac.uk/services.htm. Accessed 21 October 2004.

Phillips, Margaret E. 1998. *Towards an Australian Digital Library*. Available at: http://www.nla.gov.au/nla/staffpaper/mphillips4.html. Accessed 13 May 2004.

Popham, Michael. 2004. Interview by author. METS. Oxford, the United Kingdom, 31 August.

Russell, Kelly. 2000. Digital Preservation and the Cedars Project Experience. Available at: http://www.rlg.org/events/pres-2000/russell.html. Accessed 5 May 2004.

Smith, Terence R. 1996. "The Meta-information Environment of Digital Libraries," *D-Lib Magazine* (July/August). Available at: http://www.dlib.org/dlib/july96/new/07smith.html. Accessed 25 June 2003.

Tennant, Roy. 1999. *Digital v. Electronic v. Virtual Libraries*. Available at: http://sunsite.berkeley.edu/mydefinitions.html. Accessed 22 March 2004.

Xiao, Long, and Chen Ling. n.d. *Designing and Implementation of Chinese Metadata Standards: A Case Study on Metadata Applications in Peking University Rare Book Digital Library*. Available at: http://www.idl.pku.edu.cn/5/page.htm. Accessed 24 May 2004.

Young, Jeffrey R. 2004. "Google Teams up with 17 Colleges to Test Searches of Scholarly Materials," *The Chronicle of Higher Education* (4 April). Available at: http://chronicle.com/free/2004/04/2004040901n.htm. Accessed 21 May 2004.

Appendix: GILS Data Elements and Corresponding USMARC Tags

GILS Data Element	USMARC Tag
Title	245$a
Control identifier	001
Abstract	520
Purpose	500
Originator	710$a
Access constraints	506
Use constraints	540

Distributor

Distributor name	270$p [proposed field]
Distributor organization	270$p [proposed field]
Distributor street address	270$a [proposed field]
Distributor city	270$b [proposed field]
Distributor state	270$c [proposed field]
Distributor zip code	270$e [proposed field]
Distributor country	270$d [proposed field]
Distributor network address	270$m [proposed field]
Distributor hours of service	301$a [proposed field]
Distributor telephone	270$k [proposed field]
Distributor fax	270$l [proposed field]

Available resource description	037$f
Available order process	037$c
Available technical prerequisites	538
Available time period—structured	045$c
Available time period—textual	037$n [proposed field] (for nonelectronic resource)
	856$z (for electronic resource)
Available linkage	856$u
Available linkage type	856 1st indicator/856$2
Point of contact	856$m (for electronic resources)
Contact name	270$p [proposed field]
Contact organization	270$p [proposed field]
Contact street address	270$a [proposed field]
Contact city	270$b [proposed field]
Contact state	270$c [proposed field]
Contact zip code	270$e [proposed field]
Contact country	270$d [proposed field]
Contact network address	270$m [proposed field]
Contact hours of service	301$a [proposed field]
Contact telephone	270$k [proposed field]
Contact fax	270$l [proposed field]
Record source	040
Date last modified	005
Agency program	500
Sources of data	537 [proposed field]
Index terms—Controlled	650
Thesaurus	650 1st indicator/ 650$2
Local subject term	653$a
Methodology	567
Bounding rectangle	255$c
Westernmost	034$d
Easternmost	034$e
Northernmost	034$f
Southernmost	034$g

Geographic Name

Geographic key word name	651
Geographic key word type	655

Time period—structured	045$c
Time period—textual	513
Cross-reference title	787$t
Cross-reference linkage	787$w
Cross-reference type	856 1st indicator/856$2
Original control identifier	035
Supplemental information	500

NOTE

U.S. Department of Commerce. National Institute of Standards and Technology, *Approval of Federal Information Processing Standards Publication 192, Application Profile for the Government Information Locator Service (GILS)*, http://www.dtic.mil/gils/documents/naradoc/fip192.html (accessed 3 October 2003).

References

American Library Association. Association for Library Collections & Technical Services. 2002. *Announcements and reports*. Available at: http://www.libraries.psu.edu/tas/jca/ccda/ann0210.html. Accessed 16 May 2007.

American Library Association. Association for Library Collections & Technical Services. 2005. *AACR3: The Next Big Thing in Cataloging*. Available at: http://www.ala.org/ala/alcts/alctsconted/alctsceevents/alctsannual/AACR3prog.htm. Accessed 16 May 2007.

American Library Association. Committee on Cataloging: Description and Access. 1998b. *Task Force on Metadata and the Cataloging Rules. Final Report, Section 6*. Available at http://www.ala.org/Content/NavigationMenu/ALCTS/Division_groups/MARBI/Next_Section_6.htm. Accessed 14 May 2003.

ANZLIC Metadata Working Group. 2001. *ANZLIC Metadata Guidelines: Core Metadata Elements for Geographic Data in Australia and New Zealand*. Version 2. Available at: http://www.anzlic.org.au/download.html?oid=2358011755. Accessed 17 December 2003.

Arms, William. 2003. *Digital Libraries. Chapter 1: Background*. Available at: http://www.cs.cornell.edu/wya/DigLib/new/Chapter1.html. Accessed 19 March 2004.

Arms, William Y, Christophe Blanchi, and Edward A. Overly. 1997. "An Architecture for Information in Digital Libraries," *D-Lib Magazine* (February). Available at: http://www.dlib.org/dlib/february97/cnri/02arms1.html. Accessed 10 October 2003.

Associated Universities Inc. 1999. XML *in 10 points. Version 1.9, Build 275. Introduction*. Available at: http://aips2.nrao.edu/docs/reference/Coding/node39.html#SECTION0281210000 0000000000. Accessed 3 February 2004.

Association of Research Libraries. 1995. *Definition and Purposes of a Digital Library*. Available at: http://www.arl.org/sunsite/definition.html#1. Accessed 5 May 2004.

Australian Government. National Archives of Australia. n.d. *AGLS*. Available at: http://www.naa.gov.au/recordkeeping/gov_online/agls/summary.html. Accessed 18 June 2004.

Baca, Murtha, and Patricia Harpring, eds. n.d. *Introduction*. Available at: http://www.getty.edu/research/conducting_research/standards/cdwa/index.html. Accessed 10 October 2003.

Baker, Thomas. 2002. *DCMI Usage Board Review of Application Profiles*. Available at: http://dublincore.org/usage/documents/profiles/. Accessed 9 March 2004.

Barton, Jane, Sarah Currier, and Jessie M. N. Hey. 2003. "Building Quality Assurance into Meta-data Creation: An Analysis Based on the Learning Objects and e-Prints Communities of Practice." In *DC-2003: Proceedings of the International DCMI Conference and Workshop*, September 28–October 2, 2003, Seattle, Washington, 39–48. Syracuse, N.Y.: Information Institute of Syracuse.

Bearman, David. 2003. *NISO/CLIR/RLG Technical Metadata for Images Workshop, April 18–19, 1999*. Available at: http://www.niso.org/news/events_workshops/imagerpt.html. Accessed 9 October 2003.

Bearman, David, and Ken Sochats. 2004. *Metadata Requirements for Evidence*. Available at: http://www.archimuse.com/papers/nhprc/BACartic.html. Accessed 28 January 2004.

Beckett, Dave. 2004. *RDF/XML Syntax Specification (Revised): W3C Recommendation 10 February 2004*. Available at: http://www.w3.org/TR/2004/REC-rdf-syntax-grammar-20040210/. Accessed 2 March 2004.

Berners-Lee, Tim. 1997. *Metadata Architecture*. Available at: http://www.w3.org/DesignIssues/Metadata.html. Accessed 25 February 2003.

Bos, Bert. 2001. *XML in 10 Points*. Available at: http://www.w3.org/XML/1999/XML-in-10-points.html.en. Accessed 9 February 2004.

Bray, Tim, Jean Paoli, C. M. Sperberg-McQueen, Eve Maler, and François Yergeau. 2004. *Extensible Markup Language (XML) 1.0: W3C Recommendation 04 February 2004*, 3rd ed. Available at: http://www.w3.org/TR/REC-xml/. Accessed 14 October 2005.

Burnard, Lou. 2004. *Digital Texts with XML and the TEI*. Available at: http://www.tei-c.org/Talks/OUCS/2004–02/One/teixml-one.pdf. Accessed 23 February 2004.

Burnard, Lou. n.d. What is SGML and How Does It Help? Available at: http://www.oasis-open.org/cover/burnardw25-index.html. Accessed 20 October 2004.

Burnard, Lou, and Richard Light. 1996. *Three SGML Metadata Formats: TEI, EAD, and CIMI: A Study for BIBLINK Work Package 1.1*. Available at: http://www.ifla.org/documents/libraries/cataloging/metadata/biblink2.pdf. Accessed 3 February 2004.

Calanag, Maria Luisa, Shigeo Sugimoto, and Koichi Tabata. 2001. "A Metadata Approach to Digital Preservation." In *DC-2001: Proceedings of the International Conference on Dublin Core and Metadata Applications 2001*, National Institute of Informatics, 143–150. Tokyo, Japan: Nihon Printing Co., Ltd. Available at: http://www.nii.ac.jp/dc2001/proceedings/product/paper-24.pdf. Accessed 28 January 2004.

California Digital Library. 2001. *California Digital Library Digital Object Standard: Metadata, Content, and Encoding*. Available at: http://www.cdlib.org/news/pdf/CDLObjectStd-2001.pdf. Accessed 30 January 2004.

Campbell, Debbie. 1997. *The MetaWeb Project*. Available at: http://www.dstc.edu.au/Research/Projects/metaweb/timeline.html. Accessed 27 April 2004.

Campbell, Debbie. 1999a. *Dublin Core Metadata and Australian MetaWeb Project*. Available at: http://www.nla.gov.au/nla/staffpaper/dcampbell1.html. Accessed 28 April 2004.

Campbell, Debbie. 1999b. *The MetaWeb Project*. Available at: http://www.dstc.edu.au/Research/Projects/metaweb/. Accessed 27 April 2004.

Canadian Heritage Information Network. 2002. Standards for encoding metadata. Available at: http://www.chin.gc.ca/English/Standards/metadata_encoding.html. Accessed 3 February 2004.

Caplan, Priscilla. 1995. "You Call It Corn, We Call It Syntax: Independent Metadata for Document-like Objects." *The Public-Access Computer Systems Review* 6 (4). Available at: http://info.lib.uh.edu/pr/v6/n4/capl6n4.html. Accessed 25 February 2003.

Caplan, Priscilla. 2003. *Metadata Fundamentals for All Librarians*. Chicago, Ill.: The American Library Association.

Centre for Educational Technology Interoperability Standards. 2004. *ISO SC36 'Metadata for Learning Resources' Working Group Approved*. Available at: http://www.cetis.ac.uk/content/20030204163914. Accessed 12 October 2003.

Coleman, Anita. 2002. *Metadata Standards*. Available at: http://www.asu.edu/ecure/2002/coleman/coleman.ppt. Accessed 11 October 2003.

Day, Michael. 1997. *Extending Metadata for Digital Preservation*. Available at: http://www.ariadne.ac.uk/issue9/metadata/. Accessed 12 October 2003.

Day, Michael. 1999. "Metadata for Digital Preservation: An Update," *Ariadne* 22 (December). Available at: http://www.ariadne.ac.uk/issue22/metadata/#1. Accessed 28 June 2004.

Day, Michael. 2001a. "Metadata for Digital Preservation: A Review of Recent Developments." In *Research and Advanced Technology for Digital Libraries: 5th European Conference on the Digital Libraries, September 2–49, 2001, Darmstadat, Germany*, eds. P. Constantopoulos and I. T. Solvberg, 161–172. Berlin, Germany: Springer-Verlag. Availble at: http://www.ukoln.ac.uk/metadata/presentations/ecdl2001-day/paper.html. Accessed 14 April 2007.

Day, Michael. 2001b. "Metadata in A Nutshell." *Information Europe* 6 (2): 11. Available at: http://www.ukoln.ac.uk/metadata/publications/nutshell/. Accessed 11 April 2007.

Day, Michael. n.d. *CEDARS: Digital Preservation and Metadata*. Available at: http://www.ercim.org/publication/ws-proceedings/DELOS6/cedars.rtf. Accessed 16 January 2004.

DeCandido, GraceAnne A. 1999. *Metadata: Always More than You Think*. Available at: http://www.ala.org/ala/pla/plapubs/technotes/metadata.htm. Accessed 11 April 2007.

DeCandido, Robert. 1999. "Metadata: What's It to You?" In *The Internet Searcher's Handbook*. 2nd ed., eds. Peter Morville, Louis B. Rosenfeld, and Joseph Janes, rev. by GraceAnn A. DeCandido, 37–49. New York: Neal Schuman.

Dekkers, Makx. 2001. *Application Profiles, or How to Mix and Match Metadata Schema*. Available at: http://www.cultivate-int.org/issue3/schemas/#ref-03. Accessed 9 March 2004.

Dempsey, Lorcan. 1996. "ROADS to Desire: Some UK and Other European Metadata and Resource Discovery Projects," *D-Lib Magazine* (July/August). Available at: http://www.dlib.org/dlib/july96/07dempsey.html. Accessed 18 December 2003.

Dempsey, Lorcan, and Rachel Heery. 1997. *DESIRE: Project Deliverable*. Available at: http://www.ukoln.ac.uk/metadata/desire/overview/overview.rtf. Accessed 30 March 2003.

Dempsey, Lorcan, and Rachel Heery. 1998. "Metadata: A Current View of Practice and Issues." *Journal of Documentation* 54 (2): 145–72.

Digital Library Federation. 1999. *Annual Report 1998–1999. Introduction*. Available at: http://www.diglib.org/pubs/AR9899p1.html. Accessed 5 May 2004.

Distributed System Technology Centre. 2003. *HotMeta: User Guide. Version 3.2.2*. Available at: http://www.dstc.edu.au/Downloads/metasuite/HMUserGuide-3.2.2.pdf. Accessed 1 October 2003.

Distributed Systems Technology Centre. n.d. *HotMeta: HotMeta Overview and Capabilities*. Available at: http://www.dstc.edu.au/cgi-bin/redirect/rd.cgi?http://archive.dstc.edu.au/RDU/HotMeta/. Accessed 28 April 2004.

Dublin Core Metadata Initiative. 2003. *Dublin Core Metadata Element Set, Version 1.1: Reference Description*. Available at: http://dublincore.org/documents/dces/. Accessed 19 December 2003.

Duval, Erik, Wayne Hodgins, Stuart Sutton, and Stuart L. Weibel. 2002. "Metadata Principles and Practicalities," *D-Lib Magazine* 8 (4). Available at: http://webdoc.sub.gwdg.de/edoc/aw/d-lib/dlib/april02/weibel/04weibel.html. Accessed 25 February 2003.

Elkington, Nancy. 2001. *NISO Technical Metadata for Digital Still Images*. Available at: http://jodi.ecs.soton.ac.uk/noticeboard/nisoimage.html. Accessed 16 January 2004.

EU-NSF Working Group on Metadata. n.d. *Metadata for Digital Libraries: A Research Agenda*. Available at: http://www.ercim.org/publication/ws-proceedings/EU-NSF/metadata.html. Accessed 23 June 2003.

European Archive Network. 2002. *European Archive Network Project: Final Report*. Available at: http://www.euan.org/euan_final.doc#_Toc23207967. Accessed 14 November 2003.

European Committee for Standardization. 1999. *Model for Metadata for Multimedia Information.* Available at: ftp://cenftp1.cenorm.be/PUBLIC/CWAs/e-Europe/MMI-DC/cwa13699–00–1999-Sep.pdf. Accessed 21 June 2004.

European Committee for Standardization. 2003. *Guidance on the Use of Metadata in eGovernment.* English version. Available at: ftp://ftp.cenorm.be/PUBLIC/CWAs/e-Europe/MMI-DC/cwa14859–00–2003-Nov.pdf. Accessed 15 June 2004.

Fast, Karl. 2003. *Metadata Harvesting: Reflections on Metadata in a Networked World.* Available at: www.asis.org/IA03/fast.ppt. Accessed 22 October 2003.

Federal Geographic Data Committee. Metadata Ad Hoc Working Group. 1998. *FGDC-STD-001–1998, Content Standard for Digital Geospatial Metadata.* Available at: http://www.fgdc.gov/standards/documents/standards/metadata/v2_0698.pdf. Accessed 16 December 2003.

Federal Geographic Data Committee. 2003. *Content Standard for Digital Geospatial Metadata (CSDGM).* Available at: http://www.fgdc.gov/metadata/contstan.html. Accessed 16 December 2003.

Fietzer, William. 2002. "Interpretive Encoding of Electronic Texts Using TEI Lite." In *Cataloging the Web: Metadata, AACR, and MARC 21*, eds. Wayne Jones, Jodith R. Ahronheim, and Joesephine Crawford, 103. Lanha, Md., and London: The Scarecrow Press, Inc.

Fleischhauer, Carl. 2003. *Audio-Visual Prototyping Project.* Available at: http://lcweb.loc.gov/rr/mopic/avprot/SoundSavings03.ppt. Accessed 10 October 2003.

Gadd, Elizabeth, Charles Oppenheim, and Steve Probets. n.d. *RoMEO Studies 6: Rights Metadata for Open Archiving.* Available at: http://www.lboro.ac.uk/departments/ls/disresearch/romeo/Romeo%20Studies%206.pdf. Accessed 26 January 2004.

Gartner, Richard. 2002. *METS: Metadata Encoding and Transmission Standard. October 2002.* Available at: http://www.jisc.ac.uk/index.cfm?name=techwatch_report_0205. Accessed 9 March 2004.

Gartner, Richard. 2003. *METS: Metadata Encoding and Transmission Standard.* Available at: http://post-ifla.sub.uni-goettingen.de/agenda/gartner.ppt. Accessed 4 May 2004.

Gateway to Educational Materials. 2003a. *GEM 2.0 Element Set and Semantics.* Available at: http://www.geminfo.org/Workbench/GEM2_elements.html. Accessed 12 October 2003.

Gateway to Educational Materials. 2003b. *Why Should Metadata Be Created for Your Educational Resources?* Available at: http://www.geminfo.org/decision.html. Accessed 12 October 2003.

Gateway to Educational Materials. n.d. *The Gateway to Educational Materials (GEM) is...* Available at: http://www.geminfo.org/index.html. Accessed 12 October 2003.

Gill, Tony, and Anne J. Gilliland. 1998. "Metadata and the World Wide Web." In *Introduction to Metadata: Pathway to Digital Information*, ed. Los Angeles: Getty Information Institute.

Goldfarb, Charles. n.d. *SGML User's Group History.* Available at: http://xml.coverpages.org/sgmlhist0.html. Accessed 9 February 2004.

Government of Ireland. 2002. *The Irish Public Service Metadata Standard: User Guide.* Available at: http://www.gov.ie/webstandards/metastandards/index.html. Accessed 19 October 2004.

Graham, Rebecca A. 2001. "Metadata Harvesting," *Library Hi Tech* 19 (3): 290–295.

Greenberg, Jane, Maria Cristina Pattuelli, Bijan Parsia, and W. Davenport Robertson. 2001. Author-generated Dublin Core Metadata for Web Resources: A Baseline Study in an Organization," *Journal of Digital Information* 2 (2). Available at: http://jodi.ecs.soton.ac.uk/Articles/v02/i02/Greenberg/. Accessed 13 June 2003.

Guenther, Rebecca. 2002a. *Library Application Profile.* Available at: http://dublincore.org/documents/2002/04/16/library-application-profile/index.shtml. Accessed 9 March 2004.

Guenther, Rebecca. 2002b. "MARC 21 as a Metadata Standard: A Practical and Strategic Look at Current Practices and Future Opportunities." In *Cataloging the Web: Metadata, AACR, and MARC 21*, eds. Wayne Jones, Jodith R. Ahronheim, and Joesephine Crawford, transc. Jina Choi Wakimoto, 41. Lanha, Md., and London: The Scarecrow Press, Inc.

Guenther, Rebecca, and Sally McCallum. 2003. "New Metadata Standards for Digital Resources: MODS and METS." *Bulletin of the American Society for Information Science and Technology* December/January: 12–15.

Hakala, Juha. n.d. *The Nordic Metadata II Project: Cataloguing, Indexing and Retrieval of Network Documents.* Available at: http://www.lib.helsinki.fi/meta/nm2plan.html. Accessed 30 April 2004.

Hakala, Juha, Preben Hansen, Ole Husby, Traugott Koch, and Susanne Thorborg. 1998. *The Nordic Metadata Project: Final Report.* Available at: http://www.lib.helsinki.fi/meta/nmfinal.doc. Accessed 28 October 2003.

Harvard University Library. Digital Repository Service. 2002. *DRS Documentation: Administrative Metadata for Digital Still Images.* Available at: http://preserve.harvard.edu/resources/imagemetadata.pdf. Accessed 19 January 2004.

Hedstrom, Margaret. 1998. "Digital Preservation: A Time Bomb for Digital Libraries," *Computers and the Humanities* 32: 189–202.

Heery, Rachel. 2003. *Registry for Educational Metadata Schemas: Final Project Report and Recommendations.* Available at: http://www.ukoln.ac.uk/metadata/education/regproj/report.pdf. Accessed 2 April 2004.

Heery, Rachel, Robina Clayphan, Michael Day, Lorcan Dempsey, and David Martin. 1996. *BIBLINK-LB 4034: D1.1 Metadata Formats.* Available at: http://hosted.ukoln.ac.uk/biblink/wp1/d1.1.rtf. Accessed 25 February 2003.

Heery, Rachel, Pete Johnston, Csaba Fülöp, and András Micsik. 2003. *Metadata Schema Registries in the Partially Semantic Web: The CORES Experience.* Available at: http://dc2003.ischool.washington.edu/Archive-03/03heery.pdf. Accessed 1 April 2004.

Heery, Rachel, and Manjula Patel. 2000. "Application Profiles: Mixing and Matching Metadata Schemas," *Ariadne* 25. Available at: http://www.ariadne.ac.uk/issue25/app-profiles/intro.html. Accessed 29 October 2003.

Hensen, Steven L. 1989. *Archives, Personal Papers, and Manuscripts: A Cataloging Manual for Archival Repositories, Historical Societies, and Manuscript Libraries.* 2nd ed. Washington, D.C.: Society of American Archivists.

Hillmann, Diane. 2001. *Using Dublin Core.* Available at: http://www.dublincore.org/documents/2001/04/12/usageguide/. Accessed 10 February 2003.

Hodge, Gail. 2001. *Metadata Made Simpler.* Available at: http://www.niso.org/news/Metadata_simpler.pdf. Accessed 22 May 2003.

Horsman, Peter. 2000. *Metadata and Archival Description. Version 1.1.* Available at: http://www.euan.org/euan_meta.html. Accessed 14 November 2003.

Howe, Denis. 1997. *Meta-data.* Available at http://foldoc.doc.ic.ac.uk/foldoc/foldoc.cgi?query = metadata. Accessed 14 May 2003.

Huber, Alexander. 2004a. Interview by author. METS. Oxford, the United Kingdom, 1 September.

Huber, Alexander. 2004b. "Re: Two more questions, plz." E-mail to Jia Liu. 4 October.

Hunter, Jane. 2000. *An XML Schema Approach to Application Profiles.* Available at: http://archive.dstc.edu.au/maenad/appln_profiles.html. Accessed 29 October 2003.

Hunter, Jane, and Carl Lagoze. n.d. *Combing RDF and XML Schemas to Enhance Interoperatiblity between Metadata Application Profiles.* Available at: http://www.org/cdrom/papers/572/index.html. Accessed 29 October 2003.

Iannella, Renato. 1996. "Australian Digital Library Initiative," *D-Lib Magazine* (December). Available at: http://www.dlib.org/dlib/december96/12iannella.html. Accessed 13 May 2004.

Iannella, Renato. 2001. "Digital Rights Management (DRM) Architectures," *D-Lib Magazine* 7 (6). Available at: http://www.dlib.org/dlib/june01/iannella/06iannella.html. Accessed 28 January 2004.

Iannella, Renato, and Debbie Campbell. 2000. *The A-Core: Metadata about Content Metadata.* Available at: http://dublincore.org/archives/2001/02/purl-dc-website/documents/notes/acore-20000719.htm. Accessed 14 January 2004.

Iannella, Renato, and Andrei Waugh. 1997. *Metadata: Enabling the Internet.* Available at: http://archive.dstc.edu.au/RDU/reports/CAUSE97/. Accessed 14 May 2003.

IFLA Study Group on the Functional Requirements for Bibliographic Records; approved by the Standing Committee of the IFLA Section on Cataloguing. 1998. *Functional Requirements for Bibliographic Records: Final Report.* Muenchen, Germany: Saur. Available at http://www.ifla.org/VII/s13/frbr/frbr.pdf. Accessed 14 April 2007.

Imperial College, Department of Computing. 1993. *FOLDOC: Free On-line Dictionary of Computing.* Available at: http://wombat.doc.ic.ac.uk/foldoc/. Accessed 22 April 2005.

Institute of Electrical and Electronics Engineers, Inc. Learning Technology Standards Committee. 2002a. *Draft Standard for Learning Object Metadata.* Available at: http://www.learninglab.de/elan/kb3/lexikon/metadaten-standards/docs/LOM_1484_12_1_v1_Final_Draft.pdf. Accessed 15 December 2003.

Institute of Electrical and Electronics Engineers, Inc. Learning Technology Standards Committee. 2002b. *Position Statement on 1484.12.1—2002 Learning Object Metadata (LOM) Standard Maintenance/Revision.* Available at: http://ltsc.ieee.org/news/20021210-LOM.html. Accessed 12 October 2003.

Institute of Scientific and Technical Information of China. 2003.*Chinese Digital Library Standards.* Available at: http://cdls.nstl.gov.cn/cdls2/w3c/. Accessed 24 May 2004.

International Standards Organization. n.d. *Geographic Information—Metadata.* Available at: http://www.iso.org/iso/en/CatalogueDetailPage.CatalogueDetail?CSNUMBER=26020&ICS1=35&ICS2=240&ICS3=70. Accessed 17 December 2003.

J. Paul Getty Trust. n.d. *Categories for the Description of Works of Art.* Available at: http://www.getty.edu/research/conducting_research/standards/cdwa/2_overview/index.html. Accessed 10 October 2003.

Johnston, Pete. 2002. *Administrative Metadata for Collection-level Description Records.* Available at: http://www.ukoln.ac.uk/cd-focus/guides/gp3/. Accessed 14 January 2004.

Johnston, Pete. 2004. *JISC IE Metadata Schema Registry.* Available at: http://www.ukoln.ac.uk/projects/iemsr/. Accessed 4 March 2004.

Kiesling, Kris. 2002. "Archival Finding Aids as Metadata: Encoded Archival Description." In *Cataloging the Web: Metadata, AACR, and MARC 21,* eds. Wayne Jones, Jodith R. Ahronheim, and Joesephine Crawford, 69. Lanha, Md., and London: The Scarecrow Press, Inc.

Kiesling, Kristi. 2001. "Metadata, Metadata, Everywhere: But Where Is the Hook?" *OCLC Systems & Services* 17 (2): 84–88.

Koch, Traugott. 1998. *Nordic Metadata Project: A Presentation.* Available at: http://www.ub2.lu.se/tk/metadata/NMDPpres.html. Accessed 29 April 2004.

Library of Congress. 1998a. *The Making of America II Testbed Project White Paper. Version 2.0.* Available at: http://sunsite.berkeley.edu/moa2/wp-v2.html. Accessed 10 October 2003.

Library of Congress. 1998b. *How to Use Structural Metadata Attributes: Digital Element Relationship Information and Page Information.* Available at: http://memory.loc.gov/ammem/techdocs/repository/rep-examples/example-1a.html#top. Accessed 12 January 2004.

Library of Congress. 2003a. *Development of the Encoded Archival Description DTD.* Available at: http://www.loc.gov/ead/eaddev.html. Accessed 24 February 2004.

Library of Congress. 2003b. *Digital Audio-Visual Preservation Prototyping Project.* Available at: http://lcweb.loc.gov/rr/mopic/avprot/avprhome.html. Accessed 10 October 2003.

Library of Congress. 2003c. *METS: An Overview & Tutorial.* Available at: http://www.loc.gov/standards/mets/METSOverview.v2.html. Accessed 5 February 2004.

Library of Congress. 2004. *Library of Congress Digital Repository Development: Core Metadata Elements.* Available at: http://www.loc.gov/standards/metadata.html. Accessed 5 May 2004.

Lynch, Clifford. 1999. "Canonicalization: A Fundamental Tool to Facilitate Preservation and Management of Digital Information," *D-Lib Magazine* 5 (9). Available at: http://www.dlib.org/dlib/september99/09lynch.html. Accessed 28 June 2004.

Mah, Carole E., and Julia H. Flanders. 2003. *The TEI Header: A Tutorial with Examples*. Available at: http://www.wwp.brown.edu/encoding/training/teiheader/teiHeader.html. Accessed 23 February 2004.

Manola, Frank, and Eric Miller, eds. 2004. *RDF Primer: W3C Recommendation*. Available at: http://www.w3.org/TR/2004/REC-rdf-primer-20040210/. Accessed 26 February 2004.

Martin, Mairéad, and Doug Pearson. 2001. *Rights Metadata: XrML and ODRL for Digital Video*. Available at: www.vide.net/conferences/mdvc2001/DRM5.ppt. Accessed 26 January 2004.

Merriam-Webster, Inc. *Merriam-Webster Dictionary*. Available at: http://www.m-w.com/cgi-bin/dictionary. Accessed 25 June 2003.

Metadata Encoding and Transmission Standard. 2003. *METS News and Announcements: Draft Rights Declaration Schema is Ready for Review*. Available at: http://www.loc.gov/standards/mets/news080503.html. Accessed 28 January 2004.

Miller, Eric. 1998. "An Introduction to the Resource Description Framework," *D-Lib Magazine* (May). Available at: http://www.dlib.org/dlib/may98/miller/05miller.html. Accessed 4 November 2003.

Miller, Paul. 1996. *Metadata for the Masses*. Available at: http://www.ariadne.ac.uk/issue5/metadata-masses/. Accessed 7 December 2003

Miller, Paul. 1999. *Lessons from An Examination of Dublin Core*. Available at: http://www.ukoln.ac.uk/interop-focus/presentations/metalib/ahds/iap-html/sld001.htm. Accessed 29 April 2003.

Miller, Paul. 2002. *The MEG Concord*. Available at: http://www.ukoln.ac.uk/metadata/education/documents/concord.html. Accessed 12 October 2003.

Miller, Paul. n.d. *The UK's Metadata for Education Group*. Available at: http://www.ukoln.ac.uk/metadata/education/. Accessed 12 October 2003.

Milstead, Jessica, and Susan Feldman. 1999. "Metadata: Cataloging by Any Other Name." *Online* (January). Available at: http://www.onlinemag.net/OL1999/milstead1.html. Accessed 20 June 2003.

MIT Libraries. 2004a. *EAD: Encoded Archival Description*. Available at: http://libraries.mit.edu/guides/subjects/metadata/standards/ead.html. Accessed 24 February 2004.

MIT Libraries. 2004b. *Metadata Reference Guide: TEI (Text Encoding Initiative) Metadata*. Available at: http://libraries.mit.edu/guides/subjects/metadata/standards/tei.html#3. Accessed 23 February 2004.

MIT Libraries and Hewlett-Packard Company. 2002a. *DSpace: Durable Digital Depository*. Available at: http://libraries.mit.edu/dspace-mit/index.html. Accessed 21 May 2004.

MIT Libraries and Hewlett-Packard Company. 2002b. *DSpace FAQ*. Available at: http://libraries.mit.edu/dspace-mit/what/faq.html. Accessed 21 May 2004.

Moe, M., and H. Blodgett. 2000. *The Knowledge Web*. Merrill Lynch & Co., Global Securities Research & Economics Group, Global Fundamental Equity Research Department. Mueller, Martin. *A Very Gentle Introduction to the TEI Markup Language*. n.d. Available at: http://www.tei-c.org/Sample_Manuals/mueller-main.htm. Accessed 24 February 2004.

Napier, Marieke. 2001. *Metadata Resources: Metadata Encoding and Transmission Standard (METS)*. Available at: http://www.ukoln.ac.uk/metadata/resources/mets/. Accessed 5 February 2004.

National Aeronautics and Space Administration. 1988. *Directory of Interchange Format Manual*. Version 1.0, July 13. NSSDC/WDC-A-R&S: 88–9.

National Digital Library Program. Digital Repository Development Project. 1998. *Structural Metadata List. Version 1.04b*. Available at: http://lcweb.loc.gov:8081/ndlint/repository/attlist.html. Accessed 13 January 2004.

National Institute of Standards and Technology. Department of Commerce. n.d. *Approval of Federal Information Processing Standards Publication 192, Application Profile for the Government Information Locator Service (GILS)*. Available at: http://www.dtic.mil/gils/documents/naradoc/fip192.html. Accessed 3 October 2003.

National Library of Australia. 2002. *Guidelines for the Creation of Content for Resource Discovery Metadata*. Available at: http://www.nla.gov.au/guidelines/metaguide.html. Accessed 13 May 2004.

National Library of Australia. 2003. *PANDORA, Australia's Web Archive: An Overview*. Available at: http://pandora.nla.gov.au/background.html. Accessed 12 May 2004.

National Library of Australia. n.d. *Electronic Information Resources Strategies and Action Plan 2002–2003*. Available at: http://www.nla.gov.au/policy/electronic/eirsap/. Accessed 13 May 2004.

Noordermeer, Trudi. 2000. "A Bibliographic Link Publishers of Electronic Resources and National Bibliographic Agencies: Project BIBLINK," *Exploit Interactive* 4. Available at: http://www.exploit-lib.org/issue4/biblink/. Accessed 16 April 2004.

OASIS. 2004. *Extensible Markup Language (XML)*. Available at: http://xml.coverpages.org/xml.html. Accessed 10 February 2004.

OASIS. n.d. *Standard Generalized Markup Language (SGML)*. Available at: http://xml.coverpages.org/sgml.html/. Accessed 8 February 2004.

OCLC/RLG Working Group on Preservation Metadata. 2001. Preservation Metadata for Digital Objects: A Review of the State of the Art . Available at: http://www.oclc.org/research/pmwg/presmeta_wp.pdf. Accessed 6 June 2003.

OCLC/RLG Working Group on Preservation Metadata. 2002. *A Metadata Framework to Support the Preservation of Digital Objects: Preservation Metadata and the OAIS Information Model*. Available at: http://www.oclc.org/research/pmwg/. Accessed 20 January 2004.

Open Archives Initiative Executive. 2002. *The Open Archives Initiative Protocol for Metadata Harvesting: Protocol Version 2.0 of 2002–06–01*. Available at: http://www.openarchives.org/OAI/openarchivesprotocol.htm. Accessed 10 June 2003.

Oxford Digital Library. 2002a. *Digital Collections*. Available at: http://www.odl.ox.ac.uk/collections.htm. Accessed 17 May 2004.

Oxford Digital Library. 2002b. *Services*. Available at: http://www.odl.ox.ac.uk/services.htm. Accessed 21October 2004.

Patel, Manjula, and Robina Clayphan. n.d. *Project BIBLINK: Linking Publishers and National Bibliographic Agencies*. Available at: http://www.ukoln.ac.uk/metadata/publications/biblink/proj-biblink.html. Accessed 16 April 2004.

Perkins, Alan. 2004. *Developing a Data Warehouse: The Enterprise Engineering Approach*. Available at: http://members.ozemail.com.au/~ieinfo/dw.htm. Accessed 12 January 2004.

Phillips, Margaret E. 1998. *Towards an Australian Digital Library*. Available at: http://www.nla.gov.au/nla/staffpaper/mphillips4.html. Accessed 13 May 2004.

Pilling, Dennis. 2001. Quoted in McCallum, Sally H. "MARC harmonization report" *MARC listserv:* MARC@listserv.loc.gov.

Popham, Michael. 2004. Interview by author. METS. Oxford, the United Kingdom, 31 August.

Powell, Andy. 2000. *The BIBLINK Demonstrator*. Available at: http://hosted.ukoln.ac.uk/biblink/wp11/. Accessed 16 April 2004.

Powell, Andy, and Harry Wagner, ed. 2001. *Namespaces Policy for the Dublin Core Metadata Initiative (DCMI)*. Available at: http://dublincore.org/documents/dcmi-namespace/. Accessed 4 March 2004.

Project RoMEO. n.d. *Final Report*. Available at: http://www.lboro.ac.uk/departments/ls/disresearch/romeo/. Accessed 28 January 2004.

Research and Development Group of UKOLN. 1999. *DESIRE Metadata Registry*. Available at: http://desire.ukoln.ac.uk/registry/. Accessed 10 March 2004.

Research Libraries Group. Working Group on Preservation Issues of Metadata. 1998. *Final Report*. Available at: http://www.rlg.org/preserv/presmeta.html. Accessed 19 January 2004.

Ross, Seamus. 1997. "Consensus, Communication and Collaboration: Fostering Multidisciplinary Co-operation in Electronic Records." In *Proceedings of the DLM-Forum on Electronic*

Records, Brussels, 18–20 December 1996, INSAR: European Archives News, Supplement II, 330–336. Luxembourg: Office for Official Publications of the European Communities.

Rusbridge, Chris. 1999. *Rights Metadata: Why and Why Now? Models 10*. Available at: www. ukoln.ac.uk/dlis/models/models10/cr-mod10.ppt. Accessed 26 January 2004.

Russell, Kelly. 2000. Digital Preservation and the Cedars Project Experience. Available at: http:// www.rlg.org/events/pres-2000/russell.html. Accessed 5 May 2004.

Rust, Godfrey. 1998. "Metadata: The Right Approach: An integrated Model for Descriptive and Rights Metadata in e-Commerce." *D-Lib Magazine* (July/August). Available at: http:// www.dlib.org/dlib/july98/rust/07rust.html. Accessed 4 November 2003.

Rust, Godfrey, and Mark Bide. 2000. *The <indecs> Metadata Framework: Principles, Model and Data Dictionary*. Available at: http://www.indecs.org/pdf/framework.pdf. Accessed 25 June 2003.

Schwab, Eric. 2003. *Visual Resources Association*. Available at: http://vraweb.org/index.html. Accessed 10 October 2003.

Seadle, Michael. 2002. "METS and the Metadata Marketplace," *Library Hi Tech* 20 (3): 255–257.

Smith, Terence R. 1996. "The Meta-information Environment of Digital Libraries," *D-Lib Magazine* (July/August). Available at: http://www.dlib.org/dlib/july96/new/07smith.html. Accessed 25 June 2003.

Society of American Archivists. 1999. *Standards for Archival Description: A Handbook*. Available at: http://www.archivists.org/catalog/stds99/index.html. Accessed 14 November 2003.

Society of American Archivists. 2002. *Encoded Archival Description Tag Library. EAD Elements: <eadheader> EAD header*. Available at: http://www.loc.gov/ead/tglib/elements/eadheader. html. Accessed 24 February 2004.

Sperberg-McQueen, C. M., and Lou Burnard, eds. 2003a. *The XML Version of the TEI Guidelines. 1, About These Guidelines*. Available at: http://www.tei-c.org/P4X/AB.html#ABTEI. Accessed 23 February 2004.

Sperberg-McQueen, C. M., and Lou Burnard, eds. 2003b. *The XML Version of the TEI Guidelines. 5, The TEI header*. Available at: http://www.tei-c.org/P4X/HD.html. Accessed 23 February 2004.

Sperberg-McQueen, C. M., and Lou Burnard. n.d. *TEI P3. Chapter 2, A Gentle Introduction to SGML*. Available at: http://www-sul.stanford.edu/tools/tutorials/html2.0/gentle.html. Accessed 9 February 2004.

State Records Authority of New South Wales. 2000. *New South Wales Recordkeeping Metadata Standard.*Available at: http://www.records.nsw.gov.au/publicsector/rk/rib/rib18-en.pdf. Accessed 23 September 2003.

SUB Goettingen. 2002. *Metadata Server: Metadata at SUB Goettingen*. Available at: http:// www2.sub.uni-goettingen.de/sub_en.html#meta. Accessed 5 May 2003.

Tennant, Roy. 1999. *Digital v. Electronic v. Virtual Libraries*. Available at: http://sunsite.berkeley. edu/mydefinitions.html. Accessed 22 March 2004.

Text Encoding Initiative. 2001. *Welcome to the TEI Website*. Available at: http://www.tei-c.org/. Accessed 23 February 2004.

Text Encoding Initiative. 2002. *A Gentle Introduction to XML. May 2002*. Available at: http:// www.tei-c.org/Guidelines2/gentleintro.html#Note2. Accessed 10 February 2004.

Thomas, Charles F., and Linda S. Griffin. 1998. *Who Will Create the Metadata for the Internet?* Available at: http://www.firstmonday.dk/issues/issue3_12/thomas/index.html. Accessed 17 May 2003.

Treasury Board of Canada Secretariat. 2003. *TBITS 39: Treasury Board Information Management Standard. Part1: Government On-Line Metadata Standard*. Available at: http://www. tbs-sct.gc.ca/its-nit/standards/tbits39/crit391_e.asp. Accessed 17 June 2004.

Turner, M. James. n.d. *What is Metadata?* Available at: http://mapageweb.umontreal.ca/turner/ meta/english/metadata.html. Accessed 21 May 2003.

UK Office for Library and Information Networking. 1998. *Administrative Metadata: Sample Solutions.* Available at: http://www.ukoln.ac.uk/web-focus/metadata/seminar-materials/ exercises/admin-metadata/admin-metadata-solution.pdf. Accessed 14 January 2004.

UK Office for Library and Information Networking. 2004. *Metadata Watch Report #3. Section 2, The Concept of Application Profiles.* Available at: http://www.schemas-forum.org/ metadata-watch/third/section2.html. Accessed 26 August 2004.

United Kindom. Stationery Office Limited. 1988. Copyright, Designs and Patents Act, c. 48.

User Guide Committee. 2001. *Dublin Core Metadata Glossary: Final Draft.* Available at: http:// library.csun.edu/mwoodley/dublincoreglossary.html. Accessed 30 June 2004.

Visual Resources Association. 2002. *VRA Core Categories. Version 3.0.* Available at: http://www. vraweb.org/vracore3.htm. Accessed 10 October 2003.

Walsh, Norman, and Leonard Muellner. 2002. *DocBook: The Definitive Guide. 1, Getting Started with SGML/XML.* Available at: http://www.docbook.org/tdg/en/html/ch01.html. Accessed 9 February 2004.

Waters, Donald. 1998. *Current Issues in Digital Preservation: A Perspective from the Digital Library Federation.* Available at: http://ssdoo.gsfc.nasa.gov/nost/isoas/dads/presentations/ Waters/sld001.htm. Accessed 23 January 2004.

Weibel, Stuart. 1995. "Metadata: The Foundations of Resource Description." *D-Lib Magazine* (July). Available at: http://www.dlib.org/dlib/July95/07weibel.html. Accessed 18 December 2003.

Weibel, Stuart. 2003. *State of the Dublin Core Metadata Initiative.* Available at: http://post-ifla. sub.uni-goettingen.de/agenda/weibel1.ppt. Accessed 24 June 2004.

Weibel, Stuart, Jean Godby, and Eric Miller. 1995. *OCLC/NCSA Metadata Workshop Report.* Available at: http://www.oasis-open.org/cover/metadata.html. Accessed 15 September 2005.

Weibel, Stuart, and Carl Lagoze. 1997. "An Element Set to Support Resource Discovery." *International Journal on Digital Libraries* 1: 176–86.

Wood, Andrew. 1997. *Metadata: The Ghosts of Data Past, Present, and Future.* Available at: http://archive.dstc.edu.au/RDU/reports/Sympos97/metafuture.html. Accessed 25 June 2003.

World Wide Web Consortium. 1999. *Terms and Definitions.* Available at: http://www.w3.org/ TR/1999/WD-xhtml-building-19990910/terms.html. Accessed 3 February 2004.

World Wide Web Consortium. 2003. *HyperText Markup Language Activity Statement.* Available at: http://www.w3.org/MarkUp/Activity. Accessed 20 February 2004.

World Wide Web Consortium. 2004. *HyperText Markup Language (HTML) Home Page.* Available at: http://www.w3.org/MarkUp/. Accessed 20 February 2004.

Xiao, Long, and Chen Ling. n.d. *Designing and Implementation of Chinese Metadata Standards: A Case Study on Metadata Applications in Peking University Rare Book Digital Library.* Available at: http://www.idl.pku.edu.cn/5/page.htm. Accessed 24 May 2004.

Young, Jeffrey R. 2004. "Google Teams up with 17 Colleges to Test Searches of Scholarly Materials," *The Chronicle of Higher Education* (4 April).Available at: http://chronicle.com/ free/2004/04/2004040901n.htm. Accessed 21 May 2004.

Index